APSLEY HOUSE
WELLINGTON MUSEUM

Simon Jervis & Maurice Tomlin

THIS GUIDE IS SPONSORED BY

Published by the
Victoria and Albert Museum
London SW7 2RL

© The Trustees of the
Victoria and Albert Museum, 1984

ISBN 0 905209 68 0

Photography by Ken Jackson, Jeremy
Whitaker, Richard Bryant.

The drawings illustrated on pages 6 and 45
are reproduced by permission of the
Trustees of Sir John Soane's Museum.

Designed by Leonard Lawrance

Printed and bound by Four Winds Press

Front cover

*Apsley House, principal façade facing
south, with a glimpse of the base of the
Wellington Monument (1888) by Sir
Joseph Boehm*

Frontispiece

*Arthur Wellesley, First Duke of
Wellington (1769-1852) by Sir Thomas
Lawrence, P.R.A., about 1815*

Back cover

*Plate from the Saxon Service of Meissen
porcelain showing Apsley House, about
1818*

FOREWORD

IN 1947 the Seventh Duke of Wellington generously offered to the Nation his famous London residence, Apsley House, together with much of its contents and other items connected with the First Duke. The government gratefully accepted the offer and the terms of the gift were incorporated in the Wellington Museum Act of 1947, by which the property became part of the national treasure. The gift comprised Apsley House itself, in which certain apartments are kept permanently by the Wellington family, and the magnificent collection of paintings, plate, porcelain, batons, orders and decorations, furniture and personal relics.

The Wellington Museum, Apsley House, was first opened to the public on 19th July 1952. It is administered by the Victoria and Albert Museum, whose present Director placed it under the Department of Furniture & Woodwork in 1976. Since then extensive alterations have been made in order to restore Apsley House, insofar as is possible, to its appearance under the First Duke, and further improvements to this end are planned.

This new guidebook, a distant successor to the pamphlet guides issued by the Second Duke of Wellington in 1853, records these changes. It owes much to the guidebook by Charles Gibbs-Smith, first published in 1952 and subsequently revised through seven editions by Victor Percival, Officer-in-Charge from 1947 to 1981. But there is much also that is new in text, illustrations and format, and it is to be hoped that this fresh approach may draw wider attention to this great house.

I must express my thanks to my Director, Sir Roy Strong, and to His Grace the Duke of Wellington, both of whom have supported and assisted our efforts at Apsley House over the past few years. The work of planning and writing the guidebook has been shared between my Deputy Keeper, Simon Jervis, responsible for Apsley House since 1976, and Maurice Tomlin, Officer-in-Charge since 1981. We are extremely grateful to Mobil whose generosity has made its publication possible.

Peter Thornton, Keeper
Department of Furniture and Woodwork
Victoria and Albert Museum

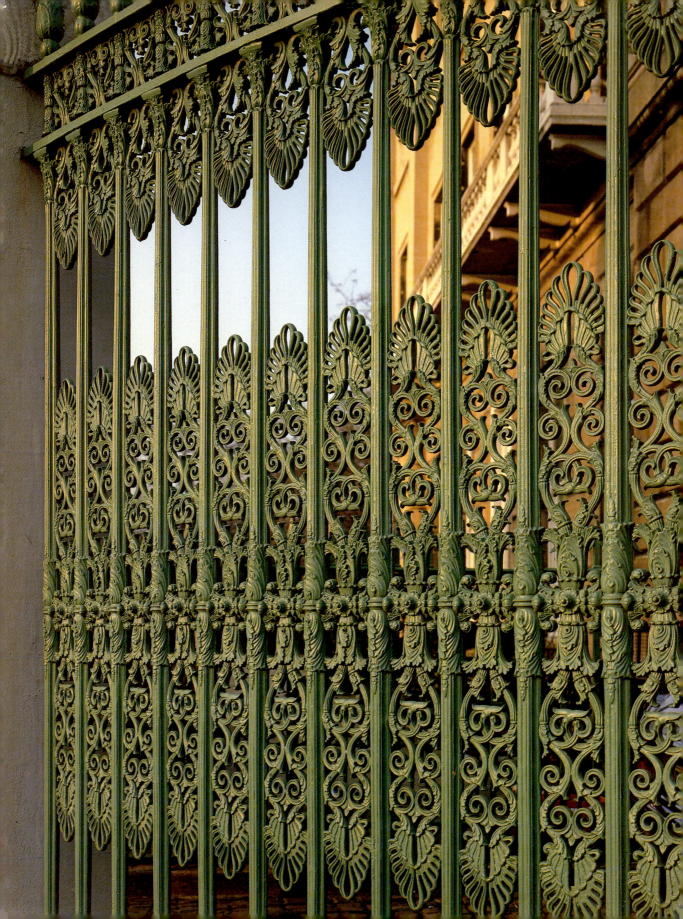

APSLEY HOUSE

Arms of the Duke of Wellington, from the Prussian Service, Berlin porcelain, about 1819

View of Hyde Park Corner showing Apsley House, about 1900. Frances Frith Collection

APSLEY HOUSE was built between 1771 and 1778 for the second Earl of Bathurst (1714-1794). It takes its name from the title, Baron Apsley (created 1771), he held before succeeding his father as Earl Bathurst in 1775. It was designed by the neo-classical architect Robert Adam (1728-1792), many of whose designs for the building and its decoration and furniture are preserved in Sir John Soane's Museum. The house was originally faced in red brick and comprised five bays. Built on the site of a lodge to Hyde Park, it was the first house to be encountered after passing the toll gates at the top of Knightsbridge, a conspicuous position which must be responsible for its popular nickname, 'No. 1 London'.

In 1807 Apsley House was bought by the Marquess Wellesley (1760-1842) from the third Earl Bathurst for £16,000. Wellesley, the First Duke of Wellington's elder brother, had returned from India in 1805 a wealthy man, and employed the fashionable architect James Wyatt (1746-1813), assisted by Thomas Cundy (1765-1825), to carry out alterations and improvements. By 1816 Wellesley was in pecuniary difficulties and it was fortunate for him that he was able in 1817 to sell Apsley House to his brother for £42,000.

Wellington had then returned from duties as Ambassador to France, with a dazzling reputation as a soldier and with a political career in view. He was advised on the purchase by his former secretary, the architect Benjamin Dean Wyatt (1775-1850), son of James Wyatt. In 1818 Benjamin Dean Wyatt carried out repairs and installed the Canova statue of Napoleon. In 1819 he built the classical Dining Room in the North-East corner, where the Waterloo Banquets were held from 1820 to 1829.

In about 1827 the Duke of Wellington seems to have set aside any plans to build a Waterloo palace with the £200,000 voted him by Parliament, and determined to enlarge Apsley House into a London residence appropriate to his status and collections. Benjamin Dean Wyatt was therefore employed to enlarge the house by two bays to the West, incorporating a great picture gallery, to add a Corinthian portico, and to encase the whole in Bath stone. The entrance screen and gates were replanned at the same time, to accord with the adjoining Ionic Hyde Park Screen designed by Decimus Burton (1800-1881) in about 1825. (In 1982 the iron gates and railings were repainted the original bronze-green colour.) For the interior of the new gallery Wyatt employed the Lous XIV or 'Versailles' style of ornament, which his brother Matthew Cotes Wyatt (1777-1862) had pioneered at Belvoir Castle in 1824, and which he himself used at York House (later Stafford House, and now Lancaster House) from 1825.

By 1831 the Duke had spent about £64,000 on improvements, an expense about which he complained bitterly. Plasterwork was carried out by the firms of Bernasconi and George Jackson & Sons; metalwork was supplied by

Design for the ceiling of the second drawing-room (the Portico Drawing Room) by Robert Adam, 1775. Sir John Soane's Museum

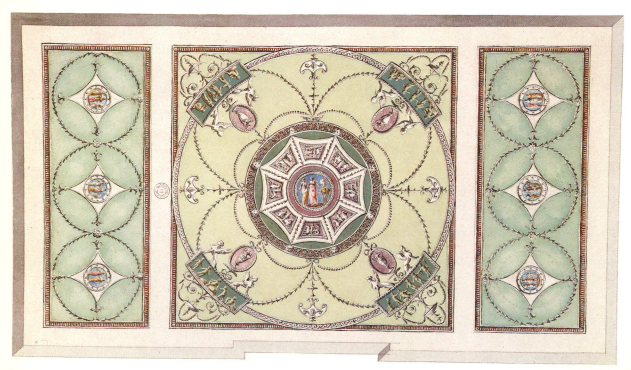

J. Bramah & Sons and furniture by Thomas Dowbiggin & Co. Dowbiggin's successors, Holland & Sons, carried out the arrangements for the Duke's funeral in 1852 and made an inventory of Apsley House in 1854. The Second Duke of Wellington (1807-1884) allowed the public to visit the principal apartments of the house from 1853 onwards; they were open three days a week, but admission was allowed only in answer to written application. The Second Duke made some alterations on the ground floor but the main rooms remained substantially intact until the house was presented to the nation by the Seventh Duke of Wellington (1885-1972) in 1947. In World War II a bomb and a flying bomb had fallen nearby: their damage and the effects of time were put right by a major renovation carried out by the Ministry of Public Building and Works in time for the public opening on July 19th 1952. In 1961 to 1962 a road was built to the East, separating the House from Piccadilly. The new east façade was then faced with Bath stone and pierced with windows, the coach house removed and the forecourt rendered symmetrical.

View of Hyde Park Corner (with Apsley House in the foreground) by Edward Dayes, 1810

The Inner Hall

The Seventh Duke of Wellington, K.G., by Peter Greenham, R.A. Lent by His Grace the Duke of Wellington

The Inner Hall, described thus in the 1854 Inventory and as the Waiting Hall leading to Grand Staircase (sic) in the 1857 Inventory, was remodelled by Wyatt in about 1830: before then it was the entrance hall. The ceiling is plain, the walls are painted to resemble Siena marble, and the doors are mahogany. The mosaic floor, along with the cast-iron radiator covers, was probably installed by the Second Duke of Wellington in about 1860. The three French mahogany side-tables with gilt-bronze mounts and granite tops date from about 1810 and were in this room under the First Duke along with, among other items, 'a hexagon lantern with three burners . . . a Pembroke- and a sofa-table and 2 mahogany chairs with leather seats'. The bronze statuette of Prince von Blücher (1742-1819) by Christian Daniel Rauch (1777-1857) is a reduction of Rauch's destroyed monument to Blücher set up in Breslau in 1827: it was probably in the Inner Hall under the First Duke, along with other bronzes and many marble busts. Now present are marble busts of the Duke of Wellington by Joseph Nollekens (1737-1823), 1813, Colonel John Gurwood, C.B., by Samuel Joseph (1791-1850), 1840, Sir Frederick Cavendish Ponsonby, K.C.B., (sculptor unknown), the Duke of Wellington by George Gamon Adams (1821-1898), 1859, and a once celebrated first century B.C. bust of Cicero from the Mattei collection, which the Duke purchased in 1816. A showcase fitted into a former door into the Hall contains items of uniform belonging to the First Duke of Wellington, lent by the present Duke.

On the stairs to the Basement may be seen a state portrait by Peter Greenham R.A., painted in about 1952, of the Seventh Duke of Wellington (1885-1972), who gave Apsley House to the nation in 1947. The Seventh Duke succeeded to the title on the death of his nephew in action in 1943. As Lord Gerald Wellesley he had become an authority on artistic matters, serving as Surveyor of the King's Works of Art from 1936 to 1943. A particular interest was the Regency period and he was one of the leaders of the Regency Revival of the 1930s, as writer, collector and architect. He was an expert on his great-grandfather, the first Duke, publishing an *Iconography* (1935) and editing his letters (1965). The Seventh Duke also served as a Trustee of the National Gallery and as a member of the Advisory Council of the Victoria and Albert Museum.

The paintings are as follows:

NORTH WALL

Colonel John Gurwood, C.B. (1790-1845).
By James Hall (1797-1854).
Dated 1837.
Private secretary to the Duke of Wellington; edited the *Wellington Despatches;* wounded at Waterloo.

Overpage: The Battle of Waterloo, by Felix Philipotteaux, 1874. Victoria and Albert Museum

The Inner Hall, about 1900

William Pitt (1759-1806).
By Gainsborough Dupont (1754-1797).
Prime Minister 1783-1801 and 1804-1806.

Horatio, Viscount Nelson (1758-1805). After Sir William Beechey, R.A.
(1753-1839).

*Prince von Blücher, by Christian Daniel
Rauch, bronze, 1824*

EAST WALL

William II, King of Holland (1792-1849), when Prince of Orange.
By John Singleton Copley, R.A. (1737-1815).

Field-Marshal August Neidhardt, Count of Gneisenau (1760-1831).
By George Dawe, R.A. (1781-1829).
Prussian soldier; served under General Blücher against Napoleon.

Field-Marshal Prince von Blücher (1742-1819).
By George Dawe, R.A. (1781-1829).
Commander of the Prussian Army; combined with Wellington to win the
Battle of Waterloo.

General Miguel Ricardo de Alava (1771-1843).
By George Dawe, R.A. (1781-1829).
Signed and dated 1818.
Spanish officer attached to Wellington's staff in the Peninsular War and
Waterloo. Later ambassador to England.

The Battle of Waterloo.
By Felix Philipotteaux (1815-1884).
Historical reconstruction painted in 1874. Lent by the Victoria and Albert
Museum.

SOUTH WALL

Stapleton Cotton, Field-Marshal Viscount Combermere G.C.B., K.S.T.,
(1773-1865).
By John Hayter (1800-c.1891). Signed and dated 1839.
Served in India and in the Peninsular War; second in command under
Wellington at Salamanca.

WEST WALL

William Henry West Betty, the "Young Roscius" (1791-1874). Artist
unknown. British school, about 1805.
Famous juvenile actor.

Self-portrait, wearing glasses. After Sir Joshua Reynolds, P.R.A. (1723-1792).
Contemporary copy of the self-portrait, painted in 1788, in the Royal
Collection at Windsor Castle.

The Duke of Wellington visiting the Outposts at Soignies.
By Hippolyte Lecomte (1781-1857). Signed.
Soignies, between Waterloo and Brussels, was the site of the British camp in
1815.

The Hall

A selection of flags presented by Napoleon to the French Departments on June 1st 1815

The Hall, described as the Front Hall in the 1854 Inventory and as the Entrance Hall in the 1857 Inventory, was created by Wyatt in about 1830, when he moved the entrance one bay westward. Before that it was a drawing-room. The ceiling is plain, the walls and columns are painted to resemble Siena marble, and the doors are mahogany. As in the Inner Hall the mosaic floor and radiator covers were probably installed by the Second Duke of Wellington in about 1860, along with the black marble fireplace. Under the First Duke the contents included 'a hexagon lantern with 3 burners . . . 6 hall chairs, a porter's hall chair, a kneehole writing-table and an eight-day bracket clock'. The Hall contains the following busts: the Duke of Wellington by Benedetto Pistrucci (1784-1855), heroic size, 1832, by Sir Francis Chantrey, R.A. (1781-1841), 1823, and by Sir John Steell (1804-1891), 1846, the Marquess of Londonderry, K.G., by Chantrey, George Canning by Joseph Nollekens, R.A. (1737-1823), Napoleon Bonaparte by A. Triscornia (1797-1867) after Canova, and Richard, Marquess Wellesley, K.G., by John Francis (1780-1861), 1818, after Nollekens. On the east wall is a plaque erected in 1930 to commemorate the visit of the Venzuelan patriot Simon Bolivar (1783-1830) in 1810 to the Marquess Wellesley, then Foreign Secretary. Above the showcase hang some of the silver-embroidered French flags presented by Napoleon to the French Departments on the occasion of the great assembly known as the *Champ de Mai*, held on the Champ de Mars on June 1st 1815. The showcase contains costumes kindly lent by the present Duke of Wellington.

The Duke of Wellington, by Benedetto Pistrucci, 1832

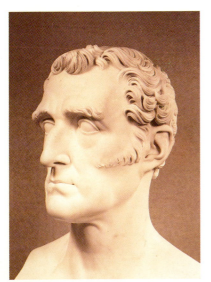

The paintings are as follows:

WEST WALL

His Last Return from Duty.
By James W. Glass (1825-1857).
Signed and dated 1853.
The Duke is shown riding from his office at the Horse Guards for the last time as Commander-in-Chief.

The Duke of Wellington.
By Spiridone Gambardella (?1815-1886).
After a portrait by Lawrence, about 1825, now at Wellington College.

EAST WALL

The Duke of Wellington.
By John Simpson (1782-1847).
About 1835.

The Plate and China Room

Under the First Duke of Wellington the Plate and China Room occupied the north-west corner of Apsley House. After his death in 1852 the Second Duke moved the room to its present position in the south-west corner, sweeping away some small ground-floor bedrooms to create the space. The new room had a very similar character to its predecessor, and the Second Duke moved his father's rosewood showcases in, adapting one to incorporate the door. He also installed the black marble fireplace. In 1981 new showcases were introduced, two in the outer window bays in the west wall, and a carpet was laid, woven to resemble that in interior watercolours of 1852 and 1853. In 1854 the room, sometimes called the Museum, contained, as well as many of the objects shown now, the Portuguese centre-piece (see p.65), bronze busts of Turenne and Condé, now at Stratfield Saye, two Indian drums, and a 'Wax Bust of the Duke on japan'd pedestal stand and glass shade'.

The large showcase on the North wall contains the Wellington Shield, designed by Thomas Stothard, R.A. (1755-1834) and made by Benjamin Smith for Green, Ward & Green in about 1822. Its central group, Wellington crowned by Victory, is surrounded by ten reliefs of scenes from his career. Flanking the Shield are Standard Candelabra by Benjamin Smith, dated 1816 to 1817. These are supported by figures of a Sepoy, a Portuguese soldier, and a Spanish guerilla (left) and an English, a Scottish, and an Irish soldier (right). Shield and Candelabra were presented to the Duke by the Merchants and Bankers of the City of London.

Tureen from the Deccan Service, silver, London, 1806, made by John Edwards

The Plate and China Room, watercolour by Thomas Shotter Boys, 1853

The rosewood case (1981) in the centre of the room contains the Sèvres Egyptian Service, purchased from the present Duke of Wellington by the Victoria & Albert Museum in 1979. The Service was made by the Sèvres porcelain factory from 1809 to 1812 as a divorce present from Napoleon to the Empress Josephine. She rejected it and in 1818 it was presented to Wellington by Louis XVIII of France. The book on Egypt (1802) by Dominique Vivant Denon (1747-1825) supplied the models for the monumental centre-piece, based on the Temples of Karnak, Dendera, and Philae, and for the views on the sixty-six plates. Three large cases on the east and south walls contain part of an even larger service made by the Berlin porcelain factory from 1816 to 1819 and presented to Wellington by King Frederick William III of Prussia (1770-1840). The sixty-four plates of this Prussian Service depict the Duke's life and campaigns, while its centre-piece includes a green porcelain obelisk with his orders and titles, and white

Plate from the Egyptian Service, Sèvres porcelain, painted by J.-F.-J. Swebach, with a view of the Sphinx, 1811

Vase from the Prussian Service, Berlin porcelain, about 1819

Ice-cream pail from the Egyptian Service,
Sèvres porcelain, painted and gilt by
Micaud, 1811

The Wellington Shield, designed by Thomas Stothard and made by Benjamin Smith, 1822, Detail

Part of the centrepiece from the Egyptian Service, Sèvres porcelain, 1809 to 1812

biscuit porcelain river gods appropriate to his career. The second large case on the south wall contains elements from the Saxon Service of Meissen porcelain, made in about 1818 and presented to the Duke by King Frederick Augustus IV of Saxony, and pieces from the Austrian Service of Vienna porcelain presented by the Emperor Francis I of Austria in 1820 (see also pp.68-69).

Of the two projecting cases on the west window wall the larger contains parts of the Deccan Service, which comprised some 125 pieces of silver parcel gilt, made in London in 1805 to 1807 by John Edward; it was presented to the Duke, when Major-General Sir Arthur Wellesley, by officers who had served in the division under his command in the Indian campaigns of 1803. This case also contains a silver centre-piece made by Paul Storr (1771-1844) in 1811 to 1812 and presented to the Duke by the Field Officers of the Peninsular Army. The smaller projecting case contains another Storr centre-piece, dated 1810 to 1811 and presented by the General Officers of the Peninsular Army, and the silver Waterloo Vase of 1824 to 1825, designed by Thomas Stothard and presented to the Duke in 1826 by a group of noblemen and gentlemen, to commemorate the Battle of Waterloo.

Figure of Britannia from the Prussian Service, Berlin porcelain, about 1819

Detail of an ice-bucket from the Prussian Service, Berlin porcelain, about 1819

By the window are watercolours by Thomas Shotter Boys (1803-1874) showing the original Plate and China Room in 1852 and 1853. The case (1981) in the former window bay to the South contains in its lower part a selection of the Duke's Campaign Plate, an assemblage of relatively simple functional silver, English, French, Spanish and Portuguese. Its upper part is devoted mainly to the foreign orders conferred on the Duke by the grateful rulers of Europe from 1811 onwards. Its contents are as follows (left to right):

Military Order of Willem (Netherlands: conferred in 1815), Order of St Januarius (The Two Sicilies: conferred in 1817), Order of the St Esprit

Snuff box, St Petersburg, presented by the Emperor Alexander I of Russia in about 1820

Snuff box, London, 1812, presented with the Freedom of the Borough of Plymouth in 1812

Standard candelabrum made by
Benjamin Smith about 1816

(France: conferred in 1815), Grand Cross of the Order of Fidelity (Baden: conferred in 1815), Royal Military Order of Maximilian Joseph (Bavaria: conferred in 1815), Order of the Elephant (Denmark: conferred in 1815), Order of St Alexander Nevsky (Russia: conferred in 1816), Royal Military Order of St Hermenegildo (Spain: conferred in 1816), Royal Military Order of St Ferdinand (Spain: conferred in 1812), Order of the Green Crown (Saxony: conferred in 1815), Imperial Military Order of Maria Theresa (Austria: conferred in 1814), Royal Military Order of St Ferdinand and of Merit (The Two Sicilies: conferred in 1817), Imperial Military Order of St George (Russia: conferred in 1814), Royal Hanoverian Guelphic Order (Hanover: conferred in 1816), Order of the Black Eagle (Prussia: conferred in 1815), Order of St Andrew (Russia: conferred in 1815), Supreme Order of the Annunziata (Savoy: conferred in 1815), Order of the Red Eagle of Brandenburg (Prussia: conferred in 1815), Order of the Lion (Baden: conferred in 1815), Order of the Crown (Württemberg: conferred in 1815), Royal Military Order of the Sword (Sweden: conferred in 1814), English Peninsular Medal, inscribed SALAMANCA, Spanish medal commemorating the restoration of the Spanish monarchy in 1812, Spanish medal commemorating the Battle of Vitoria, 1813, English Peninsular

Order of the Golden Fleece, Spain,
conferred in 1812

Medal, inscribed Rolica, Vimieiro, Talavera, 1808-9, Order of the Lion d'Or of Hesse Cassel (Hesse Cassel: conferred in 1815), leather box for the gold box presented by King Maximilian I of Bavaria, Order of the Golden Fleece (Spain: conferred in 1812).

The case in the northern window bay contains in its lower part a pair of the Duke's pistols, lent by the present Duke of Wellington, together with telescopes, a dressing case, a powder horn and other mementos of the First Duke. Its upper part contains the Duke's English orders, comprising the Order of the Garter (collar, garter and small George: conferred March 4th 1813) and the Order of the Bath (collar: conferred September 1804), together with a Collar of Honour designed by Sir George Nayler and presented by George IV in 1825. There are also the keys of Ciudad Rodrigo and Pamplona, and orders written at Waterloo on prepared slips of vellum, along with the Duke's Peninsular Medal, the only example with all nine clasps, and his own Waterloo Medal, as given to all present at the battle.

Above the fireplace is a frame (1981) containing ten of the Duke's batons — British (three, one presented by the Prince Regent in 1813), Portuguese

The Royal Hanoverian Guelphic Order,
Hanover, conferred in 1816

Right: Baton of Field Marshal in the British Army, made by Rundell, Bridge and Rundell and presented by George IV to Wellington in 1821

(1809), Hanoverian (1844), Dutch, Spanish (1808), Austrian (1818), and Prussian, together with his staff as High Constable of England (1837 to 1838). Three further wall frames (1981) contain respectively thirteen gold and silver snuff-boxes presented by English and Irish cities and Allied sovereigns, and swords and daggers. The most notable among the latter are, on the left, Napoleon's court sword, taken from his carriage after the Battle of Waterloo and later acquired by the Duke, the Duke's own Waterloo sword, a plain example by Napoleon's goldsmith, Biennais, and, on the right, Tippoo Sahib's sword and dagger, said to have been taken from his body after the capture of Seringapatam in 1799. Above these cases and at the opposite end of the room are more of the French Departmental flags already noted in the Hall.

Baton of Field Marshal of Hanover, by W. Lameyer of Hanover, 1844

Hilt of Napoleon's court sword, by Martin Guillaume Biennais, about 1809

The Basement

A small display area in the Basement contains the Wellington Museum Reference Collection, a group of miscellaneous articles connected with Apsley House or the Duke of Wellington, and acquired subsequent to the gift of Apsley House in 1947. Also shown is an exhibition of political cartoons of the First Duke, on loan from the Victoria and Albert Museum. The present arrangement of the Basement is, in the main, a consequence of the Hyde Park road improvement scheme of 1961 to 1962. It is hoped (1984) that a further rearrangement of the Basement may incorporate a gallery to display the Reference Collection to better advantage, together with some of the Wellington relics at present in the Inner Hall and Hall, and to include a documentation of the recent restoration of Apsley House.

The objects now on view include a Panorama of Wellington's Funeral, engraved by Henry Alken and George Augustus Sala, published in 1853, a programme of the Funeral printed on silk, and a coloured lithograph by T. Picken of the Funeral Procession passing Apsley House, after the original painting by Sir Lewis Hague (1806-1885). In a case are various relics and mementos of the Duke, some presented by the Royal United Services Institution, and others, collected by the boot blacking firm, John Oakley & Sons (1833-1964), given by Mr C.A. Oakley. Exhibits are from time to time added to this collection, including, for instance, a silk rosette worn at the Duke's Funeral, given in 1983.

Panorama of Wellington's Funeral, engraved by Henry Alken and George Augustus Sala, 1853; detail with the Prince Consort's coach

The parts of the Basement not on view, and now altered and adapted for staff use, formerly included the Servants' Hall and the Kitchen.

The Piccadilly Drawing Room

The Piccadilly Drawing Room was designed in 1774 by Robert Adam, whose frieze, doors, ceiling ornament, and marble chimney piece remain, the latter inspired by an engraving by G.B.Piranesi (1720-1778). In 1828 Benjamin Dean Wyatt transformed the room into his 'First Drawing Room', sweeping away the columns and niches in Adam's apse, and introducing the present white and gold colour scheme, restored in 1980. The curtains and wall-hangings are copies of the original 'Yellow Silk Tabaret', the carpet is also a copy of the original, and mirrors have been reintroduced in the pilasters of the apse. The mirror above the chimney piece was not here in 1854, but was present in 1857; it follows a Wyatt design and may well be original to the room. The magnificent chandelier was here in 1854, as were the armchairs, kindly lent by the present Duke of Wellington. In 1854 there was also 'a couch, a corner ottoman, a square ottoman . . . 12 Italian chairs with cane & willow seats . . . a pedestal table, a marble-topped centre table, a sofa-table, 2 card tables, a bookcase with marble top and an Octagon Pianoforte' among other items.

A Musical Party, by Pieter de Hooch, about 1675

*Chelsea Pensioners reading the Waterloo
Despatch, by Sir David Wilkie, R.A.,
1822*

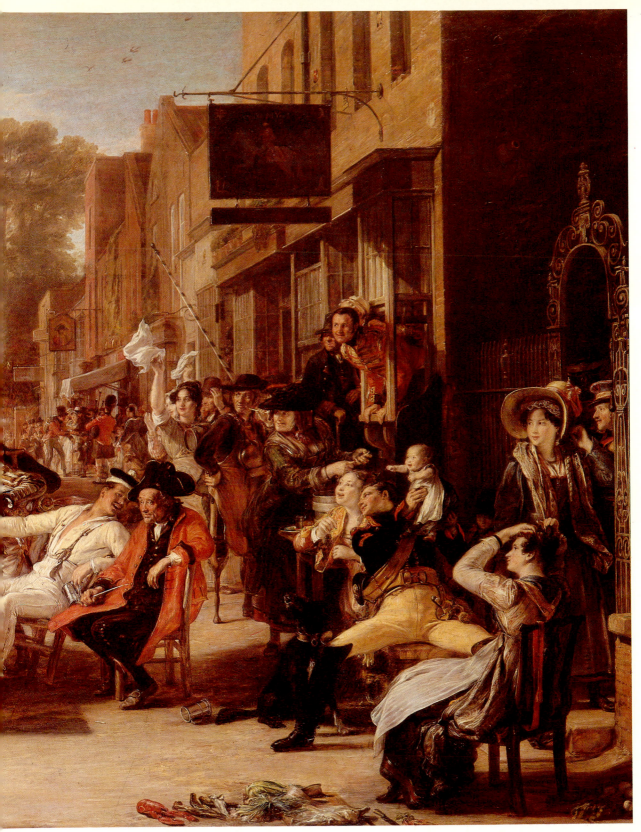

The paintings are as follows:

NORTH WALL (left to right)

† *Dutch shipping in a river.*
By Abraham Storck (1644-after 1704).
Signed *A. Storck.*

† *Landscape with classical ruins and figures.*
By Bartholomeus Breenbergh (1598/1600-1657).

Interior with a Cavalier drinking and a couple embracing.
By Willem van Mieris (1662-1747).

⋆ *Chelsea Pensioners reading the Waterloo despatch.*
By Sir David Wilkie, R.A. (1785-1841).
Signed *David Wilkie, 1822.* Commissioned by the Duke of Wellington
in 1816.

† *An Encampment.*
By Jacques François Joseph Swebach, called Fontaine (or Swebach-
Desfontaines) (1769-1823).
Signed *Swebach dit font* (aine) *1796.*

A Village Scene.
By Jan Victors (1620-about 1676).
Signed *Jan Victors Fect 1654.*

⋆ *The Greenwich Pensioners commemorating Trafalgar.*
By John Burnet, F.R.S. (1784-1868).
Signed *Jno. B/Oct.21/18* (sic).

A lady at her toilet.
By Caspar Netscher (1635/6-1684).
Signed *G. Netscher f.*

† *The river bank: landscape with figures and cattle.*
By Karel Du Jardin (1621/2-1678).
Signed (?) *K.D.*

† *Self-portrait of an unknown painter.*
Netherlandish School, 1596.

† *A Shipwreck.*
After Claude-Joseph Vernet (1714-1789).

† *Landscape with St Hubert and the stag.*
By Paul Bril (1554-1626).
Signed *PA-- BRIL.*

† *A Harvest Scene.*
By David Teniers the younger (1610-1690).
Signed *D Teniers F.*

EAST WALL (left to right)

† *Landscape with shepherds and a distant view of a castle.*
By David Teniers the younger (1610-1690).

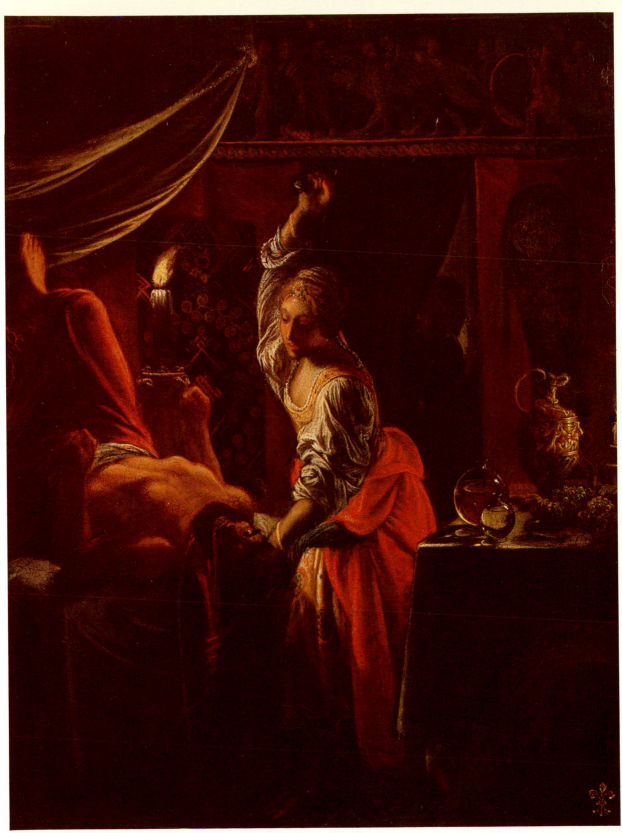

Judith slaying Holofernes, by
Adam Elsheimer, about 1603

† *A lime-kiln with figures.*
By David Teniers the younger (1610-1690).
Signed *D. TENIERS F.*

Landscape with travellers resting.
By Johannes Lingelbach (1622-1674).
Signed *LB* (monogram).

A village merrymaking at a country inn.
By David Teniers the younger (1610-1690).
Signed and dated *D. TENIERS. FIC. 1655.*

† *Landscape with two shepherds, cattle and ducks.*
By David Teniers the younger (1610-1690).
Signed *D. TENIERS F.*

† *Peasants playing bowls in front of an inn by a river.*
By David Teniers the younger (1610-1690).
Signed *D. TENIERS F.*

† *Judith slaying Holofernes.*
By Adam Elsheimer (1578-1610).
Bought from the estate of Rubens by Don Francisco de Rochas for
Philip IV of Spain.

† *The Holy Family with St Elizabeth and St John.*
After Sir Peter Paul Rubens (1577-1640).
17th century copy of a painting by Rubens in the Wallace Collection.

† *The Last Supper, with the institution of the Eucharist and Christ washing
the Disciples' feet.*
Workshop of Juan de Flandes (active 1496; died before 1519).
One of a series of 47 small panels recorded as having belonged to
Queen Isabella of Spain (died 1504).

SOUTH WALL

The rape of Proserpina.
By Jan van Huysum (1682-1749).

† *Camp scene with bugler and farrier's booth.*
By Philips Wouverman (1619-1668).
Signed *PHLS* (monogram) *W.*

* † *Card Players.*
Ascribed to Antiveduto Grammatica (about 1571-1626).
Formerly attributed to Caravaggio.

† *View of the artist's house "De Dry Toren" near Perck.*
By David Teniers the younger (1610-1690).
Signed *D.T.F.* (DT in monogram).

† *The angels guiding the shepherds to the Nativity.*
By Cornelis van Poelenburgh (about 1595-1667).
Signed *C.P.*

† *Landscape with figures crossing a brook.*
By Peeter Gysels (1621-1690/1).
Signed *p. gijsels.*

The intruder: a lady at her toilet, surprised by her lover.
By Pieter de Hooch (1629-after 1684).
Signed *P.D.Hooch.*
Bought by the Duke of Wellington before 1821 (not, as stated elsewhere, captured at Vittoria).

WEST WALL

A warship at anchor in a rough sea.
By Ludolf Bakhuizen (1631-1708).
Signed *L. BAKHUYZEN F.1685.*

The Milkwoman.
By Nicolaes Maes (1634-1693).
Signed *N. MAES.*

★ *The Smokers.*
By Adriaen Brouwer (1606?-1638).
Signed *Braw . . .*

A Flemish village festival.
By David Teniers the younger (1610-1690).
Signed *DAVID TENIERS FC 1639.*
Possibly from the Spanish royal collection; bought for the Duke in 1840.

★ *A musical party.*
By Pieter de Hooch (1629-after 1684).
Signed *P.D.HOO(GE).*

† *Landscape with deer.*
By François van Knibbergen (1597-after 1665).
Signed *F. KNIBBERGEN.*

The Eavesdropper.
By Nicolaes Maes (1634-1693).
Signed *N. MAES. P.*

The physician's visit.
By Jan Steen (1625/6-1679).
Signed *J. Steen.*

The Portico Drawing Room

The Portico Drawing Room originally faced Hyde Park to the West. Robert Adam designed the smaller doors and door-cases, the chimney piece, and the decoration of the ceiling whose frieze incorporates stags suggested by those supporting the Bathurst coat-of-arms. Benjamin Dean Wyatt created the present windows in the south wall under his portico when those to the West had to be closed to allow the addition of the Waterloo Gallery. This is entered through a new door by Wyatt, detailed to match those by Adam, but on a much grander scale. Wyatt replaced the predominantly green Adam colour scheme on walls and ceiling with a white and gold scheme similar to that in the Piccadilly Drawing Room. He also designed the mirror frames and the two side-tables. The Wyatt scheme was restored in 1978, when the curtains were reconstructed and a copy of the original carpet was supplied.

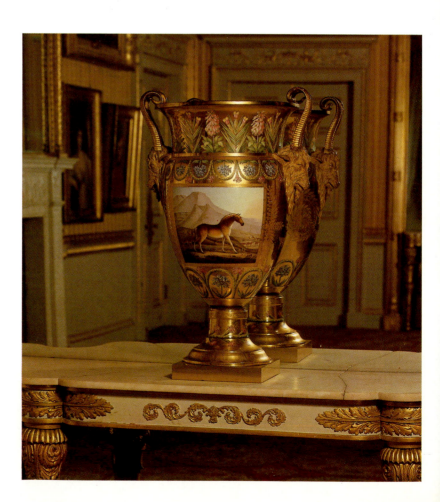

Vase painted with a quagga, Sèvres porcelain, 1814

42

In the 1854 Inventory the Portico Drawing Room was called the 'Large Drawing Room'; its contents included, in addition to the existing side-tables, four more side-tables, a circular and an octagonal pedestal table, two large sofas, seven elbow chairs and twelve 'Italian' chairs. The two great Sèvres porcelain vases on the side tables have always been in the room. Made in 1814, they are painted with, respectively, a quagga and a gnu, animals derived at second hand from aquatints illustrating Samuel Daniell's *African Scenery and Animals,* 1804.

The paintings are as follows:

WEST WALL (left to right)

* *William Pitt, M.P.* (1759-1806).
  By John Hoppner, R.A. (1758-1810).
  Prime Minister 1783-1801 and 1804-1806.

* *The illicit Highland whisky still.*
  By Sir Edwin Landseer, R.A. (1802-1873).
  Commissioned by the Duke.

* *Copy of Raphael's "Madonna with the fish".*
  By Féréol Bonnemaison (active 1796; died 1827).
  The frame is a modern copy of the original frame of the Bonnemaison 'Holy Family' (opposite).
  Given by the Duke of Wellington in 1980.

* *Marshal Nicolas Jean de Dieu Soult, Duc de Dalmatie* (1769-1852).
  By George Peter Alexander Healy (1808-1894).
  Served under Napoleon in the Peninsular War and at Waterloo.

* *Spencer Perceval* (1762-1812).
  By George Francis Joseph, A.R.A. (1764-1846).
  Prime Minister 1809 to 1818, when assassinated.

* *Copy of Raphael's "Christ carrying the Cross".*
  By Féréol Bonnemaison (active 1796; died 1827).
  The frame is a modern copy of the original frame of the Bonnemaison 'Holy Family' (opposite).
  Given by the Duke of Wellington in 1980.

NORTH WALL

* *Frederick William, Duke of Brunswick* (1771-1815).
  German School, about 1810-15.
  Brother of Queen Caroline; fought with the British Army in the Peninsular War; killed fighting Napoleon at Quatre Bras.

* *The Rt. Hon. Charles Arbuthnot, M.P.* (1767-1850).
  By Spiridone Gambardella (?1815-1886).
  Dated (on the back) 1849.
  Diplomat and politician.

Chimneypiece of the Portico Drawing Room, designed by Robert Adam, about 1775

'Chimney Piece for the 2d. Drawing room at Apsley House', by Robert Adam, about 1775. Sir John Soane's Museum

EAST WALL

* *Pope Pius VII* (1742-1823).
  By Robert Lefèvre (1755-1830).
  Signed *Robert Lefèvre ft. 1805 à Paris.*

* *Copy of Raphael's "Holy Family", called "La Perla".*
  By Féréol Bonnemaison (active 1796; died 1827).
  Given by the Duke of Wellington in 1980.

* *Napoleon Bonaparte* (1769-1821) as First Consul.
  By Laurent Dabos (1761-1835).

  Pauline Bonaparte, Princess Borghese (1780-1825).
  By Robert Lefèvre (1755-1830).
  Signed *Robert Lefèvre ft. 1806.*
  Sister of Napoleon; married, first, General Leclerc, later Prince Borghese.

* *Copy of Raphael's "Visitation, with the baptism in the distance".*
  By Féréol Bonnemaison (active 1796; died 1827).
  The frame is a modern copy of the original frame of the Bonnemaison 'Holy Family' (left of fireplace).

* *The Empress Josephine* (1763-1814).
  By Robert Lefèvre (1755-1830).
  Signed *Robert Lefèvre/ft. 1806.*

  Napoleon Bonaparte (1769-1821).
  After Baron François-Pascal-Simon Gérard (1770-1837).

* *Napoleon in the prison of Nice in 1794.*
  By Edward Matthew Ward, R.A. (1816-1879).
  Signed *EMW 1841.*

The Madonna del Pesce; copy by Féréol Bonnemaison after Raphael, about 1817

Chimney Piece for the 2.d Drawing room at Apsley House

45

The Waterloo Gallery

The Waterloo Gallery was designed by Benjamin Dean Wyatt in 1828 for the display of the Duke of Wellington's magnificent collection of paintings, many captured at the Battle of Vitoria in 1813 and subsequently presented to the Duke by King Ferdinand VII of Spain. From 1830 to 1852 the annual Waterloo Banquets were held here; that of 1836 is shown in a print after William Salter, R.A. (1804-1875), displayed on an easel. The Gallery, 90 feet (27.43 metres) long, is in Wyatt's 'Louis XIV' style; the windows are fitted with sliding mirrors which transform it, at night, into an evocation of Louis XIV's Galerie des Glaces at Versailles. The white and gold ceiling incorporates the badge and collar of the Order of the Garter, the Duke's crest, and his coat-of-arms. His friend, Mrs Arbuthnot, claimed to have assisted Wyatt on the design of such ornaments as the gilt cornices above doors and windows. The plasterwork was by the firm of Bernasconi, the other ornaments, of 'paste composition' on a wood base, by George Jackson & Sons. Wyatt also designed the three rococo style chimney pieces, executed in a yellow Siena marble which echoes the gold so prominent in the rest of the Gallery's decorations, and the elaborate parquetry border to the floor.

The Gallery was even more gold under the First Duke because, against the advice of Mrs Arbuthnot and Wyatt, he chose yellow silk damask hangings for the walls. The Second Duke changed this to the present red, but it is hoped (1984) to revert to the First Duke's colour, when the paintings will be hung, as in his day, from gilt chains. The furniture comprises a set of English gilt seat furniture, which was probably supplied in about 1760 to the Duke's country house, Stratfield Saye, and which is listed in the Gallery in the 1854 Inventory. There are also two ottomans for public use (1982). The Gallery also contains two great candelabra of grey Siberian porphyry given to the First Duke by the Emperor Nicholas I of Russia, and two vases of Swedish porphyry, on loan from the present Duke, which were presented by King Charles John XIV of Sweden (Marshal Bernadotte); the latter support porcelain candelabra from the Prussian Service (see p.18). The chandelier, English about 1830, has always been at Apsley House, although not always in this room. The carpet (1978) is a copy of the original, as shown in Salter's painting of 1836.

The hanging of the paintings, revised in 1980, reflects the original scheme as recorded in the watercolour by Joseph Nash illustrated here, and in other visual or documentary records. However the First Duke is said to have had about 130 paintings in the Gallery, as opposed to the 70 now present, and his top tier has been necessarily omitted. The positions of the three large paintings above the chimney pieces, the Van Dyck of King Charles I, the Moro of Queen Mary Tudor ('Bloody Mary', as the First Duke called her), and the Hans von Aachen of the Emperor Rudolf II ('Rodolph of

Hapsburgh'), had already been decided before the Gallery was built. They have elaborate frames designed by Wyatt and made by Thomas Temple & Son. By contrast the Goya equestrian portrait of the Duke was disliked by its subject and kept by him in store at Stratfield Saye.

The paintings are as follows:

SOUTH WALL

★   *A man of rank embarking at Amsterdam.*
By Ludolf Bakhuizen (1631-1708).
Signed *L. Bakhuyzen F.1685.*

★   *The Egg Dance: peasants merrymaking in an inn.*
By Jan Steen (1625/6-1679).

★   *The courtyard of an inn with a game of shuffleboard.*
By Adriaen van Ostade (1610-1685).
Signed *A v Ostade 1677.*
Formerly in the collection of the Duc de Choiseul.

★   *The Emperor Rudolf II* (1552-1612).
By Hans von Aachen (1552-1615).

†   *River scene with boats and figures.*
By Jan Brueghel I (1568-1625).
Signed *BRVEGHEL 16(?06).*

† *Entering the Ark.*
By Jan Brueghel I (1568-1625).
Signed *BRVEGHEL 1615.*

★ † *Large ships and boats in a calm.*
By Willem van de Velde the younger (1633-1707).
Signed *WVV.*

† *Venus and Adonis.*
Ascribed to Carlo Cignani (1628-1719).

★ *A Wedding Party.*
By Jan Steen (1625/6-1679).
Signed *J. Steen 1667.*

WEST WALL

† *Virgin and Child.*
Italian School, about 1600.

† *The Virgin and Child with St Carlo Borromeo.*
Ascribed to Francesco Trevisani (1656-1746).

† *The Expulsion from Paradise.*
By Giuseppe Cesari, called Il Cavaliere d'Arpino (1568-1640).

† *Saint Catherine of Alexandria.*
By Claudio Coello (1642-1693).
Inscribed *CLAUD. COELL. FA. PICT. REG. ANNO 1683.*

★ † *The departure of a hawking party.*
By Philips Wouverman (1619-1668).
Signed *P.H.* (monogram) *W.*

The Agony in the Garden, by Antonio Allegri, called Correggio, about 1525

† *The Holy Family with the Infant St John.*
By a follower of Bernardino Luini (active 1512; died 1532).

Architectural fantasy, with the Old Town Hall, Amsterdam.
By Jan van der Heyden (1637-1712).
Signed *V. Heyde f.*

Landscape with the Flight into Egypt.
Traditionally ascribed to Sir Joshua Reynolds, P.R.A. (1723-1792).

★ † *The Annunciation.*
By Marcello Venusti (1512/15-1579).

★ † *An unknown lady, called "Titian's mistress".*
By a follower of Titian (Tiziano Vercellio) (about 1482-1576).

★ † *La Carcasse: a witch being drawn on the skeleton of a monster.*
Traditionally ascribed to Jusepe de Ribera, called Lo Spagnoletto (1591-1652).

Portrait of a man.
Italian School.

Queen Mary Tudor, after Antonio Moro;
the frame designed by Benjamin Dean
Wyatt and made by Thomas Temple &
Son, about 1830

51

Saint Rosalie, by Sir Anthony Van Dyck, 1624

Ana Dorotea, daughter of Rudolf II, by Sir Peter Paul Rubens, 1628

Head of St Joseph.
By Guido Reni (1575-1642).
From the Spanish Royal Collection; presented to the Duke by the Intendant of Segovia in 1812.

† *Head of an old man.*
By Sir Peter Paul Rubens (1577-1640).

A sainted nun.
Italian School, 16th century.
From the Spanish Royal Collection; presented to the Duke by the Intendant of Segovia in 1812.

★ *The Château of Goudestein, on the River Vecht, near Maarsen.*
By Jan van der Heyden (1637-1712).
Signed *J V D Heyde/1674.*

★† *Pastoral landscape with the Ponte Molle, Rome.*
Ascribed to Claude Gellée, called Le Lorrain (1600-1682).

† *The Virgin and Child with St Elizabeth and the infant St John.*
By Giovanni Battista Salvi, called Sassoferrato (1609-1685).

★† *The return from the chase.*
By Philips Wouverman (1619-1668).
Signed *PH* (monogram) *W.*

NORTH WALL

An unknown lady.
Venetian School, 16th century.

★ *Mars as a warrior.*
By Guercino (1591-1666).

★† *The Mystic Marriage of St Catherine.*
After Parmigianino (1503-1540).

★† *Virgin and Child.*
By Giovanni Battista Salvi, called Sassoferrato (1609-1685).

★ *Queen Mary I of England (1516-1558).*
After Anthonis Mor (Antonio Moro) (about 1519-1576/7).

† *Travellers on a country road, with cattle and pigs.*
By Jan Brueghel I (1568-1625).
Signed *BRVEGHEL. 1616.*

† *Road scene with travellers and cattle.*
By Jan Brueghel I (1568-1625).

† *Country road scene with figures: a man praying at a shrine.*
By Jan Brueghel I (1568-1625).

Doge Marcantonio Memmo (1536-1615).
Ascribed to Leandro Bassano (1557-1622).

Venus and Cupid.
By Guercino (1591-1666).

* *The Mystic Marriage of St Catherine.*
  By Giuseppe Cesari, called Il Cavaliere d'Arpino (1568-1640).

*† *The Agony in the Garden.*
  By Antonio Allegri, called Correggio (about 1494-1534).
  Praised by Vasari (1568); the Duke's favourite painting.

EAST WALL

* *The entry of Philip IV into Pamplona.*
  By Juan Bautista del Mazo (about 1612/16-1667).

† *River view: evening.*
  By Aert van der Neer (1603/04-1677).
  Signed *AV DN* (two monograms).

*† *Pope Innocent X.*
  Ascribed to Diego Velazquez (1599-1660).

*† *The Holy Family with the Infant St John.*
  By Anton Raphael Mengs (1728-1779).
  Signed *ANTONIUS. RAPHAEL. MENGS. SAX. FACEB.
  MDCCLXV.*

*† *Battle scene with classical colonnade.*
  By Salvator Rosa (1615-1773).
  Signed *SR* (monogram).

*† *Interior of a cowshed.*
  By David Teniers the younger (1610-1690).

*† *Two young men eating at a humble table.*
  By Diego Velazquez (1599-1660).

*† *A Spanish gentleman, probably José Nieto, Chamberlain to Queen
  Mariana of Austria, wife of Philip IV.*
  By Diego Velazquez (1559-1660).

† *Hercules wrestling with Achelous in the form of a bull.*
  After Sir Peter Paul Rubens (1577-1640).
  Companion piece to *Hercules and the Nemean lion* (to the right).

*† *The Infant Christ appearing to St Anthony of Padua.*
  By Anton Raphael Mengs (1728-1779).

* *Francisco Gomes de Quevedo y Villegas (1580-1645).*
  Studio of Diego Velazquez (1599-1660).

A Musician.
  By Cecco del Caravaggio (active c.1600-1620).
  Traditionally known as *The Conjuror.*

*† *The Waterseller of Seville.*
  By Diego Velazquez (1599-1660).
  The most famous of the *bodegones* painted by Velazquez in Seville in
  about 1620.

Hercules and the Nemean lion.
  After Sir Peter Paul Rubens (1577-1640).

Companion piece to *Hercules wrestling with Achelous in the form of a bull* (to the left).

★ *The Crucifixion, with the fall of the rebel angels.*
By Cornelius van Poelenburgh (about 1595-1667).
Signed *CP.*

★ *St James the Great.*
By Jusepe de Ribera, called Lo Spagnoletto (1591-1652).

★ *Charles I (1600-1649) on horseback with M. de St Antonie.*
After Sir Anthony van Dyck (1599-1641).
The original, painted for St James's Palace in 1633, now at Buckingham Palace.

★ *The Virgin and Child.*
After Raphael (1483-1520).
Copy, with variations, of his *Madonna della Sedia* in the Palazzo Pitti, Florence.

St Rosalie crowned with roses by two angels.
By Sir Anthony van Dyck (1599-1641).

★ *St Francis receiving the stigmata.*
By Bartolomé Esteban Murillo (1617-1682).

★ *Orpheus enchanting the animals.*
Ascribed to Alessandro Varotari, Il Padovanino (1588-1648).

An unknown man.
Ascribed to Bartoleme Esteban Murillo (1617-1682).

★ *The Virgin with the standing Child.*
Ascribed to Bernardino Luini (active 1512; died 1532).
A replica of Luini's *Virgin of the Columbine* in the Wallace Collection.

Ana Dorotea, Daughter of Rudolf II, a nun at the Convent of the Descalzas Reales, Madrid.
By Sir Peter Paul Rubens (1577-1640).

St John the Baptist.
By Jusepe de Ribera, called Lo Spagnoletto (1591-1652).
Signed *Jusepe de Ribera/espanol/F.1650.*

★ *The Colbert family.*
By Adam François van der Meulen (1632-1690).

French generals arriving before a town.
By Adam François van der Meulen (1632-1690).
Signed *F.V.MEULEN 1678.*

Louis XIV at a siege.
By Adam François van der Meulen (1632-1690).

★ *The Dissolute Household.*
By Jan Steen (1625/6-1679).
Signed *J.Steen.*

Equestrian portrait of the Duke of Wellington.
By Francisco de Goya (1746-1828).

The Yellow Drawing Room

The Yellow Drawing Room, called the Small Drawing Room in 1854 and the North West Drawing Room in 1857, occupies the site of Robert Adam's Third Drawing Room; only his doorcases to the Portico Drawing Room remain. The two large doorcases were designed by Benjamin Dean Wyatt, together with the white marble chimney piece and the cornice with its paired gilt consoles. The chandelier is English, about 1830. The two tables, with red porphyry tops supported on lion monopodia, are French about 1810. That by the window supports a delicate marble bust by Antonio Canova (1757-1822) of a dancer. This was given by Canova to Wellington in 1817, in recompense for his efforts to restore to Rome art treasures taken by the French to Paris. In 1854 the room also contained a Grecian couch, ten chairs, a writing-table and two other tables, a small cabinet and five stands. It is hoped (1984) to restore carpet and curtains.

The paintings are as follows:

WEST WALL

St Paul preaching at Athens.
By Giovanni Paolo Panini (or Pannini) (1691/2-1765?).
Signed *I.P.P. 1737.*
Companion piece to St Paul at Malta.

Passage of the Danube by Napoleon, by J.F.J. Swebach, 1810

Landscape with peasants driving cattle: evening.
David Teniers the younger (1610-1690).
Signed *D. TENIERS FEC.*

Isaac blessing Jacob (Genesis XXVII, 18-29).
By Bartolemé Esteban Murillo (1617-1682).

The Death of Cleopatra.
By Johann Georg Platzer (1704-1761).

A Cavalier with a grey horse.
By Abraham van Calraet (1642-1722).
Signed *AC.*

Shepherd and cattle.
By Philipp Peter Ross, called Rosa da Tivoli (1655/7-1706).

A festival in the Piazza di Spagna, Rome, 1727.
By Giovanni Paolo Panini (or Pannini) (1691/2-1765?).
Signed: *I.P. Panini Placentus Romae 1727.*

A musical party.
By Willem Cornelisz Duyster (c. 1599-1625).
Signed *W.C.D.A. 1634.*

Two wings of a triptych: The Virgin and the Angel of the Annunciation.
By Marcellus Coffermans (active 1549-1578).

Boys with a trapped bird.
By Aert van der Neer (1603/4-1677).
Signed *E. Van der Neer.*

† *Landscape with bleaching grounds.*
By a follower of Jacob van Ruisdael (1628/9-1682).
Indistinctly signed (?) *Gi . . . or Ri . . . .*
Traditionally attributed to Jan Vermeer van Haarlem (1628-1691).

St Paul at Malta, grasping the viper.
By Giovanni Paolo Panini (or Pannini) (1691/2-1765?).
Signed *I.P.P. 1735.*
Companion piece to *St Paul at Athens.*

Passage of the Danube by Napoleon before the Battle of Wagram.
By Jacques François Joseph Swebach, called Fontaine (or Swebach-Desfontaines) (1769-1823).

† *An encampment with soldiers playing cards.*
By Lambert de Hondt (d. before 1665).
Signed *L.D. Hondt. F.*

Anthony and Cleopatra at the Battle of Actium.
By Johann Georg Platzer (1704-1761).

SOUTH WALL

Samson and Delilah (Judges XVI, 19).
By Luca Giordano (1634-1705).

King William IV, by Sir David Wilkie,
R.A., 1833

Sunset: view over a bay with figures.
By Claude-Joseph Vernet (1714-1789).
Painted in 1742.

Athenian girls drawing lots to determine which seven among them shall be sent to Crete for sacrifice to the Minotaur.
By Jean Francois-Pierre Peyron (1744-1814).

A Flemish Village: the river landing stage.
By Peeter Gysels (1621-1690/1).
Signed *p.gÿsels.* (sic)

A Flemish Village with river view.
By Peeter Gysels (1621-1690/1).
Signed *Petrus Geysels.*

EAST WALL

Joseph Bonaparte, King of Spain (1768-1844).
By Robert Lefèvre (1755-1830).
Eldest brother of Napoleon. Defeated by Wellington at the Battle of Vittoria, 1813.

The Empress Josephine (1763-1814).
By Robert Lefèvre (1755-1830).
Signed *Robert Lefèvre/ft. 1806.*

★ *Alexander I, Emperor of Russia* (1777-1825).
By George Dawe, R.A. (1781-1829).
Signed *Geo. Dawe RA 1825 pinxt.*

★ *King William IV* (1765-1837).
By Sir David Wilkie, R.A. (1785-1841).
Signed *David Wilkie f. Brighton 1833.*
Presented to the Duke of Wellington by William IV in 1833.

Joseph Bonaparte, King of Spain (1768-1844).
By Baron François Pascal-Simon Gérard (1770-1837).
Signed *F. Gérard.*
Eldest brother of Napoleon. Defeated by Wellington at Battle of Vittoria, 1813.

Frederick Augustus Duke of York and Albany, K.G. (1763-1827).
By Henry Wyatt (1794-1840).
Commanded British forces in Flanders 1793-5; appointed Commander-in-Chief of the army 1798.

The Duke of Wellington looking at a bust of Napoleon.
By Charles Robert Leslie, R.A. (1794-1859).

★ *Richard, Marquess Wellesley, K.C.* (1760-1842).
By C. Fortescue Bates after Sir Martin Archer Shee (1769-1850).
Lent by His Grace the Duke of Wellington.

The Striped Drawing Room

The Striped Drawing Room, called by the name in 1854 and the North Drawing Room adjoining Dining Room in 1857, was created by Benjamin Dean Wyatt in about 1828 from Robert Adam's bedroom and Etruscan dressing-room of the 1770s. The ceiling, cornice, frieze and chimney piece were all designed by Wyatt. The English cut-glass chandelier dates from about 1830. The two ormolu and malachite side tables and the malachite centre table were given to the Duke of Wellington by Emperor Nicholas of Russia. Above the chimney piece hangs a silk French tricolor standard lent by Her Majesty the Queen. A similar standard is presented to the Sovereign by the Dukes of Wellington on each anniversary of the Battle of Waterloo. They are kept in the Waterloo Chamber at Windsor Castle.

The Striped Drawing Room, watercolour by Thomas Shotter Boys, 1852

A watercolour of 1853 on display in the room shows it hung with what the 1854 Inventory calls 'rose coloured striped taboret', similar to that now

*The Battle of Waterloo, 1815, by Sir
William Allan, 1843*

present, the ottomans round the walls with upholstery and valances in the
same material, and the same carpet as elsewhere at Apsley House. It is
planned (1984) to restore the original form of the upholstery and the carpet.
In his 1853 *Apsley House and Walmer Castle* Richard Ford called this room
the 'Walhalla' and noted the presence of many portraits of the Duke's
'comrades of his arms'. There seems little doubt that the striped taboret and
ottomans were intended to reinforce this martial theme, producing the effect
of a striped military tent, an echo of a famous tent room in Napoleon's
apartment at Malmaison, designed by Percier and Fontaine. On the side
tables are busts of the Prime Ministers Spencer Perceval (1762-1812) and
William Pitt (1759-1806), both by Joseph Nollekens (1737-1823). In 1854 the
room also contained a central ottoman, a large sofa . . . a writing-table, a loo
table and an Ecarté table.

The paintings are as follows:—

WEST WALL

★ *Major-General Sir Henry Willoughby Rooke, C.B., K.C.H. (1782-1869).*
By John Hoppner, R.A. (1758-1810).
Assistant Adjutant General at Quatre Bras and Waterloo.

★ *General Rowland Hill, Viscount Hill, G.C.B., G.C.H. (1772-1842).*
By Jan Willem Pieneman (1779-1853).
Signed *JWP/Apsly (sic) House/London/1821*.
Served in the Peninsular War and at Waterloo; in 1828 appointed
Commander-in-Chief of the army.

* *General Lord Edward Somerset, K.C.B.* (1776-1842).
By Jan Willem Pieneman (1779-1853).
Signed *JWP/Apsly House/London/1821*.
Served in the Peninsular War; commanded the household brigade of cavalry at Waterloo.

* *Lt. General Sir Thomas Picton, G.C.B.* (1758-1815).
By Sir William Beechey, R.A. (1753-1839).
Served in the Peninsular War and at Waterloo, where he was killed.

* *The Battle of Waterloo.*
By Sir William Allan (1782-1850).
Signed *William Allan Pinxt, 1843*.
This shows the battle from the French side, at 7.30 p.m. on 18 June 1815. It represents "the last desparate effort of Napoleon (seen on the right) to force the left centre of the allied army and turn their position". In the centre are the advancing battalions of the Imperial Guard, led by Marshall Ney, which are being successfully attacked on three sides by the British. The Duke of Wellington can be seen on the rising ground to the left. He is said to have commented of this painting, 'Good — very good; not too much smoke'.

SOUTH WALL

* *General Miguel Ricardo de Alava* (1771-1843).
By Jan Willem Pieneman (1779-1853).
Signed *JWP/Apsly House/London/1821*.
Spanish soldier and diplomat; served under the Duke in the Peninsular War and at Waterloo.

Lieut.-Colonel William Thornhill (died 1850).
By Jan Willem Pieneman (1779-1853).
Signed *JWP/Apsly House/London/1821*.
Served in the Peninsular War and at Waterloo.

* *Thomas Graham, Lord Lynedoch, G.C.B., G.C.M.G.* (1748-1843).
By Sir Thomas Lawrence, P.R.A. (1769-1830).
Served in the Peninsular War.

Major-General Sir Frederick Cavendish Ponsonby, K.C.B. (1783-1837) and *Major-General Sir Colin Campbell, K.C.B., K.C.H.* (1776-1847) (on the left).
By Jan Willem Pieneman (1779-1853).
Signed *JWP/Apsly House/London/1821*.
Both officers served in the Peninsular War and at Waterloo.

* *Field Marshal Sir John Colborne, 1st Baron Seaton, G.C.B., G.C.H.* (1778-1863).
By Jan Willem Pieneman (1779-1853).
Signed *JWP/Apsly House/London/1821*.
Served in the Peninsular War; played a major part in the defeat of Napoleon's Old Guard at Waterloo.

General Sir George Cooke, K.C.B. (1768-1837).
By Jan Willem Pieneman (1779-1853).
Signed *JWP/Apsly House/London/1821*.
Served in the Peninsular War, at Quatre Bras and Waterloo.

The First Marquess of Anglesey, K.G., by
Sir Thomas Lawrence, P.R.A., 1818

★ *Major-General John Fremantle, C.B.* (died 1845).
By Jan Willem Pieneman (1779-1853).
Signed *JWP/Apsly House/London/1821*.
Served in the Peninsular War; was A.D.C. to Wellington at Waterloo.

★ *Lt.-General Sir Edward Barnes, G.C.B.* (1776-1838).
By George Dawe, R.A. (1781-1829).
Served in the Peninsular War and at Waterloo.

★ *William Carr, Viscount Beresford, G.C.B.* (1768-1854).
By Sir Thomas Lawrence, P.R.A. (1769-1830).
Served in the Peninsular War as commander of the Portuguese army;
later made a general and Master of the Ordnance.

★ *Field Marshal Lord Fitzroy James Henry Somerset, 1st Baron Raglan,*
G.C.B. (1788-1855).
By Jan Willem Pieneman (1779-1853).
Signed *JWP/Apsly House/London/1821*.
Served in the Peninsular War and at Waterloo; commanded the British
troops in the Crimea.

Field Marshal Henry William Paget, 1st Marquess of Anglesey, K.G.
(1768-1854).
By Jan Willem Pieneman (1779-1853).
Signed *JWP/Apsly House/London/1821*.
Served at Waterloo; later, Master General of the Ordnance and Lord
Lieutenant of Ireland.

EAST WALL

Arthur Wellesley, 1st Duke of Wellington (1769-1852).
By Sir Thomas Lawrence, P.R.A. (1769-1830).
Painted about 1815.

★ *Henry William Paget, 1st Marquess of Anglesey, K.G.* (1768-1854).
By Sir Thomas Lawrence, P.R.A. (1769-1830).
Served at Waterloo; later, Master General of the Ordnance and Lord
Lieutenant of Ireland.

NORTH WALL

★ *Lieut.-General Sir John Elley, K.C.B., K.C.H.* (died 1839).
By Jan Willem Pieneman (1779-1853).
Signed *JWP/Apsly House/London/1821*.
Served in the Peninsular War and at Waterloo.

General Sir James Shaw Kennedy, K.C.B. (1788-1865).
By Jan Willem Pieneman (1779-1853).
Signed *JWP/Apsly House/London/1821*.
Served in the Peninsular War and at Quatre Bras and Waterloo.

★ *General Sir Colin Halkett, G.C.B., G.C.H.* (1774-1856).
By Jan Willem Pieneman (1779-1853).
Signed *JWP/Apsly House/London/1821*.
Served in the Peninsular War and at Waterloo.

The Dining Room

The Dining Room was created by Benjamin Dean Wyatt in 1819.
Approached through a mirrored lobby (called the 'Octagon Passage' by
Wyatt in 1829), it has a masculine classical interior with buff walls, oak
doors, dado, sideboard, plate-warmer and chairs, and an oak-grained cornice
supported by massive Corinthian pilasters of Siena scagliola, with gilt bases
and capitals. The sideboard, probably supplied by Messrs. Dowbiggin,
incorporates a central support for the Wellington Shield (see p.17), which
was displayed here at Waterloo Banquets up to 1829. The present carpet
and red wool curtains were supplied in 1982. The cut-glass chandelier is
English, about 1830.

On the mahogany table stands the 26 feet (7.92 metres) long centrepiece of
the Portuguese Service. The complete Service, of silver and silver-gilt,
originally consisted of some thousand pieces. It was presented to the Duke
of Wellington in 1816 by the Portuguese Council of Regency. Designed by

The Dining Room, watercolour by
Thomas Shotter Boys, 1852

The Dining Room

King George IV, by Sir David Wilkie, R.A., 1830

D.A. de Sequeira (1768-1857) and made in the Military Arsenal at Lisbon from 1812 to 1816, it is the single great monument of Portuguese neo-classical silver. The central ornament of the centrepiece shows the Four Continents paying tribute to the united armies of Britain, Portugal and Spain. The dancing figures which surround the plateau were originally linked by garlands of silk flowers.

The paintings, since 1982 all in their original positions, are as follows:

WEST WALL

* *Louis XVIII, King of France* (1755-1824).
  By Baron François-Pascal-Simon Gérard (1770-1837).
  Presented to the Duke of Wellington by Charles X in 1826.

* *Francis II, Emperor of Austria* (1768-1835).
  By Anton Einsle (1801-1871).
  Signed *Anton Einsle K.K.* (Kaiserlich Koniglicher) *Hofmaker in Wien 1841.*
  Given to the Duke of Wellington by Ferdinand, Emperor of Austria, in 1842.

EAST WALL

* *Frederick William III, King of Prussia* (1770-1840).
  By Wilhelm Herbig (1787-1861).
  Signed *Herbig pint.*
  Given to the Duke of Wellington by the King of Prussia in 1818.

* *King George IV* (1762-1830).
  By Sir David Wilkie, R.A. (1785-1841).
  Signed *David Wilkie 1830.*
  The Highland dress was worn by the King on his visit to Edinburgh in 1822.

* *Alexander I, Emperor of Russia* (1777-1825).
  By Baron François-Pascal-Simon Gérard (1770-1837).
  Presented to the Duke of Wellington by Alexander I of Russia in 1817.

SOUTH WALL

* *William I, King of Holland* (1772-1843).
  By François Joseph Navez (1787-1869).
  Signed *F.J. Navez, 1823.*
  Presented to the Duke of Wellington by William I of Holland in 1824.

The central feature of the centrepiece of the Portuguese Service, silver parcel gilt, Lisbon, about 1816

The Passage

Showcase containing pieces from the Portuguese Service (Lisbon, about 1816) and supporting a porcelain vase from the Austrian Service (Vienna, about 1815), with a portrait of the Emperor Francis I

Fruit bowl and stand, silver-gilt, from the Ambassador Service, by Paul Storr, London, 1810-11

The Passage, so called from at least 1829 onwards, was originally a service passage for the Dining Room, fitted with fold-down trays. As a consequence of the Hyde Park road scheme of 1961 to 1962 three new windows were introduced. However in 1981 these were filled by built-in showcases with fanlights above, and the original proportions of the Passage were restored. Also in 1981 the Passage was oak-grained with gilt and painted decorations on its vaulted ceiling, reproducing the original scheme; the carpet was laid at the same time. On the showcases are five massive Viennese porcelain vases bearing the names of protagonists at the Congress of Vienna in 1815, King George IV of England (Prince Regent in 1815), Emperor Francis I of Austria, King Frederick I of Prussia, Viscount Castlereagh, and Prince von Blücher.

Tureen from the Ambassador Service, about 1814

Déjeuner, Dihl and Guérard factory, Paris, about 1810

The contents of the showcases are as follows:

CASE I (East side)

A selection from the Ambassador Service, which consists of some 650 pieces of silver and silver-gilt plate used by the Duke of Wellington when he was British Ambassador to the Court of France in 1814. Below are two Déjeuner Sets, one of Sèvres porcelain, painted by Langlacé in 1813, awarded a prize in 1815, and presented to the Duke by King Louis XVIII of France, the other, of porcelain made at the Dihl and Guérard factory in Paris in about 1810, taken from the coach of Joseph Bonaparte after the Battle of Vittoria in 1813.

CASE II (East side)

A selection from the Portuguese Service (see p.32).

CASE III (East side)

The majority of a set of 48 *gros bleu* porcelain dessert plates made at the Sèvres factory from 1821 to 1822, for presentation to the Duke of Wellington by King Louis XVIII, and delivered to the Duke in 1823. The plates display views in France, including one of the Sèvres porcelain factory, painted by Langlacé. Below is a small group of green, gold and white porcelain produced by a Paris factory in about 1820.

CASE IV (West side)

Above is a group of plates from the Saxon Service of Meissen porcelain, made in about 1818 and presented to the Duke of Wellington by King Frederick Augustus IV of Saxony. Below are elements of the Austrian Service of Vienna porcelain, presented to the Duke by Emperor Francis I of Austria in 1820.

CASE V (West side)

A further selection from the Saxon Service of Meissen porcelain, including two centrally placed plates with views of Apsley House as built by Robert Adam, before its enlargement by Benjamin Dean Wyatt for the Duke of Wellington.

The Rest of the House

The rest of Apsley House, apart from certain parts of the Basement used for administrative purposes, was reserved under the Wellington Museum Act of 1947 for the use of the Seventh Duke of Wellington and his successors who are, happily, still in occupation. Certain changes in function and decoration have taken place in some of these private rooms, particularly under the Second Duke of Wellington, but the appearance of the First Duke's own rooms was recorded in the illustrations to Richard Ford's *Apsley House and Walmer Castle*, 1853, reproduced here.

'The Duke's Bed Room', after Thomas Shotter Boys, from Richard Ford, 'Apsley House and Walmer Castle', 1853

'The Duke's own Room', after Thomas
Shotter Boys, from Richard Ford, 'Apsley
House and Walmer Castle', 1853

'The Secretary's Room', after Thomas
Shotter Boys, from Richard Ford, 'Apsley
House and Walmer Castle', 1853

Life of the Duke of Wellington
1769-1852

"A Wellington Boot or the Head of the Army"; cartoon by Paul Pry, London, 1827. Victoria and Albert Museum

A WELLINGTON BOOT
or the Head of the Army.

Extract from a letter to Lord Nugent, dated 1830, from the Duke of Wellington. Victoria and Albert Museum, Forster Collection

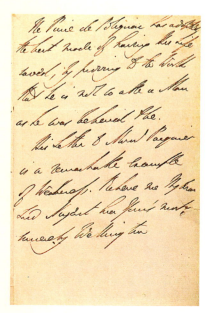

The future Duke of Wellington was born at 24 Upper Merion Street, Dublin, on 29 April (or 1 May?) 1769. He was Arthur Wellesley, the fourth son of Garret Wellesley (or Wesley), first Earl of Mornington, and his wife Anne, the eldest daughter of Viscount Dungannon. Just over three months later Napoleon Bonaparte was born at Ajaccio in Corsica, on 15 August.

Wellington was educated first at Brown's preparatory school in Chelsea, and then at Eton from 1781 to 1784. His father died in 1781 and three years later his mother removed him from Eton and took him to Brussels, where his education was continued privately with Louis Goubert, a barrister.

Early impressions of the boy show him as aloof and rather aggressive, with talents for mathematics and music — he played the violin when young — but otherwise "not very attentive to his studies". His mother decided that the best thing for him was the army, although his constitution was not too robust.

This severe but practical woman remarked that her "ugly boy Arthur" was "fit food for powder". So in 1786 he went to Pignerolle's military academy at Angers in France where he stayed a year. His brief stay there brought him new friends, the devotion of a "little terrier called Vic" and a useful fluency in French.

In 1787 his brother, Lord Mornington, obtained a commission for him in the 73rd (Highland) Regiment — he was gazetted Ensign on 7 March — and then, after the fashion of the time he advanced through five different regiments and became Lieutenant (1787) and Captain (1791). On 30 April 1793, he purchased the commission of major in the 33rd Foot (now the Duke of Wellington's Regiment) and on 30 September of the same year the

Lieutenant-Colonelcy of the regiment. He sailed with it for the Continent in June 1794 to join the Allied armies behind the River Dyle in Belgium.

It was at Boxtel, near Bois-le-Duc in Holland, that Wellesley first saw action, when he distinguished himself by halting a French force which was driving back the Allies. He fought through the months of retreat to the mouth of the Weser (assuming the command of a brigade) where the army embarked for England in the spring of 1795.

During this early period (1787-95) he saw little military service in the strict sense, as he was Aide-de-Camp to two Lords Lieutenant of Ireland, and represented the Irish constituency of Trim in Parliament from 1790 to 1795.

After other minor adventures, he went to India in 1796, being now a Colonel. He had persuaded his eldest brother, Lord Mornington (afterwards Marquess Wellesley) to take the Governor-Generalship of India, and acted as his unofficial adviser. India was to be his true training ground, both as a soldier and a statesman; for he had now decided to take his military career seriously, working strenuously to train himself in all branches of military science. He gave up card-playing and even music — he had burnt his violin in 1793 — in order to devote himself to his work.

In 1799 Wellesley took part in the invasion of Mysore against Tippoo Sultan and was appointed Governor of Seringapatam when it was captured, later being put in charge of the civil administration of Mysore State. He next fought and defeated Dhoondiah, a freebooter who invaded the territory with a large army (1800). After being prevented by illness from going as second in command of the expedition to Egypt — an illness which saved his life, because the troopship was sunk with all hands in the Red Sea — he continued to administer Mysore, during which time he was promoted to Major-General (1802).

When hostilities broke out against the Mahratta tribes (1803), Wellesley took a leading part in the war and inflicted severe defeats on the enemy at Assaye, Argaum and Gawilghur, and afterwards negotiated the treaties which saw the end of the campaign. He received the thanks of Parliament, and the people of Calcutta presented him with a sword of honour. He was now anxious to return to England; "I think I have served as long in India as any man ought who can serve anywhere else", he said. It was during this formative period of life in India that he grew to be an outstanding soldier and a shrewd statesman; his experience had been wide and varied, and he had mastered every department of civil and military administration, as well as proving himself an excellent field commander.

After further minor actions in India, and after declining command of the Bombay army, he resigned his appointments, civil and military (24 February 1805) and sailed for England, where he arrived on 10 September.

After his return to England he commanded a brigade in Lord Cathcart's expedition to Hanover, which returned after Napoleon's victory at Austerlitz (1805); was made Colonel of the 33rd Foot; was given a brigade at Hastings; was re-elected to Parliament (1806) and made Irish Secretary; went to Denmark in 1807 and took part in the surrender of Copenhagen; and was promoted Lieutenant-General on 25 April 1808, the year of commencement of the Peninsular War. He was married 10 April 1806 to the Hon. Catherine Pakenham, second daughter of Edward, second Baron Longford. She died 24 April 1831, in London, and is buried at Stratfield Saye.

A selection of the Campaign Plate

In July 1808 he sailed for Portugal in command of a force of some 9,000 men to assist the Portuguese and Spaniards against the French, and was joined later by reinforcements both from England and from the Portuguese themselves. After winning the Battles of Roliça and Vimieiro, he was made the scapegoat for the unpopular Convention of Cintra, and returned to England on 6 October 1808. Sir John Moore was then appointed to command the army in Portugal. After Moore's glorious death at Corunna (1809) Wellesley was re-appointed to the Command and arrived in Mondego Bay, Portugal, in April 1809.

Wellesley's first successes in the Peninsula were the forcing of the passage of the Douro, and the defeat of Soult's army at Oporto (12 May 1809). He then crossed the Spanish border and, with the help of the Spanish army, again beat the French at Talavera (27-28 June). For these victories he was raised to the peerage and took the titles of Baron Douro of Wellesley and Viscount Wellington of Talavera, this title being chosen by his brother William because Wellington is near Wellesley in Somerset, from which the family originally took its name.

Masséna was appointed by Napoleon to command the French, now reinforced, in the Peninsula. With the arrival of these new French forces, Wellington was forced to withdraw and finally took up positions on the lines of Torres Vedras, outside Lisbon, after defeating Masséna at the Battle of Busaco (27 September 1810).

But Masséna, finding the lines too strong to attack, and running short of supplies, was forced to fall back, followed and harried by Wellington. Actions were fought at Pombal, Redinha, Cazal Nova, Foz d'Aronce and Sabugal (3 April 1811) — this last signalling the end of the French

invasion of Portugal and the retreat of their armies to Salamanca. Wellington now received the confidence and thanks of Parliament and prepared to drive the enemy out of the whole Peninsula. He went over to the offensive, and defeated the French at Fuentes de Onoro, Almeida and Albuera (16 May 1811); but the siege of Badajoz in June was unsuccessful and was raised by the French generals Marmont and Soult. Having once failed to take Ciudad Rodrigo, Wellington again attacked the city and by a brilliant action captured it on 19 January 1812 — an achievement for which he was made an earl and received the acclaim of his own country and of Spain, the latter making him Duke of Ciudad Rodrigo.

The next objective was Badajoz which, at severe cost in lives, was besieged and captured on 6 April 1812. Three months later Wellington defeated Marmont at the Battle of Salamanca (22 July) — "this battle was Wellington's masterpiece" as one writer said — and then went on to occupy Valladolid. On 12 August he entered Madrid. He next marched northwards, but failed to capture Burgos after a month's siege (October) and later fell back to the Portuguese frontier, where the allied armies, British, Spanish, and Portuguese, were brought together in preparation for the campaign of 1813.

Honours were now heaped upon Wellington, of which the most important were his elevation to Marquess (August 1812) with a grant of £100,000 from Parliament; the award of the Order of the Garter (March 1813); and his appointment as generalissimo of the Spanish armies (September 1812).

He opened the campaign of 1813 by advancing into Spain in two columns, one by the north bank of the Douro, the other to Salamanca. The columns pressed forward and joined forces at Toro on 4 June, and advanced upon

Burgos, which the French then abandoned. On 21 June was fought the great Battle of Vitoria in which the French lost about five thousand men, together with most of their guns, stores and loot. Joseph Bonaparte's baggage train, captured with the rest, contained many works of art stolen from the Spaniards, which King Ferdinand afterwards presented to Wellington (see p. 83). For this victory he was promoted to Field Marshal, and received from Spain the estate of Soto de Roma, near Granada.

The French army retreated across the Pyrénées — after continuous and heavy fighting during July and August 1813 — and soon they only had the armies of Aragon and Catalonia left in Spain, with garrisons in Pamplona and San Sebastian, which were blockaded and besieged by the Allies. San Sebastian was finally stormed, and surrendered (9 September); and Pamplona gave in a few weeks later (31 October).

With the war in Germany now settled by the defeat of Napoleon at Leipzig (16-19 October 1813), Wellington advanced into France, driving the French back to Bayonne after the Battles of the Nivelle (16 November) and Nive (9-13 December). Leaving two divisions to blockade Bayonne, Wellington pursued Marshal Soult with the rest of the allied armies. There followed the Battle of Orthez (27 February 1814) and, after lesser actions, the Battle of Toulouse (10 April). Two days later Wellington heard that Napoleon had abdicated; and the convention by which hostilities came to an end was signed on 18 April 1814. After being summoned to Paris, Wellington visited King Ferdinand at Madrid and then returned to England, landing there on 23 May. His home-coming was a triumphal procession, and amidst a fresh shower of honours he was created Marquess Douro and Duke of Wellington, with an extra grant from Parliament of £400,000.

He was, strangely enough, appointed Ambassador to France (5 July 1814), and after much controversy left in February of 1815 to take Lord Castlereagh's place at the Congress of Vienna. But Napoleon returned to France from the Island of Elba on 1 March, and Europe was again in a turmoil. Wellington was appointed Commander of the Anglo-Netherland and Hanoverian forces in Europe (28 March) and by early June held, with Blücher's Prussians, a ninety-mile front just behind the Belgian frontier. Napoleon, with his Grand Army, hoped to drive a wedge between Wellington and Blücher and deal with them piecemeal before help could arrive from the Austrians and Russians. The French attacked on 16 June, defeating the Prussians on the right flank but being beaten at Quatre Bras on the left. Wellington then pulled his forces back at Waterloo to which Blücher promised to send two corps, and there the great battle was fought. On 18 June Napoleon began his main assault on Wellington's army but, after repeated attacks and fierce fighting, failed to overcome the British and was beaten back. The Prussians then attacked from the north-east and the French were routed, losing about half their army and most of their guns. Napoleon reached Paris on 21 June and abdicated on the 22nd. He finally surrendered to the British on 15 July.

After the French defeat, Wellington took a major part in the peace negotiations and was subsequently made commander of the allied occupation army. His command lasted until 15 November 1818, when the armies were evacuated, and he returned to England. The Parliamentary Commissioners had, in 1817, bought for him the estate of Stratfield Saye, in North Hampshire.

The Duke re-entered politics in December 1818, and was made Master-

Silk rosette worn at the Funeral of the Duke of Wellington, 1852

General of the Ordnance, a post which carried Cabinet rank. He was also appointed Lord Lieutenant of Hampshire in December 1820, and Lord High Constable at the Coronation of George IV — an office he later held at the crowning of William IV and Victoria. In September 1822, he took Lord Londonderry's place at the Congress of Verona, where he stood for non-intervention in the affairs of Spain, but failed to persuade his allies.

After a brief mission to Russia in 1826, he was appointed Commander-in-Chief in January 1827, at the same time retaining his Cabinet position; both of which he resigned, however, on 12 April after a dispute with Canning. He was reappointed on 22 August by Lord Goderich, after Canning's death. On 9 January 1828, Wellington became Prime Minister, although he had no desire for the post, and resigned command of the army.

His period of office was a stormy one, and is perhaps best remembered for the difficult but successful passage of the Catholic Emancipation Bill. The Government fell in November 1830. During the Grey administration which followed, the Duke opposed the Reform Bill and became very unpopular with large sections of the public. The windows of Apsley House were broken by a mob on 27 April 1831, and again later on. These occurrences caused him to fit iron shutters to the windows of Apsley House, which remained there until his death. But this unpopularity did not last for long. A happier occasion was his election to the Chancellorship of Oxford University in 1834.

In November 1834 William IV dismissed Melbourne (who had taken Grey's place) and in the Peel administration which followed the Duke served as Foreign Secretary. After four months the Government fell and Peel and the Duke were again in opposition.

When Peel returned to power in 1841 the Duke (whose health had been failing since 1837) was given a seat in the Cabinet, but without office. On 15 August 1844, he was again appointed Commander-in-Chief, a post he continued to hold after the Peel Government fell in June 1846.

From that time he ceased to take a prominent part in public life, although he once again came into national prominence when he organized the military defence of London against the threat of Chartist riots in April 1848. But he took an informed and active interest in foreign and domestic affairs and he is particularly remembered as an admired, admiring, and almost daily visitor to the Great Exhibition of 1851, where he was once nearly mobbed by an enthusiastic crowd.

On 14 September 1852 he died peacefully at Walmer Castle, Kent, his official residence as Lord Warden of the Cinque Ports. His body lay in state there until 10 November, when it was brought to London. It again lay in state for five days in Chelsea Hospital, where 200,000 people paid homage to the great Duke. The funeral was one of the great spectacles of the century, with over a million and a half people lining the route from the Horse Guards to St Paul's Cathedral, where he was buried on 18 November.

Titles, Offices and Appointments of the Duke

Obelisk with Wellington's orders and titles from the centrepiece of the Prussian Service, Berlin porcelain, about 1819

Ensign, *7 March 1787*

Lieutenant, *25 December 1787*

Captain, *30 June 1791*

Major, *30 April 1793*

Lieut.-Colonel, *30 September 1793*

Colonel, *3 May 1796*

Major-General, *29 April 1802*

Knight Companion of the Bath, *1 September 1804*

Colonel of the 33rd Regiment of Foot (later the Duke of Wellington's Regiment), *30 January 1806 (to December 1812)*

Irish Secretary, *3 April 1807 (resigned April 1809)*

Privy Councillor, *8 April 1807*

Lieutenant-General, *25 April 1808*

Marshal-General of the Portuguese Army, *6 July 1809*

Baron Douro of Wellesley and Viscount Wellington of Talavera, *26 August 1809*

Member of the Regency in Portugal, *August 1810*

General, *31 July 1811*

Conde de Vimieiro and Knight Grand Cross of the Tower and Sword (Portugal), *26 October 1811*

A grandee of Spain, with the title of Duque de Ciudad Rodrigo, *February 1812*

Earl of Wellington, *18 February 1812*

Order of the Golden Fleece (Spain), *1 August 1812*

Generalissimo of the Spanish Armies, *August 1812*

Marquess of Wellington, *18 August 1812*

Marquez de Torres Vedras (Portugal), *August 1812*

Duque da Victoria (Portugal), *18 December 1812*

Colonel of the Royal Regiment of Horse Guards, *1 January 1813 (to 1827)*

Knight of the Garter, *4 March 1813*

Field Marshal, *21 June 1813*

Marquess Douro and Duke of Wellington, *3 May 1814*

Ambassador to the Court of France, *5 July 1814 (to November)*

Prince of Waterloo (Netherlands), *18 July 1815*

Commander-in-Chief of the Allied Armies of Occupation in France, *22 October 1815*

Field Marshal in the Austrian, Russian and Prussian Armies, *October 1818*

Master-General of the Ordnance, *26 December 1818*

Governor of Plymouth, *9 December 1819*

Colonel-in-Chief of the Rifle Brigade, *19 February 1820*

Lord High Constable (at the Coronations of George IV, William IV and Victoria), *1821, 1831, 1838*

Constable of the Tower of London, *29 December 1826*

Colonel of the Grenadier Guards, *22 January 1827*

Commander-in-Chief, *22 January 1827*

Prime Minister, *15 February 1828 (resigned October 1830)*

Lord Warden of the Cinque Ports, *20 January 1829*

Chancellor of the University of Oxford, *30 January 1834*

Secretary of State for Foreign Affairs, *December 1834 (resigned April 1835)*

Master of Trinity House, *22 May 1837*

Ranger of Hyde Park and St James's Park, *31 August 1850*

Miscellany

Peninsular Cross, about 1814, the only example with nine clasps, inscribed 'General the Marquis of Wellington'

There is a pillar near Wellington in Somerset, an obelisk in Phoenix Park, Dublin, and a monument by Marochetti outside the gates of Stratfield Saye House. Of the many busts the most interesting are perhaps that by Guillaume (Willem) Geefs (1805-1883) in the village church of Waterloo, that by Nollekens at Apsley House, which the Duke's wife and elder son thought the best likeness, and the one in the guardroom of Windsor Castle, over which hangs a French banner, replaced annually by the Dukes of Wellington on Waterloo Day (18 June) as a condition of the tenure of the estates voted to the Duke by Parliament. Among the many subject paintings in which the Duke figures are the Meeting of *Wellington and Blücher* by T.J. Barker, the wall-painting of the same subject by David Maclise in the Houses of Parliament and Robert Thorburn's large miniature showing the Duke in the library at Stratfield Saye with his grandchildren.

The Duke's funeral on 18 November 1852 was perhaps the most elaborate funeral ever held in this country. It was decided to mount the coffin on an elaborate *Triumphal Car,* which was designed and built in some three weeks. It was designed by the Government School of Design (now the Royal College of Art) under the supervision of Henry Cole and Richard Redgrave and was made of the metal of guns captured at Waterloo. It was constructed by eight firms and the great embroidered pall was worked by women students of the School of Design. The six-wheeled car was 20 feet long and 17 feet high (so that, with the added height of coffin and bier, it could just clear Temple Bar) and bore a large Wellington coat of arms on the front and elaborate trophies of actual weapons on the front and sides.

Stretched above the coffin and removable bier was a canopy. The car,

now at Stratfield Saye House, was drawn by twelve black horses along the route from the Horse Guards — whence the body had been moved from Chelsea Hospital, the scene of the lying-in-state — to St Paul's Cathedral by way of the Mall, Buckingham Palace, Hyde Park Corner, Piccadilly, St James's Palace, Pall Mall, Charing Cross, the Strand and Fleet Street. An enormous crowd lined the route and some 20,000 specially invited people were seated in the Cathedral on temporary stands.

The Cathedral was blacked out and the four-hour service took place by the light of gas jets. The coffin and wheeled bier were let down into the crypt exactly under the centre of the dome and placed on top of Nelson's tomb, from which the upper part had been removed. It remained there for a year (until 22 November 1853) by which time the Wellington tomb was ready to receive it. This was placed in the crypt, to the east of Nelson's tomb. The *Tomb* is a simple and massive structure of Cornish porphyry resting on a base of Peterhead granite. It was designed by F. C. Penrose, and finally completed in August 1858.

In 1857 a competition was held for a large *Monument to the Duke* to be placed in the Cathedral proper. The winner was Alfred Stevens, who designed an impressive monument to include both a recumbent effigy and an equestrian figure. The original model is in the Victoria and Albert Museum. But owing to interminable delays and acrimonious controversies the tomb was not finished until 1878; even then it was placed in the south-west Chapel (the present Chapel of St Michael and St George) although designed for the north aisle. It was transferred to its proper position in 1892. Even then it was incomplete, as another — and absurd — controversy had led to the omission of the crowning equestrian figure on the grounds of the unsuitability of allowing a horse in the Cathedral. However, the bronze figure was ultimately completed by John Tweed from the model left by Stevens (who had died in 1875), and was placed in position in 1912. It is the largest monument in St Paul's Cathedral, and the bronze recumbent effigy is particularly fine.

The *Wellington Arms* (see p. 5): quarterly: 1st and 4th gules, a cross argent, between five plates, in saltire, in each quarter, for Wellesley; 2nd and 3rd, or, a lion rampant, gules, for Colley; and as an honourable augmentation, in chief an escutcheon, charged with the crosses of St George, St Andrew, and St Patrick, conjoined, being the union badge of the United Kingdom of Great Britain and Ireland. The *Crest:* out of a ducal coronet, or, a demi-lion rampant gules, holding a forked pennon of the last, flowing to the sinister, one-third per pale from the staff, argent, charged with the cross of St George. The *Supporters:* two lions gules, each gorged with an eastern crown, and chained or. The *Motto* is: *Virtutis Fortuna Comes* (Fortune the Companion of Valour).

The title *"Wellington"* is taken from the manor of Wellington in Somerset which was given to the Duke by the Nation in 1812. The name has been given to countless buildings, streets, squares and open spaces throughout the country — there being twenty-six streets, etc., in the London area alone. The two most famous buildings bearing the Duke's name are Wellington Barracks, London, and Wellington College, Berkshire. *Wellington Barracks,* in Birdcage Walk, was built in 1834 and is the headquarters of the Brigade of Guards. *Wellington College,* which is near Sandhurst, was built by public subscription as a national memorial to the Duke, to form a public school for the sons of officers. The sum of £100,000 was raised, and the first stone was laid on 2 June 1856 by Queen Victoria, who opened the College on 29 January 1859. The Capital City of New Zealand — Wellington — was named after the Duke on 28 November 1840 by Edward Gibbon Wakefield, the founder of the colony. Also called Wellington are a mountain in Tasmania; three towns and a lake in Australia; a town in Canada; a town in South Africa; a channel in the Arctic regions of Canada; an island off Chile; etc. There have been a number of warships of the Royal Navy named *Duke of Wellington, Wellington,* and *Wellesley;* as well as various merchant ships. The Royal Air Force has had two famous bombers named, respectively, *Wellesley* and *Wellington.*

Wellington Boots were of two kinds — the high boots covering the knees in front and cut away behind, and a shorter kind worn under the trousers. More lately the title has been applied to the familiar high rubber boots. Keats wrote in 1821: "Miss's comb is made a pearl tiara, and common Wellingtons turn Romeo boots." The first printed reference to Wellington boots was by Moncrieff in 1817. The *Wellington Coat* was "a kind of half-and-half great coat and under-coat . . . meeting close and square below the knees" (Creevey, 1828). *Wellington Trousers* were referred to by Sir Walter Scott (1818): "the equally fashionable latitude and longitude of the Wellington trousers." The *Wellington Apple,* a cooking apple, was named by Richard Williams in 1821: "a very handsome and long keeping variety" as the Transactions of the Horticultural Society said in 1822. Perhaps the most distinguished use of the name is the *Wellingtonia,* the popular name in England for the giant Californian sequoia tree, the *sequoia gigantea,* given it by the English botanist John Lindley. The *Gardener's Chronicle* (1853) says: "Wellington stands as high above his contemporaries as the Californian tree above all

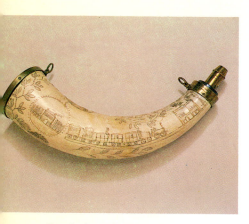

Powder-horn. Lent by the Duke of Wellington

surrounding foresters. Let it then bear henceforward the name of *Wellingtonia gigantea.*"

The name *"Waterloo"* is also popular as a name for streets of which the best known is Waterloo Place — where the Duke had stones erected to assist the clubmen to mount their horses — and there are, of course, Waterloo Station and Waterloo Bridge (the original bridge was opened in 1817); and another Waterloo Bridge across the River Conway in Gwynedd, opened in 1815. There is also the Waterloo Tower, built to commemorate the battle, by Sir Watkin Wynn in Wynnstay Park, Clwyd. In the Cemetery of Brussels, a Waterloo monument was erected, at the wish of Queen Victoria, over the graves of the officers and men who fell in the campaign of 1815. It was unveiled by the Duke of Cambridge, 26 August 1890. It was suggested, and rejected that four London churches projected before 1815 and finished afterwards should be called the 'Waterloo Churches'. The name has stuck although the then Chancellor of the Exchequer stated that "the idea of appropriating churches to commemorate our triumphs did not appear to him to be one that could be entertained". The four churches are: St Matthew's, Brixton; St Mark's, Kennington; St Luke's, Norwood; and St John's, Waterloo Road (damaged by a bomb and rebuilt in 1950 to be the 1951 "Festival Church").

The Waterloo Chamber in Windsor Castle was built in 1830 by George IV to display portraits, mostly by Sir Thomas Lawrence, of those men chiefly responsible for the overthrow of Napoleon, and includes one of the Duke bearing the Sword of State.

The Duke of Wellington never met Napoleon; and met Nelson only once, and that by chance, in September 1805 at the Colonial Office. Nelson was

killed at the Battle of Trafalgar the month after, on 21 October. Napoleon, after his defeat at Waterloo, abdicated on 22 June 1815, and surrendered to Captain F. L. Maitland on 15 July on board H.M.S. *Bellerophon* at Rochefort (France). He was taken in this ship to Plymouth. On 7 August he sailed in H.M.S. *Northumberland* for the island of St Helena where he died on 5 May 1821, at the age of fifty-one.

At the suggestion of the Duke, the *Silver Waterloo Medal* was given "not only to the higher officers, but to all ranks alike, a thing unprecedented".

There is no authority for believing the Duke ever made the oft-quoted exhortation at the Battle of Waterloo, "Up Guards and at them!"; or for his alleged remark that the Battle of Waterloo was won on the playing fields of Eton.

The origin of the words, 'Iron Duke', is uncertain, but the Duke was certainly called this during his lifetime. The earliest known use in print is in *The Mechanics Magazine* in 1845, although *Punch* referred to him in 1842 as "the Wrought-iron Duke". It was long ago suggested that this sobriquet derived from his installation of iron shutters on Apsley House; or, alternatively, that it referred to his face and bearing. Most evidence points to the former origin. Tennyson, in his "Ode" on the Duke's funeral (1852), referred to "their everloyal iron leader's fame"; and thereafter the Duke was constantly called the Iron Duke, even in serious works. An earlier reference is another possibility. In 1822 the Duke became deaf in the left ear as a result of an incompetent doctor's attention. He complained saying, "Even the strength of my iron constitution tells now against me." A number of merchant ships have been called *Iron Duke*, although at first the name appears to have been a kind of nickname when iron ships were superseding wood vessels. But two battleships of the Royal Navy have borne the name; the first launched in 1870, the second Admiral Jellicoe's flagship at the Battle of Jutland in 1916, launched in 1912.

The Duke fought one duel, on 21 March 1829, when he was Prime Minister. The Earl of Winchilsea had publicly accused him of dishonesty over the Catholic Emancipation Bill, and was challenged by the Duke. The duel took place at 8 a.m. in Battersea Fields (now Battersea Park). The Duke apparently intended to aim for his opponent's legs but missed: whereupon Lord Winchilsea fired into the air. After which he apologized to the Duke. "I was amazed yesterday morning", wrote Mrs Arbuthnot, "by the Duke walking in while I was at breakfast and telling me he had been fighting Lord Winchilsea . . . The Duke went afterwards to Windsor and saw the King, who thought he was quite right."

Portraits: a selection of the more important, excluding those at Apsley House:

Sir Joseph Boehm (1834-1890), Bronze equestrian statue, 1846, opposite Apsley House.

Sir Francis Chantrey (1781-1841), Bronze equestrian statue, erected 1844, opposite the Royal Exchange.

Francesco Goya (1746-1828), Painting, 1814, National Gallery.

Benjamin Robert Haydon (1786-1846), Painting, 1839, Stratfield Saye House.

Thomas Heaphy (1775-1835), Drawing, 1813, National Portrait Gallery.

Robert Home (1752-1835), Painting, 1804, National Portrait Gallery.

John Hoppner (1758-1810), Painting, about 1795, Strafield Saye House.

Sir Thomas Lawrence (1769-1830), Painting, 1814, Windsor Castle, Waterloo Chamber.

Baron Marochetti (1805-1867), Bronze equestrian statue, 1844, Glasgow.

Count Alfred d'Orsay, Painting, 1845, National Portrait Gallery.

Sir John Steell (1804-1891), bronze equestrian statue, 1852, Edinburgh.

Alfred Stevens (1817-1875), Bronze recumbent effigy and bronze equestrian statue, 1857 (completed by John Tweed (1869-1933)), Wellington Monument, St Paul's Cathedral.

Sir David Wilkie (1785-1841), Painting, 1834, Merchant Taylors' Hall.

Franz Winterhalter (1806-1873), The First of May, 1851, a painting showing the Duke with Queen Victoria, the Prince Consort and the Duke's godson, Prince Arthur, Windsor Castle.

Plaster cast of the Duke's death mask, National Portrait Gallery.

Linked with Apsley House are four familiar monuments.

The *Constitution Hill Arch* was designed by Decimus Burton and erected in 1828 in front of the present entrance to Hyde Park. In 1846 there was placed on it a huge equestrian statue of the Duke of Wellington by M. C. Wyatt. In 1883 the arch was moved to its present position at the top of Constitution Hill, and the statue sent to Aldershot, where it still stands on a knoll near Wellington Avenue. It was not until 1912 that the present group of Peace in a Quadriga (four-horse chariot) by Adrian Jones was placed on it. To replace the Wyatt statue, the present *Equestrian Statue in Bronze,* on a granite base, was placed directly opposite Apsley House in December 1888. The group is the work of Sir J. E. Boehm, R.A. At each corner of the

The Restoration of Apsley House

pedestal stands the figure of a soldier — a Grenadier, 42nd Royal Highlander, 23rd Royal Welch Fusilier, and 6th Inniskilling Dragoon. The Duke is shown on his horse Copenhagen. This chestnut charger, ridden by the Duke at Waterloo, was born in 1808. He died 12 February 1836 at Stratfield Saye, and was buried with military honours. A headstone marks the grave, inscribed:

*God's humble instrument, though
   meaner clay,
Should share the glory of that
   glorious day.*

The *Achilles* statue, which stands inside Hyde Park and just to the north-west of Apsley House, was erected in June 1822. The pedestal bears the inscription: "To Arthur, Duke of Wellington, and his brave companions in arms this statue of Achilles cast from cannon taken in the victories of Salamanca, Vitoria, Toulouse and Waterloo is inscribed by their country-women." The eighteen-foot statue of Achilles, by Sir Richard Westmacott, is a bronze adaptation of one of the antique Horse-tamer figures on the Quirinal Hill, Rome. It cost £10,000.

Marble Arch (at the north-east corner of Hyde Park) was designed by John Nash, to the order of George IV, both as a memorial to the victories of Trafalgar and Waterloo, and as a Royal entrance to Buckingham Palace. But the sculptural decorations were not included when the arch was erected in front of the Palace in 1833; they were incorporated instead in the exterior of the Palace itself, and the arch was no longer regarded as a victory memorial. It was transferred to its present position in 1851. The original model, with scenes not only of Waterloo but of the Duke receiving the Order of the Garter (the latter sculpture never being carried out), is in the Victoria and Albert Museum.

Since 1976 the Department of Furniture and Woodwork in the Victoria and Albert Museum, already responsible for Ham House and Osterley Park, has administered Apsley House. After careful research the firm decision was taken to restore the house, insofar as possible, to its appearance under the First Duke of Wellington. This process, still incomplete, has included work in the Portico Room (1978), the Piccadilly Room (1980), the Waterloo Gallery (1980), the Plate & China Room (1981), the Staircase (1982) and the Dining Room (1982). Further improvements are planned, including work on the Striped Drawing Room, the Inner Hall and the Hall.

Restoration has involved work with documents such as the inventories of the house taken in 1854 and 1857, surviving bills, published accounts by Richard Ford and others and early watercolours and photographs of the interiors. Physical research has included the examination of paint sections and scrapes to establish original colours. The discovery of surviving fragments of the original carpets and wall-hangings has in some cases allowed their accurate reproduction. Where evidence is insufficient or unavailable an attempt has been made to discover and follow appropriate contemporary models, having regard to the particular character and circumstances of Apsley House.

One of the main results of the programme of restoration so far carried out has been the elimination of museum show-cases from the state rooms of Apsley House. At the same time the adoption of a more concentrated method of display has reduced to a small range the number of objects in store. When the programme is complete Apsley House will be arranged and decorated to match, as closely as possible, its appearance when it was the London palace of the First Duke of Wellington.

Curtain pole from the Piccadilly Drawing Room, 1980

The Paintings

Fragment of original carpet found in the attics of Stratfield Saye and presented by the present Duke of Wellington

Tassel from the Piccadilly Drawing Room, 1980

In 1812 the Intendant of Segovia, in recognition of Wellington's liberation of Spain from the French, gave him twelve paintings from the Palace of Ildefonso. The final expulsion of the French from Spain followed Wellington's victory at the battle of Vitoria on 21 June 1813. After that battle Joseph Bonaparte, who had been made King of Spain in 1808, fled. His coach was captured and proved to contain over 200 paintings appropriated from the Spanish Royal Collections. They had been detached from their stretchers and rolled up. Wellington sent them to London to the custody of his brother, Lord Maryborough. In 1814, when they had been catalogued and their importance and royal provenance discovered, Wellington not only had them restored but also offered to return them to the King of Spain. A further offer in 1816 produced the response from Count Fernan Nunez, Spanish Minister in England that: "His Majesty, touched by your delicacy, does not wish to deprive you of that which has come into your possession by means as just as they are honourable".

Eighty-three of these paintings are now at Apsley House. They range in date from the Juan de Flandes Last Supper, which was painted for Queen Isabella of Castille before her death in 1504, to the Mengs Holy Family dated 1765, and include works by such masters as Correggio, Elsheimer, Rubens, Velazquez, and Van Dyck.

After the end of the war the Duke bought some important old master paintings, mainly Dutch, in Paris at the La Peyrière sale (April 1817) and the Le Rouge sale (April 1818) and from the dealer, painter and restorer, Féréol Bonnemaison (1818). From the same period onwards he also collected modern portraits of his comrades-in-arms by Lawrence, and others, and portraits of Napoleon and his family mainly by Lefèvre. Portraits of the allied sovereigns came as gifts. Wellington's most important modern purchase was Wilkie's Chelsea Pensioners, commissioned in 1816. The second Duke of Wellington also collected; seven of the two hundred pictures at Apsley House were acquired by him.

In recent years a programme has been underway to rehang the paintings following, insofar as possible, their arrangement under the first Duke, as recorded in descriptions and watercolours. As a result many of the paintings have been restored to the rooms where they were hung by the first Duke and several are close to their original positions. The first Duke probably had about ninety more paintings than are now in the rooms on view at Apsley House; their arrangement was therefore even richer and denser. The frames are all as supplied to the first Duke: his principal framemaker was Thomas Temple after whose bankruptcy in 1839 Robert Thick was employed.

† This symbol is used to indicate a painting captured at the Battle of Vitoria, 1813.
* This symbol is used to indicate that the painting is known to have hung in the same room under the 1st Duke of Wellington.

Stratfield Saye House

near Reading, Berks
Tel. Basingstoke (0256) 882 882

The Duke of Wellington's country house, dating from 1630 and containing paintings, furniture and relics from his time, including his Funeral Car.

Open Easter to September. Further information from the Manager, Wellington Office, Stratfield Saye House, near Reading, Berkshire RG7 2BT.

Ham House

near Richmond, Surrey
Tel. 01-940 1950

Property of the National Trust; administered by the Victoria and Albert Museum.

Originally built in 1610 by Sir Thomas Vavasour as a modest country residence, Ham House was enlarged and modernised by the Duke and Duchess of Lauderdale in the 1670s and contains most of the paintings and furniture from that period.

Open all year, Tuesday to Sunday inclusive. April to September: 14.00 to 18.00. October to March: 12.00 to 16.00.

Guided tours can be arranged through the Education Section, Victoria and Albert Museum, South Kensington, SW7 2RL. Tel: 589 6371; ext. 247 or 258.

Osterley Park House

Osterley, Middlesex
Tel. 01-560 3918

Property of the National Trust; administered by the Victoria and Albert Museum.

An Elizabethan mansion transformed into an 18th century villa. Elegant neo-classical interior decoration designed by Robert Adam for the banker Robert Child.

Open all year, Tuesday to Sunday inclusive. April to September: 14.00 to 18.00. October to March: 12.00 to 16.00.

Guided tours can be arranged through the Education Section, Victoria and Albert Museum, South Kensington, SW7 2RL. Tel: 589 6371; ext. 247 or 258.

How to get there

London Underground
Hyde Park Corner Station (Piccadilly Line) is next to Apsley House

London Transport
Buses 9, 9A, 14, 19, 22, 30, 52, 73, 74, 74B, and 137 stop at the top of Knightsbridge, very close to Apsley House.

By Car
Apsley House is easily accessible by car but there is NO PARKING whatever. The Park Lane Underground Car Park is five minutes walk away (see map).

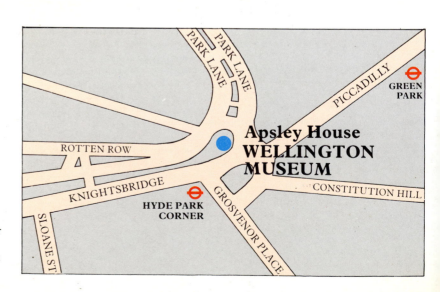

Simone Jeska

TRANSPARENT PLASTICS

DESIGN AND TECHNOLOGY

Birkhäuser

Basel | Boston | Berlin

Graphic design: nalbach typografik, Stuttgart

Translation into English: Gerd H. Söffker and Philip Thrift, Hannover

This book is also available in a German edition:
ISBN 978-3-7643-7469-3

Library of Congress Control Number: 2007933206

Bibliographic information published by Die Deutsche Bibliothek
Die Deutsche Bibliothek lists this publication in the Deutsche
Nationalbibliografie; detailed bibliographic data is available in the
Internet at http://dnb.ddb.de.

© 2008 Birkhäuser Verlag AG
Basel · Boston · Berlin
P. O. Box 133, CH-4010 Basel, Switzerland
Part of Springer Science+Business Media
Printed on acid-free paper produced from chlorine-free pulp. TCF ∞
Printed in Germany

ISBN 978-3-7643-7470-9

www.birkhauser.ch
9 8 7 6 5 4 3 2 1

CONTENTS

PREFACE

Since the mid-1990s, synthetic materials – primarily transparent or translucent plastics – have once again been making their mark on architecture. Artistically curving tension structures made from transparent plastic membranes, but also industrially manufactured plastic sheets are readily used instead of heavy glass constructions. But the transparent plastics not only represent a less costly alternative to glass. In addition, they evolve their own particular qualities that become evident through the lightness of such constructions, the variety of forms and, last but not least, their aesthetic effects – the upshot of unusual façade arrangements and structures.   ///
This book is intended to provide the reader with an overview of the potential uses of transparent and translucent plastics in architecture, and demonstrate the broad range of both constructional and architectural opportunities. Lightweight, cost-effective synthetic materials are particularly suitable for use in the façades of warehouses or temporary pavilions. Tension structures made from transparent membranes can serve as climate-control envelopes for animal enclosures, glasshouses or extensive biospheres, and are ideal for long-span atrium roofs as well as conservatories and sunspaces providing intermediate climate zones for the adjoining interior spaces. In the meantime, they have become almost a standard solution for the roofs to large sports arenas. But in housing, museums and schools, too, where high demands are placed on the imperviousness, insulation and durability of the walls, synthetic materials are being used more and more.   ///   Depending on the type of building and the interior climate requirements, single-leaf, multi-leaf or multi-layer façade constructions can be chosen. These differ from conventional wall structures and open up the way for experimentation by the architectural avant-garde. External walls are turned into air collectors or reduced to a thickness of just a few millimetres. Plastic sheets are glued to the supporting construction to form a minimalist design, membranes are attached with Velcro tape, which allows them to be removed and washed; high-tech insulation systems are available, or translucent insulation is improvised DIY-style. Façades become moving, adaptive "skins", large sections of which can be opened up to the outside, or react to solar radiation levels. New production methods are tried out on double-curvature plastic sheets, and tension structures imitate natural phenomena and become efficient minimal constructions.   ///   At the same time, transparent plastics quite obviously serve as a source of inspiration for the artistic rendition of the façade – coloured artificial light, pigments,

printing or coloured infills provide an effective advertising medium externally or a changing play of light internally. The alienation of everyday articles or the use of waste products create provocations and challenge our visual perceptions – architecture becomes art.   ///   The projects shown here represent only the beginning of a new development; the potential of synthetic materials is illustrated in the introductory chapter with the title "Transparent plastics between intellectualisation and trash culture". Plastics are not only destined to be part of the new, digital design and manufacturing process, which renders possible mass customisation in architecture, but are also ideal for use as "bionic" building materials and are being tested from the point of view of sustainability. Demands for efficient constructions and adaptive building envelopes, which adjust automatically to climatic conditions, determine the themes here and in the end lead to architectural designs that respond dynamically to dynamic processes.   ///   These tendencies in contemporary architecture, which are leading to a gradual renaissance for synthetic materials, are understandable when we consider the relationship between form and material. The chapter entitled "Form follows material?" presents an overview of developments and the change in the meaning of form and material in architecture, which has led to a breakdown in the formerly clearly defined form-material relationship. In architecture, form and material have now become autonomous parameters, opposites in the shapes of the digitally created form and a material fetishism, which focuses on the sensual qualities of the material.   ///   But the fascination of synthetic materials and the willingness of architects to experiment with such substances are not new phenomena, as the chapter "A brief history of plastic buildings" reveals. Since the mass production of plastics began in the 1920s, these materials have awakened the imaginations of architects and engineers alike. Nevertheless, their current visions of the future are less euphoric and less idealistic than those of the early pioneers of plastic buildings. Once again, it is not the material itself that dominates or constitutes the starting point for a design. Instead, architects are seeking the *right* material for their architecture, which follows conceptual design approaches or notions of form, and are aiming at atmospheric, sensual or provocative effects. In doing so, immateriality and ambiguity – the characteristics of transparent plastics – frequently harmonise well with such design approaches and make plastics the current building material of choice for the architectural avant-garde.

A BRIEF HISTORY OF PLASTIC BUILDINGS

Synthetic materials from the chemistry lab have always had something remarkable about them. Even the alchemists of old were searching for a synthetic substance supposedly more precious than gold because it would unite all the positive properties of the conventional "natural" materials. As plastics were invented in the 19th century and went into large-scale production in the early 20th, it seemed as though this vision had become reality. Architects and engineers linked their hopes and dreams to this "miracle material", which apparently could be given all conceivable characteristics. It combined lightness, strength, transparency, thermal insulation capacity, light permeability and loadbearing characteristics, and opened up a world of infinite shapes. Plastics enabled planners to think in terms of bold, futuristic architectural and urban visions and to revolutionise architecture through technoid spatial forms or organically curving engineered structures. They were likewise a symbol of a better, promising future that would know no housing shortages nor climate problems and do justice to the needs of modern society in every respect.   ///   The architectural applications conquered by the new plastics were just as diverse as the plastics themselves. Plastic sheets could be used to build folded-plate structures, or shells and panels for room modules or modular constructions; nylon ropes formed long-span nets, and membranes of every kind were inflated to form dome structures, or stretched across an existing loadbearing framework.   ///   The history of the development of plastic buildings can be understood only in the social context and by referring back to the countless experimental designs of the visionaries and artists. This is where the fascination of the synthetic material finds expression; and in the end it was mostly the bold visionaries who determined the direction of practical everyday building, whether in the formal-aesthetic or the technical-constructional aspect. In the discord between pragmatism and utopia, a number of remarkable plastic buildings emerged, each of which, however, represents a momentary respite in this ongoing journey of development.

Richard Buckminster Fuller's "Dymaxion Dwelling Machine" of 1927 was the development of his idea for a mobile, lightweight house.

1 See Joachim Krausse (ed.), *R. Buckminster Fuller*, Reinbek bei Hamburg, 1973, p. 133   **2** The idea of a lightweight, mobile and at the same time prefabricated house runs like a thread through the work of Buckminster Fuller. Using the same principle, he developed the "Streamlined Dymaxion Shelter" in 1932, a residential tower on a circular plan with a streamlined, transparent enclosing façade which shields the tower against the wind. A refinement and further development of his ideas resulted in the building of a prototype, "Wichita House", in 1945/46.   **3** Kiesler understands time-space architecture as the embedment of the chronological aspect of living into the spatial design; the house should not be divided into self-contained rooms, but rather into functional zones, whose use and size should remain flexible and changeable. Frederick Kiesler, *Notes on architecture: the Space House*, in: Siegfried Gohr, Gunda Luyken (eds.), *Frederick J. Kiesler. Selected Writings*, Stuttgart, 1996, pp. 23–28   **4** The plastic houses of the 1930s were produced by their manufacturers for advertising purposes. See Arthur Quarmby, *The Plastic Architect*, London, 1974, p. 21. In the early 1940s, with

THE BEGINNINGS: THE STUFF DREAM HOUSES ARE MADE OF

The triumphant advance of plastics in architecture began with the rapid progress in plastics research and the onset of the boom in manufacture towards the end of the 1920s. The allure of these synthetic materials provided creative minds like Richard Buckminster Fuller and Frederick Kiesler with impulses for their architectural utopias.   ///   Buckminster Fuller designed his "Dymaxion Dwelling Machine" in 1927. It was a "featherweight", mobile house that could be transported in one piece to any faraway place and set up in a few hours. The name "Dymaxion", a concoction of dynamic, maximum and tension, is the expression of his intentions. Just like the advocates of "white modernism", Buckminster Fuller was inspired by automotive and aircraft production and saw the future of architecture in the mass production of industrially prefabricated buildings. But in contrast to his colleagues, he focused on energy concepts and mobile architecture. Joachim Krausse describes this conceptual approach as follows: "Within the constructions, the distribution of building mass should make way for an organisation of energy-exchange processes, the sturdy statics supplanted by ephemeral dynamics."[1] "Dymaxion" consisted of a loadbearing aluminium mast from which the floors, hexagonal on plan, were suspended by means of steel ropes made from piano wire. The central mast simultaneously served as a service shaft not only for heat and power, but also for water and ventilation. The floors of the house were made of pneumatic membrane assemblies and the façade was conceived as a double-leaf, self-supporting plastic envelope – transparent, translucent or opaque – with a vacuum in the cavity.[2]   ///   Whereas the transportable plastic house was for Buckminster Fuller part of a global social utopia, Frederick Kiesler linked the design of an organically curving plastic house into his "time-space architecture" theory.[3] He designed the "Space House" for the Modernage Furniture Company in New York in 1933. The house was to be moulded completely in plastic so that the walls, floors, ceilings and columns would merge into one. The interior extended as a continuous space over several levels and could be subdivided into individual areas or segments as required by means of movable partitions. This streamlined building anticipated the architectural language of the plastic buildings of the 1970s, with their apt use of synthetic materials.   ///   However, the practices of everyday building in those days were in no way able to take up the ideas of the visionaries and turn them into reality. The materials had not yet been fully developed, their properties had not been verified and their structural behaviour was still uncertain. Nevertheless, from the late 1930s onwards, initial, cautious attempts were made to establish the new materials in architecture[4] – a dynamic that was interrupted by the outbreak of World War II because the plastics industry was forced to concentrate on supplying products for the war effort.

"Space House", Frederick Kiesler, 1933

a view to the impending housing shortage, the British developed concepts for prefabricated houses made from plastics consisting of self-supporting, multi-layer sheets (see "The all-plastics house", in: *British Plastics*, April 1944]   **5** Archive material on the 1946 fair: "The planned plastic house for export in order to secure food supplies and rebuilding activities" (building archives of the Berlin Academy of Arts); published in *Der Bauhelfer*, No. 6, 1946   **6** The prefabricated plastic house "Deutschland" was designed by Hans Scharoun and Karl Böttcher.   **7** Ulrich Conrads and Hans G. Sperlich, *Fantastic Architecture*, London, 1963. Goff's use of plastics is not contrary to his "organic" form of building in which he makes direct references to nature, the natural surroundings and the character of the materials.   **8** The house was funded by the *Daily Mail* newspaper and exhibited at the Ideal Home Exhibition in London.   **9** "The general conception of the house: The rooms flow into one another like the compartments of a cave, and as in a cave, the skewered passage which joins one compartment with another effectively maintains privacy." Catherine Spellman, Karl Unglaub [eds.],

PLASTIC SHELLS AND SHEETS

THE POST-WAR YEARS AND GERMANY'S ECONOMIC MIRACLE – THE PLASTIC BUILDING BETWEEN PRAGMATISM AND EXPERIMENTATION

FROM THE HOUSE TO THE ROOM MODULE /// In the industrialised countries, the shortage of housing in the post-war years led to a yearning for the prefabricated house. This method of building, which had been established after World War I, encourages standardisation, mass production, transportability and the straightforward assembly of prefabricated elements. The new synthetic materials seemed predestined for this method of building, and compared to conventional prefabricated timber and concrete elements their lower weight would help to reduce transport and erection costs – an important advantage. A certain plastics euphoria was evident; some even proclaimed it to be the dawn of the plastics age, which led to considerable research and development activities on an international scale. A building trade fair held in Berlin in 1946 exhibited a number of prefabricated plastic houses which were intended to be produced in large numbers in the following years in order to overcome the shortage of housing at home and at the same time for export in order to help German industry get back on its feet.[5] The initiator of this study was the International Committee for Building & Housing, composed of architects from the US and the UK as well as Germany. Five national teams of architects designed single-storey, modular house types made from plastic sheets with a floor area of 65 m², which could be arranged as terrace or semi-detached houses.[6] The pragmatic approach of this study was reflected in the design of the houses, which matched those of conventional house types. /// Buckminster Fuller's "Wichita House" was less conventional. It was both a prototypical prefabricated house ready for mass production and at the same time, the first time Fuller had been able to realise his vision of a lightweight, transportable house. However, the house was made chiefly of aluminium, not plastics, because Fuller had acquired a former aircraft assembly plant for the production, which was equipped for metalworking operations. The only remnant of his materials concept for "Dymaxion" was the wraparound windows made from double-leaf Perspex sheets. The industrially prefabricated aluminium and plastic elements were intended to be dispatched as a building kit to all parts of the country. Despite the great interest shown by potential buyers, mass production never got going; the plastics industry, which was primarily concerned with the manufacture of everyday articles, at that time showed no interest in the mass production of houses. ///

House in Urbana, Illinois, Bruce Goff, 1952; perspective view of garden side

The perspective view of the interior shows the spiral connecting ramp and the suspended "living spheres" (drawing: Herbert Greenberg).

Peter Smithson: Conversations with Students, New York, 2005, p. 43   **10** The architects' priority was to find new housing concepts for urban living. Besides the "House of the Future", they designed several other house types between 1956 and 1958 based on similar concepts: mass production in contemporary construction, integral garden, open-plan layout, built-in storage and working spaces, etc. are the features of their houses.   **11** The house was commissioned by Charbonnages de France together with the engineers Coulon and Magnant, and was also displayed in The Hague in 1956.   **12** The house was financed and produced by the plastics manufacturer Monsanto Chemical Co. and remained on show for 10 years at Disney World in California.   **13** Schein's mobile room module (1956) can be seen in conjunction with the growing caravan fashion. Starting in the mid-1950s, caravans made from moulded glass fibre had been produced in the UK. The mobile plastic room modules were not intended just for holiday accommodation, but could also provide living accommodation for families; furthermore, they could be equipped and used for any type of mobile task (e.g. exhibitions,

It was not until the mid-1950s, as the price of oil began to fall steadily, as the new generation of plastics started to appear and as production and machining methods underwent improvements, did it seem that the plastic house, as a mass-produced item, was within reach. The plastics industry recognised the potential in the building industry and encouraged the development of prototypes, which were exhibited at relevant trade fairs; however, the first plastic houses turned out to be merely displays of the materials of standard industrial products. /// Beyond the widespread pragmatism and the architectural approach tailored to the needs of industry, there were isolated attempts to sound out the design options that plastics offered. The "fantastic" house designed by Bruce Goff for a musician dating from 1952 can be counted among these attempts. The plastics and aluminium industries financed the project and determined the materials. Goff designed the roof as an oversized "umbrella" of transparent plastic and suspended spherical room modules from this which were linked via a ramp-like ascending plastic tube. The transparent walls of the house were to be moulded from liquid plastic which cures to form a rigid shell.[7] /// In subsequent years, the first plastic houses appeared in which both the architecture and the construction did justice to the materials themselves, which kindled a sort of for-mal-aesthetic revolution. The houses made from moulded parts, which joined together floors, walls and ceilings seamlessly, were the expression of a new image of civilisation in the increasingly prosperous and individualised society of leisure. Mobility and flexibility were the buzzwords of a new generation of architects. How life in the future would look was demonstrated by Alison and Peter Smithson in 1956 with their "House of the Future" (H.O.F.).[8] The introverted, single-storey patio house consisting of organi-cally interlinked spaces on the one hand evoked a feeling of an-cient cave shelters,[9] but at the same time the interior, with its moulded, seamless, satin gloss walls, the "O-Volving" shelving, cupboards, kitchen appliances and washing facilities, reminded the viewer of scenes from a science-fiction film. Even though the whole design was based on the new plastic materials (the house was intended to be moulded in glass fibre), the materiality was more an inspiration than the actual focus of the design.[10] In that same year, Ionel Schein presented his "Maison en Plastique" in Paris at the Salon des Arts Ménagers.[11] This "expanding" house had a spiral form on plan to which extra rooms could be added if required – thus anticipating society's demands for flexibility. De-spite the complex plan geometry, the rooms were made from iden-tical segments produced from prefabricated, folded plastic sheets. In contrast to the organically curving science-fiction vi-sion of the Smithsons, the structure of this house employed a conventional form of construction in which the walls, loadbearing structure and roof are clearly separate items. /// A sensa-tional breakthrough in the building of plastic houses was achieved by the American architects Hamilton and Goody in 1957 with the

"House of the Future", Alison and Peter Smithson, 1956; bedroom

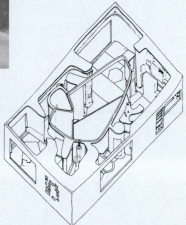

"House of the Future". Cut-away view

mobile hospitals, building site accommodation, etc.]. **14** 1957: The "Plastic House" by Hubert Hofmann and Wassili Luckhardt and the "Owopor House" made from plastic sandwich panels and exhibited at the Interbau fair in Berlin, plus any number of additive plastic cubes measuring 4.8 x 4.8 m by Cesare Pea at the Triennale in Milan. 1958: A plastic house as a weekend retreat made from a self-supporting shell construction by Rudolph Doernach at the "Plastics Conquer the World" exhibition in Stuttgart. 1959: Troisdorfer plastic house from the Dynamit-Nobel A/G company. **15** The Congrès Internationaux d'Architecture Moderne (CIAM) held in 1956 discussed issues of mobility, growth, organic "cluster formation" and communication (*Bauwelt*, No. 38, 1956). **16** The founding members of the group were David Georges Emmerich, Yona Friedman, Jean Pecquet, Jerzy Soltan and Jan Trapman. In addition, the German architects Frei Otto, Günter Günschel and Günther Kühne also took part in the meetings. **17** "The expression 'architecture mobile' signifies not only the mobility of the whole construction, but also its adaptability to meet the changing needs of a

Monsanto "House of the Future".[12] The curved plastic shells raised above ground level were joined together seamlessly to form the roof, walls and floor of the four square rooms that radiated out from a central square space. The construction of the nearly 5 m wide, cantilevering glass fibre-reinforced plastic shells represented the limits for this material, and it was therefore a perfect demonstration vehicle for the plastics industry. In terms of architecture, aesthetics and construction, the house staked out the route that would be taken by the future development of plastic houses. Another equally pioneering project was the plastic room module conceived by Ionel Schein, which could be used as a mobile beach-house, a hotel chalet or for other functions. It contained a small bathroom unit and a double bed, which during the day could be converted into a couch and table. These minimal accommodation units could be easily transported on a goods vehicle and set up as interconnected structures.[13] Further plastic houses, the majority conceived as holiday chalets, followed in the footsteps of these early examples.[14]   ///   The growing trend towards lightweight, mobile room modules found an outlet in new urban concepts. Inspired by the CIAM Congress held in Dubrovnik in 1956,[15] young architects in Paris founded the "Groupe d'Ètudes d'Architecture Mobile" (GEAM).[16] Based on the realisation that people should form part of a permanent sociological and technical process of change, the architects called for flexible and variable residential structures. As an answer to these demands, they developed the "architecture mobile":[17] room modules without specific functions that could be inserted into an independent loadbearing and services structure and added to or removed depending on requirements (growing/shrinking families, relocation, etc.).[18]

SHEDS AND CANOPIES   ///   Temporary exhibition halls and canopies represented another area where the exponents of plastics architecture could experiment. Starting in the mid-1950s, plastic sheets or membranes were used to form enclosures to the delicate timber and steel loadbearing structures of single-storey sheds and to demonstrate the innovative energies of their owners.[19]   ///   Richard Buckminster Fuller played a special and pioneering role in this sector, too, with the development of his geodesic domes. Starting with his "Necklace Domes", which he built in 1948/49 together with students, the following 20 years saw him produce a multitude of dome structures covered with the most diverse synthetic materials or made from self-supporting plastic sheets. The uses and the sizes of these domes varied.[20] The early 1950s saw Fuller introduce the use of transparent membranes and plastic sheets for façades. At the same time he also demonstrated the load-carrying capacity of the new material by constructing a radome made from rhombus-shaped, self-supporting plastic shells (1954).   ///   Another option for creating large structures using loadbearing plastics was put to the test by the

Monsanto "House of the Future", Hamilton and Goody, 1957

With its cantilevering plastic shells, the Monsanto "House of the Future" demonstrated the possibilities of synthetic materials and hence heralded a new era in architecture.

The mobile room module – here as a library – which was conceived as a beach-house or hotel chalet, can be regarded as the predecessor of the modular architecture of the 1970s.

changing society." Yona Friedman in: Werk, No. 2, 1963. The group first published its ideas in 1958 (see Bauwelt, No. 21, 1958); they presented their works at an exhibition in Amsterdam in 1962. **18** See Bauwelt, No. 21, 1958   **19** Halls and canopies at the 1955 German National Garden Exhibition, the Hannover Industry fair of 1956, Interbau 1957 and the 1958 World Exposition in Brussels were built in this way. See Hansjürgen Saechtling, Amtor Schwabe, Bauen mit Kunststoffen, Berlin, 1959.   **20** Buckminster Fuller built domes with diameters up to 67 m; they were used for research centres, restaurants, swimming pools, planetariums, warehouses, aircraft hangars, exhibition halls and radar stations.   **21** Similar canopy constructions were used in the 1960s and 1970s as roofs to petrol stations or for large projects such as the airport terminal in Dubai.   **22** Sir George Thomson, quoted in Michel Ragon, Où Vivrous-nous Demain?, Paris, 1963   **23** ibid.   **24** "Why not design fully fitted houses into which one can step and simply live, complete, in much the same way as one can sit in a normal fully-fitted car and drive away?" Quarmby, The Plastic Architect, p. 132   **25** Suuronen

US pavilion at the American Exchange Exhibition in Moscow in 1959. A modular system consisting of translucent, canopy-type moulded plastic shells 6 m high and about 5 m in diameter formed the roofs to this pavilion.[21]   ///   Mobility, flexibility, modular architecture and space-travel aesthetics were the dominating themes and paradigmatic features of 1960s architecture, and elements of this could be seen in the plastic buildings of the early years.

THE 1960S – THE RIGHT-ANGLE IS A THING OF THE PAST

During the 1960s, the mobile leisure society, characterised by its enthusiasm for space travel, its belief in technology and the future, its rejection of traditions, but also its fear of the worldwide population explosion, constituted a fertile soil for the ongoing development of plastic houses. This new, lightweight material fuelled the fantasies of a whole generation; enthusiastic planners and theorists saw the cities of the future as dynamic organisms characterised by weightlessness and a diversity of forms.[22] Plastics architecture promised to liberate us from an "architecture of concrete or steel, the structure of which appears like a cage and unluckily has led to the aesthetic of the right-angle."[23] The profession was in agreement: the future of architecture belonged to synthetic materials.

ROOM MODULES AND MODULAR CONSTRUCTION   ///
In thematic terms, the use of plastics in architecture thoroughly declined in the 1960s. Room modules appeared, additive or stand-alone, made from prefabricated, self-supporting, curved plastic shells and also buildings made from modular panel systems. The fully equipped room module fitted perfectly into the idealised image of future living styles.[24] With crystalline, circular or organic forms, they were placed on stilts, anchored like tents to the ground, or floated on the water. They were placed in rows, stacked in towers, or suspended from loadbearing frameworks. The imaginations of the designers seemed to know no bounds. Within a very short period of time, more than 200 prototypes destined for mass production were developed in Europe and the US.   ///   One of the highlights in this wide assortment of plastic houses was the "Futuro" après-ski hut designed by Matti Suuronen (1968). Optimised structurally and ecologically, this mobile room module looked like a flattened plastic sphere sitting on a steel frame with four legs.[25] Sixteen identical plastic segments enclosed a floor area of 50 m². The prototype was fitted with relaxing armchairs arranged radially around a fireplace. Besides this communal room, there was a small kitchen, a bathroom and one bedroom.[26] The building, which reminded the observer of a UFO after touchdown,

The fully fitted, mobile module "Futuro" was built from 16 identical plastic segments and could be used as an après-ski hut, holiday accommodation, kiosk or petrol station building; Matti Suuronen, 1968

The flattened plastic sphere with fold-out stairs looks like a UFO after touchdown!

realised an architectural space that Frederick Kiesler had already proclaimed as an ideal space back in 1934: "Next simplified method of building: the die-cast unit... Such construction I call shell-monolith. Easily erected. Weight minimized. Mobile. Separation into floor, walls, roof, columns, is eliminated. The floor continues into the wall..., the wall continues into the roof, the roof into the wall, the wall into the floor.... The ideal house configuration with least resistance to outer and inner stress is not the ovoid but the spheroid matrix: a flattened sphere. In its equatorial section a circle, in its longitudinal section an ellipse..." Gohr, Luyken (eds.), *Frederick J. Kiesler*, pp. 23–28   **26** A detailed description of the history and construction of the "Futuro" après-ski hut can be found in Elke Genzel, Pamela Voigt, *Kunststoffbauten*, Weimar, 2005, and in Marco Home, Mika Taanila (eds.), *Futuro. Tomorrow's House from Yesterday*, Helsinki, 2002.   **27** The Feierbach family lived in the house from 1968 to 1978. By 1979, a further 35 houses had been built using this system. Genzel, Voigt, *Kunststoffbauten*, p. 189; www.feierbach.com   **28** During the 1950s Luigi Nervi, Oscar Niemeyer, Félix

was the practical manifestation of a generation enthusiastic about technology, and also the culmination of the possibilities of synthetic materials in terms of architectural language, content and construction. Patents for the system were sold worldwide and in the following years some 60 "Futuros" were built for use as kiosks, holiday homes, petrol station buildings and even watchtowers. /// Despite the great public interest in the plastics architecture of a "Monsanto" or a "Futuro", the vast majority of potential buyers was not prepared to accept the dictatorial principle of the room module. A moderate yet contemporary variation appeared in the form of the FG 2000 system by Wolfgang Feierbach, which permitted many different plan layouts. This modular building system consisting of self-supporting, glass fibre-reinforced plastic panels fitted in well with the architectural language of the 1960s. The curved panels with their rounded edges and smooth surfaces formed both the roof and the external walls of the buildings. The prototype, a rectangular plastic box standing on a masonry plinth was used by the Feierbach family itself.[27] Full-height built-in cupboards of plastic divided the open-plan layout into functional areas, and carpeted ceilings, replaceable textile wall coverings and modern plastic furniture determined the ambience of the interior. The form of construction, the plan layout and the interior were an impressive demonstration of the ideas of contemporary, modern living. /// In contrast to the majority of plastic buildings of that period, which were conceived exclusively for temporary occupation (holiday homes, ski huts, beach-houses, etc.), the FG 2000 system was approved by the authorities and consequently could be used for commercial or residential purposes. Notwithstanding, plastic buildings still did not establish themselves firmly in the marketplace; high production costs and fire protection problems were only two of the reasons for this.

The FG 2000 system consists of plastic modules that can be joined together in a number of different ways; Wolfgang Feierbach, 1968

BUILDING ON A LARGE SCALE /// A number of different types of construction became available for large-scale projects such as industrial sheds, sports halls and large-span roofs. The range included self-supporting plastic shells and folded-plate structures, structural steelwork with plastic infill panels, or pneumatic and mechanically tensioned membrane constructions. /// Folding or double curvature gave very thin plastic sheets the necessary stiffness – construction principles that had first been used successfully in the concrete buildings of the 1950s[28] – and they became self-supporting enclosures for large projects, primarily industrial utility structures. In the 1960s many systems were developed and verified structurally for these three-dimensional building envelopes.[29] Produced as modules, they were assembled to form barrel vaults, large canopies or domes. The protective roof over an industrial plant near Rome is typical of one of these self-supporting, folded-plate constructions. The transport-

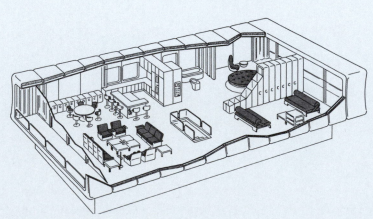

FG 2000. Cut-away view

Candela, Eero Saarinen and others had built delicate folded and curved concrete shells. **29** In the UK in particular, the Structural Plastics Research Unit, a research group at the civil engineering faculty at the University of Surrey, investigated the structural properties of folded-plate structures, and Arthur Quarmby and students at the Bradford Regional College of Art experimented with folded-plate structures that could be folded together concertina-fashion. In Italy the architect Mario Scheichenbauer investigated the development of prefabricated folded-plate structures. **30** Just like prefabricated plastic houses and pneumatic buildings, the architecture of folded-plate structures was determined by industry. Leaders in this field were the British companies Formplus Co. of Quarry Bank, Anmac Ltd. and Mickleover Transport Ltd. ("Clamp System"). **31** At the University of Surrey in the 1960s, several institutes were involved in research into 3D stressed-skin structures made from plastic pyramids: the Department of Civil Engineering headed by Prof. Z. S. Makowski and the Structural Plastics Research Unit under the leadership of R. C. Gilkie and D. Robak. In the Netherlands,

able, modular barrel vault, designed by Renzo Piano in 1966, was made up of rhombus-shaped, glass fibre-reinforced plastic elements bolted together.[30] The 3D stressed-skin structures, made up of small-format, standardised plastic pyramids, were folded-plate structures with more demanding architecture. In addition to the bolted connections, the elements were connected via a system of tubes, mostly steel or aluminium, installed inside or outside the envelope.[31] /// In other large projects the plastic shells were not used as the loadbearing elements, but rather as the façade material. One outstanding example with a resounding symbolic effect was Buckminster Fuller's US pavilion at the 1967 World Exposition in Montreal. This giant geodesic dome 61 m high and 76 m in diameter was formed by a delicate, three-dimensional network of bars with infill panels of bubble-shaped Perspex panels. As the world's largest dome construction, the pavilion became the symbol of technology's supremacy over nature.

URBAN UTOPIAS /// In the early 1960s the notion that the concrete frame would in future be replaced by modular systems with plastic room modules spread throughout the building industry;[32] plastics architecture seemed to represent an adequate answer to the emerging technological age of nuclear energy and transistors, which would give rise to the new human being – the mobile individual.[33] Architectural practices with an international outlook such as Archigram, G.I.A.P.[34] (Groupe International d'Architecture Prospective) and the Japanese metabolists took up these themes and appeared in public with urban utopias as a manifestation of complex theoretical systems. /// G.I.A.P. took up the ideas and concepts of GEAM and worked on socially relevant topics like mobility, flexibility, automation, individualisation and growth in their architectural and urban models. The result was a number of individualistic designs which, however, basically followed the same pattern: lightweight, mobile room modules "docked" at random onto a primary loadbearing and infrastructure system. The primary structure, resembling that of the "Corn on the Cob" project by Arthur Quarmby, consisted of a central concrete mast with cantilever arms, or a three-dimensional loadbearing framework, like that sketched out for the projects of Wolfgang Döring and others. As a further development of his "architecture mobile", Yona Friedman designed the "ville spatiale" (1959) and the "ville-pont" (1963) as urban megastructures. His designs consisted of large-scale, multistorey space frames supported 12 m above the ground on columns. Based on a 5 m grid, the loadbearing structure could be filled as required with any number of 25 m² room modules. The conventional apartment had been resolved into a collection of spaces made up of monolithic compartments which could be assigned to individual family members and adapted for various uses.[35] A thin, transparent membrane covering the entire living accommodation assisted the straightforward construc-

This self-supporting folded structure made from plastic modules forms a barrel-vault protective roof for an industrial plant near Rome; Renzo Piano, 1966

The spectacular geodesic dome of the American Expo pavilion consisted of a space frame with an infilling of transparent acrylic elements; Buckminster Fuller, 1967

Kisho Kurokawa designed this primary loadbearing structure for residential blocks in the form of a double helix (1961).

P. Huybers was carrying out research into pyramid systems at the University of Delft. **32** Saechtling, Schwabe, *Bauen mit Kunststoffen*, p. 511 **33** In terms of our current towns and cities, we behave like people who still clothe themselves in baggy breeches and mail-shirts in the age of radar, transistors, television, atomic centres and synthetic materials. Our current urban settlements are like old, worn-out clothes that no longer match our occupations and intentions. (Ragon, *Où Vivrous-nous Demain?*) **34** The group was founded in Paris in 1965 by Ionel Schein, Yona Friedman, Paul Maymont, Georges Patrix, Michel Ragon, Nicholas Schöffer and Walter Jonas. The intention of the founding members was to unite architects, urban planners and artists on the international stage who were examining the future of cities and architecture; ideas should be exchanged and joint exhibitions and conferences organised. The group hoped to attract international members such as Arthur Quarmby, Frei Otto, Guy Rottier, William Katavolos, Kisho Kurokawa, Stéphane du Chateau, Werner Ruhnau, Pascal Häusermann and David Georges Emmerich. The Belgian Centre d'Etudes Architecturales served

tion of the modules. Similar megastructures, but emphasizing the cyclic character of the city, are to be found in the urban utopias of the metabolists.[36] In an analogy with biological systems, their city of the future is like an organic, dynamic body subjected to changing cycles and forming an indivisible alliance between humans, machines and spaces. The different structures of a city (capsules, loadbearing structure, communication structure, transport structure) should be separated from each other according to their life cycles. Their megastructures in the form of waves ("wall clusters"), trees ("urban connectors") or double-helix molecules reflect in a very pictorial manner the biological-organic approach. The technoid, migrating cities, which the Archigram Group presented in comic-style drawings, formed the conclusion and climax of the urban utopias.[37]

The "ville spatiale" consisted of a multistorey space frame that could be fitted with any number of room modules; Yona Friedman, 1959/60

THE ROOM MODULE, A TECHNOID ORGANISM /// The futuristic urban visions were accompanied in the 1960s by architectural utopias that questioned the very essence of traditional living concepts and forms and demonstrated radical, new solutions based on the automation of fully equipped houses. Arthur Quarmby's vision of the house of the future drew a picture of a technoid organism defined by the comfort and convenience of its occupants. Lighting, colours, sounds, music, views of the outside world, odours and feelings[38] should be controlled via the touch of a button just like the movable partitions, façades and roofs. In 1965 David Greene went one step further with his "Living Pod" design. The high-tech, automated residential module with its space-travel aesthetic was fitted with electrical sliding doors, an automated "body-cleansing system", rotating cupboards for storing clothes, a mobile food-and-drink servery and integral, automatic cooker. The house had become an active, living organism – a "mother machine" that washed, clothed and fed its occupants.[39] /// Also reminiscent of a living organism was the fantastic architecture of the American philosopher and industrial designer William Katavolos. Katavolos designed a mobile, weightless plastic house made from liquid plastic moulded into torus shapes or spheres. The outcome of chemical processes, the self-cleaning windows also regulate the temperature, the rib-like, double-leaf plastic walls function as refrigerator or cooker, and the walls create everyday articles out of plastic.[40] The houses are created at random and produce – imitating the growth processes of living organisms – "blossoms" from their own integral substances in the form of everyday articles.

Self-supporting accommodation capsules suspended from a delicate structure framework; Wolfgang Döring, 1964

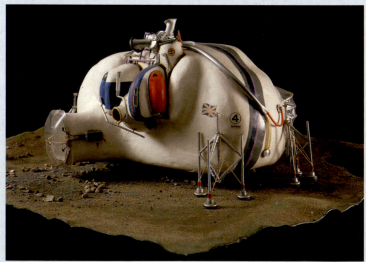

The room module as a technoid organism which cleans, clothes and feeds its occupants; "Living Pod", David Greene, 1965

as their mouthpiece, a centre which besides hosting regular avant-garde exhibitions also published a series of books defining the positions of individual members of the group. Michel Ragon, founding member of the group and architecture critic, chronicled the work of the group through publications and papers in journals. Some members of the group, e.g. Schein, Quarmby, Häusermann, dedicated themselves to investigating the possibilities of the new material in architecture.   **35** Yona Friedman, "L'Architecture Mobile", in: *Cahier du Centre d'Etudes Architecturales*, No. 3, Brussels, 1968, pp. 20–21   **36** Kisho Kurakawa founded the metabolists group in 1960 together with the architecture critic Nobru Kawazoe. In that same year they presented their ideas at the "Metabolism" exhibition in Tokyo and published their manifesto *Metabolism: The Proposals for New Urbanism*. The architecture of metabolism is an expression of the "Age of Life" and is based on cycles ("metabolic cycle"), on metamorphosis (change) and on symbiosis (the fusing of different, sometimes opposing factors and information, e.g. tradition and hi-tech, different cultures and lifestyles, etc.). Kisho Kurokawa,

THE WEIGHTLESS WORLD OF SYNTHETIC MEMBRANES

MEMBRANE TENSION STRUCTURES /// Today's plastics architecture landscape is essentially characterised by structures employing synthetic membranes. The apparently weightless forms made from transparent sheets and synthetic fabrics are the result of modern, engineered membrane construction. We should not forget that building with membranes is almost as old as humanity itself; tents with coverings of animal skins, wattle, canvas, cotton or linen have been used as accommodation since time immemorial by nomadic peoples or soldiers, as temporary banqueting halls by royal courts, and textile sunshades have been used as roofs of sports arenas and theatres since Roman times. Until the middle of the 20th century, however, the construction industry paid little attention to such membrane structures, attached little importance to them, did not regard them as elements of architecture. /// Modern membrane construction started with the development of suspended roofs.[41] Vladimir G. Shukhov built two exhibition pavilions for the 1896 pan-Russian exhibition at Nizhni Novgorod,[42] which with their suspended, mesh-like roof constructions of steel strips became exhibits themselves and excited the interest of the international audience.[43] The mesh and lattice roofs represented the breakthrough for shell structures in double curvature made from identical elements. During the 1930s, James Stewart[44] and, in particular, the French engineer Bernard Laffaille advanced the development of membrane tension structures; Laffaille's sheet-metal shells in double curvature dating from 1936 essentially formulated the nature of membrane tension structures. But it was not until the publication of *Das hängende Dach* (the suspended roof) in 1954 that the industry reached a watershed in membrane construction. Frei Otto illustrated the constructional and architectural possibilities of membrane construction and thus raised the status of architecture's "ugly duckling". Conventional tent structures became precisely designed and calculated engineered assemblies made from prestressed membranes in double curvature with diverse, complex forms, albeit initially still making use of traditional cotton materials. Again and again, trials were conducted in an attempt to replace conventional tent materials by modern fabrics because the advantages promised by the new materials were already evident. The lightweight membranes showed their potential in terms of their improved durability, higher tearing strength, better behaviour in fire and weathering resistance, and thus seemed predestined for this new field of structural engineering. /// But the first attempts ended in disaster. In 1957 the entrance arch for the German

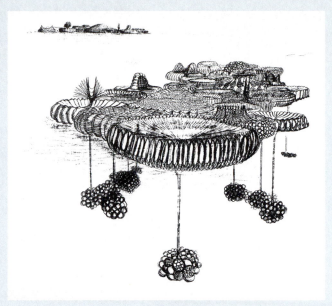

The city in the sea is the outcome of the curing processes of liquid plastics; William Katavolos, 1960

Vladimir G. Shukhov's oval pavilion at the 1896 pan-Russian exhibition was an early example of a mesh-type suspended roof construction made from identical elements.

This trial saddle-shaped arch made from sheet metal segments formulated for the first time the requirements of membrane tension structures; Bernard Lafaille, 1936

K. Kikutake, *Metabolism: The Proposals for New Urbanism*, Tokyo, 1960   **37** Archigram was founded in 1960 by the British architects Warren Chalk, Peter Cook, Dennis Crompton, David Greene, Ron Herron and Michael Webb. Up until 1974 their urban utopias such as "Walking City" or "Plug-in City" ensured plenty of attention. They first came to the notice of a wide international audience during their joint exhibition "Living City" held at the London Institute of Contemporary Arts in 1963.   **38** "I would like to be able to create an atmosphere – a mood – by varying lighting, colours, sound, music, views, smells, feeling. Why do we not build such facilities into housing?" Quarmby, *The Plastic Architect*, pp. 131–32   **39** ibid., p. 132   **40** Ragon, *Où Vivrous-nous Demain?*, pp. 102–04   **41** The Czech engineer Friedrich Schnirch invented the suspended roof in 1824 and patented it in 1826. Schnirch covered parallel purlins positioned between ridge and eaves. Georg Moller, in his "design theory" of 1828, published for the first time the use of "grid or node systems" for curved iron roof structures. He took the Gothic as his model. He built the first iron lattice dome over the east crossing

Federal Garden Exhibition in Cologne and the Bellevue Palace café at the Interbau fair, both by Frei Otto, were originally built using synthetic fabrics, but were replaced by cotton after just a short time in service because moisture damage and tears revealed the deficiencies of the plastics of that time. The changeover from cotton and linen materials to synthetic membranes in the form of textiles, sheets and meshes was only completed gradually in the 1970s as synthetic materials underwent constant improvements.   ///   Whereas the focus of interest in shell structures is the construction itself, it is the fascination of the almost immaterial material that favours the use of synthetic membranes as the façade material for temporary sheds and domes. As early as 1948, Buckminster Fuller clad his "Necklace Dome"[45] of the "Skybreak Dwelling"[46] in transparent plastic sheeting. The dome was intended to serve as a controlled-climate envelope for a mobile house, made from modular units, plus its garden. During the 1950s, other domes copied this example. However, the trade fair halls in which the sheeting was stretched over conventional loadbearing structures without taking into account the specific needs of this form of construction revealed the lack of experience in handling the new building materials.[47]   ///   The architectural and structural highlights were the tent constructions of the German pavilion[48] at the 1967 World Exposition in Montreal and the Olympics structures built two years later in Munich. In Montreal it was the graceful, playful, open roof landscape – plastic membranes in double curvature supported by a network of steel cables – that proved so popular with international visitors. The curving roofs of the Olympics structures in Munich have a covering of transparent Perspex panels which are bolted via neoprene pads to the joints of the cable-net supporting structure.

PNEUMATIC STRUCTURES   ///   Air-inflated and air-supported structures represent a special area of membrane construction. In pneumatic structures, pressure differences between the enclosed space and the exterior are responsible for giving the building its shape and also for stabilising the envelope. Although pneumatic structures had been seen in earlier centuries in the form of rafts of inflated animal skins, as the battle standards of armies in the form of air-filled kites, or as flying hot-air balloons,[49] it was not until the start of the 20th century that their use for architecture was considered. In his patents of 1917 and 1919, the British engineer F. W. Lanchester outlined the most important principles of pneumatic shed constructions (airlocks, fans for stabilising the air pressure, anchorage to the ground, stabilising network of cables) and thus created the foundation for the development of pneumatic structures in architecture. However, the patents did not bring about any notable buildings over the next 30 years and the first attempts in the 1930s to build so-called inflated domes did not get beyond the experimental stage. It was

The entrance arch for the German Federal Garden Exhibition in Cologne demonstrated the design potential of membrane structures as a new field of engineered architecture; Frei Otto, 1957

The "Necklace Dome", covered with transparent plastic sheeting, was intended to serve as a climate-controlled enclosure for a mobile house; "Skybreak Dwelling", Buckminster Fuller, 1949

The tensile shell structure of the German pavilion at the World Exposition in Montreal, with its ornate beauty and lightness, made a lasting impression on all visitors; Frei Otto, 1967

of Mainz Cathedral, although the lattice was not yet in one plane. It was Johann Wilhelm Schwedler who built the first true lattice domes (1863 onwards) in which all the members were positioned in the same plane. Rainer Graefe suspects that Shukhov was familiar with Schwedler's designs.   **42** He had already tested his mesh-like roof system on a factory building in 1894 and had applied for a patent one year later.   **43** One of his pavilions, a rotunda, consisted of two different suspended roofs. The steel mesh covered the outer perimeter of the circular building, suspended between two rings with diameters of 68.3 and 25 m. Within the inner ring, a suspended shell of riveted sheet metal formed the self-supporting roof covering.   **44** In James Stewart's suspended roof for a grain store in Albany (New York, 1932), the sheet metal panels just 2.7 mm thick spanned 36 m and thus formed a freely suspended membrane in single curvature. In contrast to prestressed shell structures in double curvature, suspended roofs are frequently only single-curvature structures and hence unstable; they achieve their stability through their high self-weight.   **45** In the "Necklace Dome" (a predecessor

the American engineer Walter Bird who achieved the breakthrough. He had been working in this field since 1946 and in 1955 he built the first spherical inflated dome for the General Electric company at Cornell University; it made use of plastic membranes and caused worldwide uproar. Just one year later, his design for a pneumatic swimming pool roof made from transparent sheets appeared on the cover of an edition of *Life Magazine*.[50] This cost-effective method of building large sheds – 1 ft² cost only 98 US cent – led in subsequent years to considerable development and production activities[51] in the industrialised countries and countless air-supported buildings with spherical and cylindrical forms appeared in the rush to achieve ever-greater dimensions.[52] These air-supported buildings were more interesting for their technical-constructional aspects than for their formal-aesthetic appeal. The lightness of these constructions seemed to be an absurd contradiction to their monstrous forms. /// The only exceptions were the sheds and pavilions of Victor Lundy, whose gracefully curving forms demonstrated the architectural potential of pneumatic structures. His exhibition hall, which he built for the United States Atomic Energy Commission in 1960, employed two adjacent domes of different height and width to create a long, cave-like structure which at the "gable" ends terminates in cantilevering, barrel-vault canopies. He managed to achieve this stroke of architectural genius through using a hybrid technique. The interior is formed according to the overpressure principle of air-inflated buildings and the outer envelope, which consists of a double-layer membrane of PVC-coated nylon fabric, has additional pneumatic stabilising. A special feature is the canopies made up of rows of air-filled, tube-shaped cushions. Cushion construction,[53] a further development of Carl Koch's theatre roof in Boston, was used here for the first time as an enclosing envelope. Koch designed the circular roof to the theatre in the form of an enormous nylon cushion, 44 m in diameter and up to 7 m deep, stretched between a circumferential steel structure. Originally, the construction was merely intended to serve as formwork for a concrete dome, but after this structure itself withstood the rigours of a hurricane in 1960, a decision was made to abandon the concrete! But for a long time, Victor Lundy's exhibition hall remained an architectural and engineering exception in pneumatic membrane architecture.

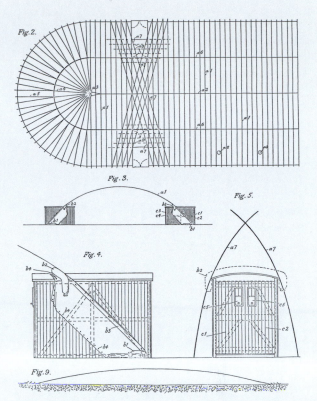

The drawings accompanying F. W. Lanchester's 1918 patent for a pneumatic shed; the patent document contained all the essential elements for modern pneumatic structures.

Walter Bird waves from the top of the first air-supported membrane dome in Cornell; Walter Bird, 1955

of his geodesic domes), the loadbearing structure of the dome is formed by straight tubes arranged in triangles, which are threaded onto wire ropes like pearls on a necklace to form a stable spherical shape. This principle is called multipolar tensegrity. **46** Fuller's students developed a "standard-of-living package" as a design exercise – a detached home for six persons, the room modules of which could be transported in one container towed behind a vehicle. **47** The Henschel company designed its cube-shaped trade fair hall using a Mero steel structure that was covered completely (walls and roof) with a 0.2 mm membrane. The barrel-vault exhibition hall for the designs of the Siemens company consisted of a mesh-like timber structure (a so-called Zollbau timber-rib construction) that was also covered with a transparent membrane (0.25 mm Gutagena sheet). The rectangular gastronomy tent at the World Exposition in Brussels had a tent-like suspended membrane (in double curvature) which looked like a prestressed shell structure; however, the membrane was not loadbearing, but simply stretched over a steel framework of suspended fish-belly girders. (Saechtling, Schwabe, *Bauen*

UTOPIA IS NOW

Utopian designs and experimental projects – maximal bubbles or minimal shelters – first revealed the fascinating appeal of "air structures". The possibility of enclosing large areas without intervening columns encouraged engineers and architects to produce futuristic designs in which transparent pneumatic domes were shown covering whole landscapes and towns. The desire to provide the needs of human beings coupled with the belief in a better future were the reasons behind these gigantic transparent enclosures creating environments with a controlled climate, and thus permitting human settlements to be established in inhospitable climates, guaranteeing a Mediterranean lifestyle worldwide, or favouring the growth of plants.   ///   Throughout the 1950s and 1960s, numerous projects – geodesic domes, cable-net structures and pneumatic buildings – were designed as climate-control envelopes covering large areas.[54] The best-known designs stem from the drawing boards of Frei Otto and Buckminster Fuller. The latter's giant transparent dome over Manhattan was published as a photomontage in 1962. Wind, rain, snow and ice, as well as emissions, were banished from the human living space. The microclimate elaborately and expensively created in each individual living space to protect against a hostile nature was now transferred into the macroclimate of the transparent dome.[55]   ///   In that same year, Frei Otto published a design for a pneumatic dome that could be built in the Antarctic to create a habitable living space and protect a whole town against the inhospitable exterior climate.[56] The background to this design was the frightening scenario of global overpopulation, a nightmare that had not lost its relevance 10 years later: in 1971 Frei Otto returned to this idea, this time together with Kenzo Tange and Ove Arup, and developed in detail a cable-supported pneumatic structure for a town in the Antarctic.

Exhibition Pavilion for the US Atomic Energy Commission; Victor Lundy, 1960 (structural engineers: Walter Bird and Severud-Elstad-Krueger)

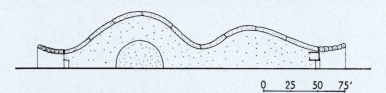

Longitudinal section; this pneumatic shed combines two construction principles: the main section is an air-supported structure stabilised by overpressure in the interior, whereas the cantilevering canopies at both ends are air-inflated structures made from air-filled tubes.

"A HOME IS NOT A HOUSE"

The book *Zugbeanspruchte Konstruktionen* (Tensile Structures) appeared in 1962, the first publication dealing in full with pneumatic structures, and was followed in 1967 by an international colloquium on this topic.[57] This special form of construction started to make more and more inroads into architecture and served the young architects on the fringe of the pop scene as a medium for their architectural experiments. The soap bubbles, as an initial starting point of the publication, illustrate impressively the weightlessness of pneumatic structures made from transparent membranes and at the same time form a link between the new building technology and the organic world of nature.   ///   The paradigmatic significance of a synthesis between technology and nature for future housing forms was demonstrated by the British

mit Kunststoffen, pp. 355–97]   **48** The pavilion was a joint composition designed by Rolf Gutbrod, Frei Otto and the structural engineer Fritz Leonhardt.   **49** Cyrano de Bergerac describes a smoke-filled balloon in his fantastic novel *L'histoire comique contenant les états et empires du soleil* (c. 1650) that carries a cabin into space. In 1709 the priest B. L. de Gusmao in Lisbon allowed himself to be transported up into the air in a hot-air balloon. And in 1731 a Russian civil servant floated above the crowns of birch trees dangling from a smoke-filled balloon. The first, spectacular flight in a manned hot-air balloon, which lasted more than 25 minutes, was achieved by the Mongolfier brothers in Paris in 1783. (Thomas Herzog, *Pneumatic Structures*, London, 1977, p. 36]   **50** Concurrently with this, G.T. Shejldahl, the founder of the Shejldahl company, built his so-called Shejldomes, likewise inflatable domes with which he could enclose swimming pools, warehouses and offices.   **51** Texair, Birdair, Shejldahl, Krupp, US Rubber and Goodyear are the best-known names from the early years of air-supported buildings. The envelopes consisted mostly of a plastic-coated nylon membrane or a polyester sheet.

architecture critic Reyner Banham with his design for an "Un-house", which he presented in 1965 in a paper entitled "A Home is not a House". Forming a contrast to monumental architecture, Banham devised his "Un-house" as a prehistoric hut in which the ingenious, highly automated infrastructure system becomes the nucleus of the living space, replacing the fireplace of ancient shelters. The infrastructure *en miniature*, as a mobile "standard-of-living package", guarantees that the occupants have everything they need (heating, cooling, ventilation, music, telecommunications, television, cooking, refrigeration), whereas a transparent, inflatable plastic dome protects them from the weather. The house is folded down to the size of a piece of luggage that the nomadic occupant can carry around with him or her ready to re-erect at any location. Technical innovations will turn human beings into the cave dwellers of the new age, living in harmony with nature.[58] /// Two years later, Haus Rucker Co[59] took up the idea of the inflatable "environment bubble" in their "Balloon for Two"[60] experiment – something between a performance and an artistic room-sized installation. The transparent plastic sheeting, including "occupants", was forced through a first-floor window of the studio, like bubblegum, and remained there suspended in the streetscape as an air-inflated room with a diameter of about 3.5 m. The background to this space experiment was the "... dream to achieve tangible control of consciousness through architectural devices."[61] Perhaps like the psychedelic drug experiences of those days, the architecture was intended to act as a "transformer", influencing the user's sensual perceptions. For this purpose, coloured, reflective patches and strips were fixed to the outside of the transparent envelope; thanks to superimposed patterns, reflections and the curvature of the façade, but also the climatic and acoustic isolation from the outside world, the picture of the outside world seen from the inside of this cocoon-type space was presented as a distorted view of reality.[62] /// Similar projects, in which the theme of the flexibility and mobility of living spaces was taken to the extreme and the architecture was transitory, continued into the 1970s.[63] These fantasies and concepts in which the architecture is resolved in entropic style, inevitably capped development in this direction.

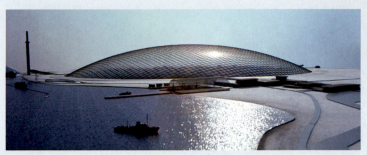

A design for a large pneumatic dome supported by a network of cables for a city in the Antarctic; Frei Otto, Kenzo Tange, Ove Arup, 1971

Photomontage: an enormous transparent dome covers a whole district of New York; inside, an environment with a controlled climate; Buckminster Fuller, 1962

---

52 Air-supported buildings were used for storage, exhibitions, radar screening, rocket assembly and as temporary roofs over swimming pools or greenhouses. Birdair's exhibition domes for the US Army had already reached a diameter of 49 m by 1958. **53** Cushion constructions are pneumatic structures in which at least two membranes are joined together along their edges and tensioned by the air pressure in the cavity between the membranes. **54** Between 1953 and 1971, Frei Otto designed numerous large-scale climate-control envelopes enclosing whole towns or landscapes. His first designs to follow this principle, dating from 1953, include an expansive glasshouse envelope spanning a complete mountain valley with cable nets and an infilling of transparent plastic sheets or corrugated Perspex panels, and also a climate envelope made from a transparent cable net for a town in the Antarctic. **55** This is an idea that Buckminster Fuller had pursued back in 1949 on a smaller scale with his "Skybreak Dwelling". The idea of a large dome over Manhattan as portrayed in the famous photomontage of 1962 probably stems from an idea he had back in 1950 in which he proved that his

DECLINE AND RENAISSANCE OF A "MIRACLE MATERIAL"

The 1970 World Exposition (EXPO) in Osaka marked the zenith and for the time being the termination of plastics architecture. Pavilions "floating" above the ground, reminiscent of UFOs, plastic capsules hanging from loadbearing frameworks, pneumatic sheds and tube-like traffic systems reflected society's fascination with technology. The EXPO was akin to the city of the future that had been propagated as the model of the future by Michel Ragon and many others during the 1960s, and for a short time transported visitors to an alien planet. Whereas the EXPO represented for many people the manifestation of their construction visions, others – even at this early date – were already criticising the inhumanity of the technoid constructions. Utopia had become "Dystopia".[64]   ///   The plastics euphoria came to an abrupt end with the oil crisis of 1973 and with the first large-scale plastic capsules. The large residential and office buildings assembled from prefabricated room modules turned out to be an anonymous and inhuman part of the built environment – the individual was degraded to an unperson in a synchronised population mass, the fully fitted capsule homes were suddenly impersonal housing cells that dictated the lifestyles of their occupants and left no room for individual expression and design. As a reaction to this, new lifestyle concepts began to emerge in society. In accordance with the catchphrase "Back to Nature!", "natural" building materials came to the fore, the intention being that they would allow individual expression and a more human interior climate. Man and machine, nature and artificiality were now inconceivable as a synthesis and as a viable model of urban living in the future. By the end of the 1970s at the very latest, plastics no longer represented progress and modernism, but instead were associated with the stigma of ugly, cheap materials, and they disappeared temporarily from the architectural landscape.   ///   Almost unnoticed and very gradually, plastics started to find their way back into architecture in the early 1990s. Unencumbered by ideology, artistically curved membrane structures made from thin plastic envelopes began to be noticed by the profession as new, transparent membranes were introduced. The efficiency of the lightweight membrane constructions is such that in the meantime enclosures and roofs of synthetic membranes are now among the standard solutions for temporary structures; transparent sheets are increasingly replacing heavy and expensive glass constructions for biospheres, animal compounds and conservatories.   ///   Furthermore, standard industrial products made from transparent plastic sheets and shells are also becoming more and more attractive as a cheap alternative to glass and are readily employed as a building material in the experiments of the avant-garde. The possibilities for plastics as building materials are being re-examined and tested, especially in terms of sustainability from the per-

Soap bubbles are an ideal way of illustrating the lightness and weightlessness of pneumatic constructions; Frei Otto's trials with models at the ILEK, Stuttgart

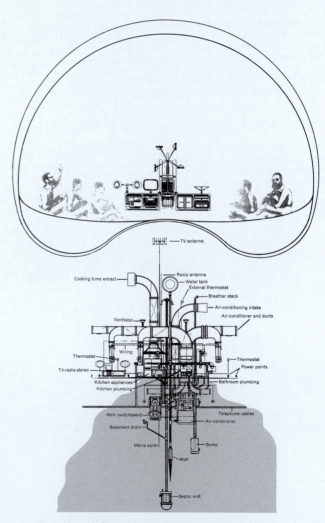

The "Un-house" of Reyner Banham (1965) consists of a complex infrastructure en miniature and a transparent pneumatic envelope.

geodesic domes could even be built in such sizes.   **56** Frei Otto, *Tensile Structures*, Cambridge, 1982   **57** Victor Lundy ("Architectural and Sculptural Aspects of Pneumatic Structures"), Walter Bird ("The Development of Pneumatic Structures. Past, Present and Future") and Heinz Isler ("Clear Transparent Roof for a Court") were among those who gave presentations at the international colloquium in Stuttgart. In: *Proceedings of the 1st International Colloquium on Pneumatic Structures*, Stuttgart University of Technology, 1967   **58** Reyner Banham, "A Home is not a House", in: *Art in America*, No. 2, 1965. The paper was written in conjunction with research carried out for the Graham Foundation in the US; Banham investigated the role of building services in modern architecture. The drawings accompanying the paper were drawn by the architect and designer François Dallegret.   **59** Klaus Pinter, Laurids and Manfred Ortner and Günter Zamp Kelp founded the Haus Rucker Co partnership in 1967.   **60** The 1972 room bubble can be seen in the form of "Oasis No. 7" at the Documenta art exhibition in Kassel.   **61** Günter Zamp Kelp, in: Heinrich Klotz (ed.), *Haus-Rucker-Co 1967 bis 1983*, Braunschweig, 1984, p. 71   **62** These fundamental considerations found their way into many of the group's projects ("Mindexpander", "Yellow Heart"), which were frequently pneumatic plastic

spective of so-called bionic architecture. /// Plastics were branded for a long time as "unmaterials" whose lack of character and undefinableness allegedly made them unsuitable for use as building materials. However, it is now precisely those properties that make them ideal for an architecture that has moved on from the traditional values of durability and standard use of materials and sees the main features as adaptability, flexibility and efficiency. As a materials experiment, the indifference of plastics and their ambiguity go hand in hand with the tendencies of contemporary architecture, which values the atmospheric, the sensual and the irritating. And that heralds the renaissance of plastics.

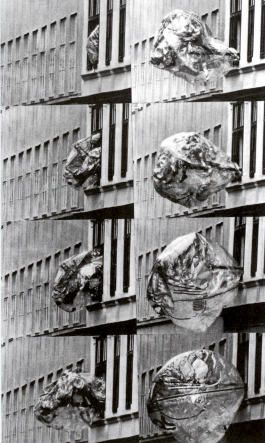

The "Balloon for Two", a transparent, pneumatic minimal space, carries its "occupants" out into the streetscape; Haus Rucker Co, 1967

structures.   **63** Guy Rottier and Denis Garnier designed the "Maison d'un jour". The house for a day consisted of a number of bubble-shaped rooms which could be created as required by the occupants like soap bubbles. After hardening, they were suitable for habitation and on the next day they could be dissolved again using a special solvent! Guy Rottier, "Recherches Architecturales", in: *Cahier du Centre d'Etudes Architecturales*, No. 8, Brussels, 1968, pp. 38–39. 1966: Gernot Nalbach designs a town of pneumatic bubbles. 1967: Haus Rucker Co designs the pneumatic, spherical housing unit "Pneumacosmic Formation", which can be docked onto an urban-type loadbearing structure, for "Interdesign 2000", an international competition. 1968: David Greene and Michael Webb develop the "Inflatable Suit House". 1974: Arthur Quarmby publishes his "House and Garden Project" with inflated, transparent domes.   **64** Takabumi Sasaki, "A passage through the Dys-topia of EXPO 1970", in: *Japan Architect*, May/June 1970, pp. 143–50

MATERIAL AND FORM – "FORM FOLLOWS MATERIAL?"

THE DUALITY OF FORM AND MATERIAL

For more than 2,000 years, the relationship between form and material in the Western world was governed by clear rules. The idea behind the form was to express the spirit, and the material had merely to serve; subsidiary to the idea, it was its manifestation.   ///   In Roman times, Vitruvius described form-finding as the result of deliberation and invention,[1] and reduced the choice of materials to economic issues and regional customs plus their constructional properties regarding durability and strength,[2] the essential criteria.[3] In the Renaissance, materials grew in importance, but continued to remain subservient to the idea. Even though Alberti basically adhered to the commentaries of Vitruvius and continued to portray durability and strength as the essential criteria when choosing materials, materials now took on the additional role of beautifying the structure.[4] The decoration and hence the specific use of the material served the consummation of architecture and underscored the form as idea.[5]   ///   The subsidiary importance of the material becomes particularly evident in sacred stone architecture over the course of the centuries; although it is always the same material, the stone appears as a cubic-closed form during the Romanesque, as delicate strutting and tracery in the Gothic, or as organically curving forms in the Baroque. The material is subjected to the whims of the designer. It was not until the 19th century, with industrialisation and the

---

1 Vitruvius, *Ten Books on Architecture*, New York, 1960   **2** Durability and strength are the features of the best building materials. Alongside appropriateness and beauty, durability belongs to the basic requirements of architecture. Durability will be assured when foundations are carried down to the solid ground and materials wisely and liberally selected. (Vitruvius, *Ten Books on Architecture*)   **3** For Vitruvius, the underlying aesthetic concepts of architecture are: order, arrangement, eurhythmy, symmetry, propriety and economy. Economy describes the proper management of materials; looked at from the point of view of cost-savings, regional building materials should be employed. Furthermore, the building materials chosen should be those that are durable and of great strength. (Vitruvius, *Ten Books on Architecture*)   **4** The grace and delightfulness, one thinks, stems from nothing other than the beauty and from the decoration. Therefore, those who wish to create something delightful must aim for greatest beauty more than anything else. If they would have wanted to do

introduction of new building materials such as concrete, glass and iron, that the relationship between form and material began to waver.   ///   In his writings, Gottfried Semper championed so-called material style in which every material should take on its appropriate form. Bricks, wood, iron especially, metal and zinc replace ashlar masonry and marble. It would be inappropriate to imitate them still further with false attestations. The material speaks for itself and appears, unveiled in the form, in the relationships that have been tried and tested by experience and science as the most appropriate for that material. Brick appears as brick, wood as wood, iron as iron, each single one according to its own laws of statics.[6] Elsewhere, he describes form-finding as the result of practical purpose, the materials used and the methods of production.[7] He therefore raised the status of the material and relieved it of its subservient function. At the same time, the latest developments in the architecture of large market halls, palm houses and exhibition buildings made from delicate iron-and-glass assemblies supplied practical evidence to back up Semper's theory and founded *de facto* a new style of building in which it was no longer the idea, but rather the material that determined the form.   ///   Architects such as Otto Wagner, Adolf Loos or Frank Lloyd Wright were following Semper's writings when they advocated a form "to suit the material". Just like Semper, Adolf Loos opposed the use of imitation and spoke up for the equality of materials. He recommended the development of form depending on material: "Every material possesses its own language of forms, and none may lay claim for itself to the forms of another material. For forms have been constituted out of the applicability and the methods of production of materials. They have come into being with and through materials."[8] Frank Lloyd Wright was of the opinion that each material had its own language and, correspondingly, every *new* material leads to a *new* form.[9]   ///   The art historians Alois Riegl and Adolf von Hildebrand took up a decidedly opposing position to this technical-material foundation for form. In his paper on the form problem in art, von Hildebrand develops a theory of form genesis from the spiritual to the material. Consequently, the form concept of the artist leads to a graphic existence form and finds its artistic expression in the materialised effect form;[10] the material, as a part of the effect form, must be subordinate to the form concept. In a similar way, Riegl bases form on the "artistic wishes" or rather the "creative thoughts" of the artist. Both Riegl and von Hildebrand banished the material to insignificance again. In the 1920s, this dispute about the predominance of form or material led to the development of the cubist architecture of the modern movement, whose protagonists, under the slogan of "material integrity", were opposed to traditional, ornamented architecture and developed their architecture of cubist spatial art on the basis of functional, economic and technical requirements.[11] However, regardless of the status of the material – whether in a secondary, subservient function or as a characterising element of the design – form and material remained inextricably intertwined, dictated by the opposing views of "artistic wishes" and "material integrity". In contrast to this, in the same period the visual arts developed approaches that led to a dissolution of the duality between material and form.

all this without the great expense of decoration and pomp, that would have been a weakly and slightly comical thing! Leon Battista Alberti, *The Ten Books of Architecture*, London, 1965   **5**   For Alberti, decoration is not just ornamentation, but likewise the wall coverings and the material. Decoration could also serve the rarity and beauty of the stone itself, we could say it was made from a type of marble. (Alberti, *The Ten Books of Architecture*)   **6**   Gottfried Semper: "Über vielfarbige Architektur und Skulptur bei den Alten", 1834, in: Hans & Manfred Semper (eds.), *Gottfried Semper. Kleine Schriften*, Mittenwald, 1979, p. 219   **7**   Gottfried Semper, "Keramisches", in: *Gottfried Semper. Kleine Schriften*, p. 24   **8**   Adolf Loos, "The Principle of Cladding", 1898, in: Adolf Loos, *Into the Void. Collected Essays 1897–1900*, Cambridge, 1982, p. 66   **9**   "Each material speaks a language of its own just as line and color speak." (p. 270) "Every new material means a new form, a new use if used according to its nature." (p. 294) Frank Lloyd Wright, "In the Cause of Architecture: Composition

THE DISSOLUTION OF THE FORM-MATERIAL DUALITY

In introducing the term formlessness in 1929, Bataille proposed the subjugation of form and hence questioned provocatively the interdependence of material and form. Just like the universe can be described as "formless", the material should not be subjected to any abstract idea. Bataille campaigned for a "materialism" that was a direct interpretation of the bare facts.[12] This approach was continued in the art of the 1950s. The intention in the works of the Japanese Gutai artists was that the material should be itself and the artist was merely a mediator.[13] In the 1960s, Robert Morris subsumed the art characterised by chance, transitoriness and process allegiance under the heading of anti-form, an expression that in the following years became a slogan for liberating the material from the dominance of form; form as an idea ceased to exist: "Arbitrary stacking, loose piling or suspending lend the material a temporary form. Chance is accepted and indeterminacy intended because another arrangement leads to a different formation. Detachment from defined, permanent forms and arrangements is seen as positive. It is part of the denial attitude of these works to continue no longer the aestheticising of form as a final measure."[14] The ephemeral and "formless" character of this art found its outlet in utopian designs and experimental plastics architecture. The "chemical architecture" of William Katavolos was produced by the curing process of liquid plastic; in an analogy to organic growth processes, his buildings created their own form.   ///   As a complement to "material art", the Russian constructivists and artists inspired by the Bauhaus movement advocated the subjugation of the material. In 1920 Naum Gabo and Antoine Pevsner called for the liberation of the sculpted body from the sealed mass,[15] and El Lissitzky described the "amaterial materialness" by means of imaginary spaces and volumes generated by linking space and time – as in "objects forced to move".[16] László Moholy-Nagy took up this approach in his book *The New Vision, from Material to Architecture* and developed the idea of architecture as spatial art, which is essentially founded on movement relationships and "fluctuating force relationships".[17] Subjugating the material aims at weightlessness, dynamic and energy, and manifests itself in kinetic sculptures, light sculptures, energy spaces and ephemeral structures. Yves Klein and Werner Ruhnau took up a radical position with regard to immaterial architecture in the 1950s with their experiments involving air (or rather energy) spaces, in which the material, in its substantial expression, vanishes completely. The air spaces were intended to be defined by different condensed airflows trying to take advantage of the thermodynamic properties of the air. Here, air as a "building material" simply represents a "spiritual principle" in which "materials" such as air, gases, fire and water are intended to be used for a dynamic and immaterial architecture. The "classic" town of tomorrow would be built using the three classic elements fire, water and air, and it would be correspondingly flexible, spiritual and immaterial.[18] Formlessness and immaterialness as thematic focuses for the art and architecture of the 20th century were united in the 1960s in

as Method in Creation", 1928, in: Bruce Brooks Pfeiffer (ed.), *Frank Lloyd Wright. Collected Writings*, vol. 1, New York, 1992   **10** Adolf von Hildebrand, *Das Problem der Form in der bildenden Kunst* (1893), Straßburg, 1913, pp. 134–36   **11** Walter Gropius, *The New Architecture and The Bauhaus*, Cambridge, Mass., 1965   **12** Georges Bataille, "Informe" and "Matérialisme", 1929, in: Charles Harrison, Paul Wood (eds.): *Art in Theory. An Anthology of Changing Ideas*, Oxford, 2001   **13** "That is illusion in which humans have burdened materials, e.g. paints, fabrics, metals, clay or marble, with false significance fraudulently so that instead of portraying their material self, they have taken on a foreign appearance ... Gutai art does not alter the material, it gives it life." Jiro Yoshihara, "Gutai Manifesto", 1956, excerpt in: Dietmar Rübel, Monika Wagner, Vera Wolff (eds.), *Materialästhetik. Quellentexte zu Kunst, Design und Architektur*, Berlin, 2005, p. 261   **14** Robert Morris, "Anti-Form", *Artforum*, April 1968, reprint in: *Materialästhetik*, Berlin, 2005, p. 269   **15** Naum Gabo, Antoine

the form of the inflatable "environment bubbles" of Reyner Banham, Haus Rucker Co and others. The climate envelopes made from transparent synthetic membranes were deprived of any formal design and apart from that were virtually immaterial.   ///   The digitising in the 1980s brought about a transformation of the material, which questioned the validity of form and material as opposites.[19] The 1985 exhibition "Les immatériaux" conceived by Jean-François Lyotard was dedicated to this phenomenon. Christine Buci-Glucksmann, in pursuing the question of the materiality of things in the age of digital production and their relationship to humans, notes that in digitising information or the "message", we have lost the classical criteria for identifying the material, which includes solid material, the materiality of the components, the permanence of space and time, stability of the subsoil, tangible reality. But although the digital "immaterials" are deprived of the definition of the material as the substantial, they are in no way immaterial, but merely differently structured. The material exists only in its smallest units, the electrons, and is hence almost identical with the spiritual, i.e. the insubstantial. The digitising of information leads to an increasingly mutual penetration of material and spirit, the effect of which is to shift the classical problem of the harmony of body and soul.[20] Because of digitisation, the form no longer manifests itself in the material, but instead as electronic information forming an analogy with the neuronal information transmission in the human brain. Structurally, the form as idea thus remains bonded to the spiritual.

FORM AND MATERIAL IN CONTEMPORARY ARCHITECTURE

As the duality of form and material started to dissolve in the 1920s, there appeared a complex weave of conditions and interdependencies which determined the material and the form in architecture. Independently from each other but nevertheless again and again interwoven, form and material follow their own laws. The material is used according to its "nature"; this "nature" contains both the constructional reality in its structural and constructional meaning and the sensual reality with its visual, haptic and atmospheric effects plus its symbolic significance, which includes emotional values. Form is the product of space and material compositions, which aim to create atmospheric effects, and the application of essential or self-elected principles – and these include the structural laws as well as the physical laws and "force fields" simulated on the computer. The form grows out of the context of topography and climate and is symbol or metaphor. In addition, social, political and ecological demands plus manufacturing and design methods influence both choice of material and also form. The individual methods of form-finding and material selection are in no way mutually exclusive and they are not adversaries either. Rather, the architectural result is frequently a conglomerate of several approaches which vary depending on the brief. The relationship between form and material can be described as a singular event that is redefined every time on the concrete artefact.[21]   ///   What is particularly clear is the independence of form and material in the formulation of their

Pevsner, "Realistic Manifesto", 1920, excerpt in: Ulrich Conrads (ed.), *Programs and Manifestoes of 20th Century Architecture*, Cambridge, Mass., 1970 **16** El Lissitzky, "K.(unst) und Pangeometrie" in: Ulrich Conrads, Peter Neitzke (eds.), *El Lissitzky, 1929. Russland: Architektur für eine Weltrevolution*, Bauwelt Fundamente, vol. 14, Braunschweig, 1989, pp. 122–29 **17** "Space creation is not primarily a question of building material … Thus a present-day space creation does not consist in putting together heavy building masses, nor in the formation of hollow bodies, nor in the relative positions of well-arranged volumes. Nor in arranging alongside of one another single cells of the same or different volume content. Space creation is today much more an interweaving of parts of spaces, which are anchored for the most part in invisible, but clearly traceable relations, moving in all directions, and in the fluctuating play of forces. The arrangement of this space creation is effected on the measurable plane by limits of bodies, and on the non-measurable by flowing fields of force.

extremes, which have established themselves as primary features of contemporary architecture with the digitising of the design and production processes and the rediscovery of the sensual qualities of the material. Form and material become antagonists leading parallel lives in contemporary architecture.

THE MATERIALNESS OF THE MATERIAL

The decline of the plastics era and the demand for "natural" materials in the 1970s brought the texture of materials within the architect's field of vision. Alvar Aalto has used the effect of material surfaces quite deliberately in his designs[22] and comes close to the nature of the material beyond its structural and building performance properties. This way of approaching the material led in the 1990s to a sort of material fetishism in which the effect of the material was paramount. Whereas architects such as Peter Zumthor and Tadao Ando looked to the sensual and atmospheric as well as the constructional character of the material plus its contextual and cultural background, others deliberately opposed precisely these features of the materials: extremely thin layers of stone bonded to a backing material negate the compressive strength property of stone so relevant to building; conventional materials are alienated and placed in a new context; materials from the aerospace industry – foreign to architecture – are used playfully in buildings; and new materials such as foams, aerogels, textiles or luminescent concrete are being tried out.   ///   The architect's willingness to experiment seems to know no bounds. The new profession of "materials consultant", who works as a "trend scout" for architects, always seeking new materials, reflects this fashion. The ways of handling materials as described in Peter Weibel's book of 1966 have become established in contemporary architecture: Regardless of whether stones or words, wood or symbols, they are materials with a rigid meaning, with an identified context. Meaning and context may be present consciously or subconsciously. Revealing subconscious contexts and meanings implies giving the material a new meaning. The materials are placed in new environments, coupled with unusual materials, and they are thereby de-identified, de-conserved. New space-time relationships, new material combinations and new symbol combinations create new meanings, are creative.[23] Façades are turned into complex three-dimensional spatial configurations through curvature and folding, are given an additional level of meaning through printing or lighting, are covered with perforated plates, metal meshes or fabrics to form multi-layer, flexible envelopes, or are reduced to textile membranes and sheets. Irrespective of the "internal workings", they claim an independence that exploits the aesthetic effects of the materials – architecture as a material art becomes an ambiguous information medium.

Thus space creation becomes the nexus of ever changing spatial entities: direct arrangement of space, pulled out of and put back into the great reservoir of all entities – a creative treatment of space, not of building materials. Building material is only an auxiliary, in so far as it can be used as carrier of space-creating and space-dividing relationships. The principal means of space creation is always the space alone, from whose laws the treatment has to proceed in all respects." László Moholy-Nagy, *The New Vision. Fundamentals of Bauhaus Design, Painting, Sculpture, and Architecture*, New York, 2005 (reprint), p. 184, 186 **18** Yves Klein, Werner Ruhnau, *Manifest zur allgemeinen Entwicklung der heutigen Kunst zur Immaterialisierung*, 1958/59 in: Heiner Stachelhaus (ed.), *Yves Klein/Werner Ruhnau. Dokumentation der Zusammenarbeit in den Jahren 1957–1960*, Recklinghausen, 1976, pp. 41–42 **19** So if we assume a material/form (*phusis/tekhn*, etc.) opposition, must this opposition not give way to the post-modernity of the immaterial? Jacques Derrida defines the material as matter

THE DIGITAL FORM

The digital form burdened with the immaterial, virtual reality of the computer world is diametrically opposed to the prevailing material fetishism. As CAD programs were introduced as design tools, the form in the planning process became completely divorced from the material, and materialisation was relegated to the background in the sequence of design and production processes. Thanks to the coupling with new production methods, which enable, and also require, digital continuity from design to production, planning the design becomes planning the product. The immaterial product has an inherent virtual form and only during manufacture do we find a reference back to the material.   ///   Robbed of its material dimension, the digital form is deprived of control and restraint by the material. Instead, the processing capacity of the computer and the options of high-end software determine the limits of form, which, however, evades the perception of the designer and presents itself as apparent boundlessness. Detached from the material in the computer world of unlimited opportunities, form as a quantity of data has added the new world of the exactly calculable freely formed surface to the language of architecture. Modelled 3D spaces with continuously curving surfaces, like walk-in sculptures, are created in virtual reality. Every conceivable form can be changed dynamically and at will in the three-dimensional, virtual model. The material as a form-giving parameter is replaced by the laws of biological, physical or statical processes, which are emulated in the computer. The dynamic of the processes is simulated and the form generated or modified accordingly – a fact that is reflected in the new terminology: the architectural avant-garde gives its architecture names like "transarchitecture", "genetic architecture" or "flowing architecture"; the design processes are like a morphogenesis and the concept of form is replaced by the term design. The form-material duality seems to have been finally banished to the pages of history. The contemporary architect is an animation designer and "materials artist" at the same time.

informed by technology, as the substance of an instrument. Jacques Derrida, "Materielles", 1985, in: Rübel, Wagner, Wolff (eds.), Materialästhetik, p. 338. Likewise: "Immaterial ... designates a structure in which the conventional opposition between spirit and material no longer has a place." Jacques Derrida in conversation with Jean-François Lyotard on 27 Oct 1984 in: Jean-François Lyotard et al., Immaterialität und Postmoderne, Berlin, 1985, p. 23   **20** "Les immatériaux" (the immaterials) is a neologism coined by Jean-François Lyotard which is made up of the words materials (matériaux) and immaterial (immatériel). Christine Buci-Glucksmann, "Entmaterialisierung", in: Rübel, Wagner, Wolff (eds.), Materialästhetik   **21** Sabine Kraft, "Werkstoffe – Eigenschaften als Variablen", in: Arch+, No. 172, 2004, p. 25   **22** Richard Weston, Materials, Form, and Architecture, London, 2003   **23** Peter Weibel, "Materialdenken als Befreiung der Produkte des Menschen von ihrem Dingcharakter", 1966, in: Rübel, Wagner, Wolff (eds.), Materialästhetik, pp. 264–65

TRANSPARENT PLASTICS BETWEEN INTELLECTUAL-ISATION AND TRASH CULTURE

Synthetic materials have re-established themselves in the experiments of the contemporary architectural avant-garde in the tension between spirit and matter, form and material.[1] Digitally generated forms on the one hand and material fetishism on the other favour the use of transparent plastics, which are characterised by immateriality and ambiguity. Their random formability plus their versatility bind the synthetic material to the digitally animated architectural form. Flexibility, efficiency and adaptability – the essential features of synthetic materials – are ideal for so-called bionic architecture. Their indifferent properties predispose them for an architecture that regards metaphor as extremely important, relies on sensuality, ambience and irritation, and takes "removal of barriers" as its key theme – specifically, the removal of barriers between inside and outside, matter and space, loadbearing structure and enclosing envelope, two-dimensionality and three-dimensionality, static and dynamic, and between space and time.

PLASTIC IS SPIRIT, PLASTIC IS FORM /// Freely formed, digital architectures and transparent plastics form a congenial symbiosis in many ways. In an analogy to the immateriality of digital forms, transparent plastics are a synonym for the subjugation of the material. As transparent and at the same time almost weightless materials, they seem closer to the spiritual world than the material world. Moulded into bubble-like shapes or

BMW Bubble, ABB Architects | Bernhard Franken, 1999

1 The renaissance of plastics – and especially transparent plastics – in architecture is based on the dissolution of the form-material relationship and the associated paradigm change in design approaches and concepts. Detached from the material, form is generated digitally, or the architecture is understood as a material art.　**2** Roland Barthes, "Plastic", 1957, in: Roland Barthes, *Mythologies*, London, 1972
3 "Shape is buoyant. The hollowness of shape also produces (and requires) an effect of buoyancy. While massive, the projects seem to be made of Styrofoam, sponge, or aero-gel...", Robert E. Somol,

designed as cushions of air, they take on spherical dimensions. /// The spiritual content, as an intrinsic characteristic of synthetic materials, has from time to time been a theme in the writings of artists and intellectuals over the course of the 20th century. Roland Barthes characterised the new material as the very "spectacle of its end-products" and defined the spiritual content of plastics by means of their "quick-change artistry". Plastic is "more than a substance, plastic is the very idea of its infinite transformation [...] Plastic, sublimated as movement, hardly exists as substance."[2] The versatility (in terms of both chemistry and form) and the resulting infinite configuration options, which lead to the invention of forms, are features of the computer-generated forms and the artificial material alike. /// Robert E. Somol has given us a link between digital forms and synthetic materials based on associations. Responsible for this is "hollowness" as a property of the computer-generated form, making a project appear as if made from polystyrene, sponges or aerogels.[3] Digitally shaped architecture can obviously express itself adequately in formal terms in the weightless world of plastics, an association that is helped by the form of the mostly "anti-architectural" morphogenetic architecture. /// Beyond the metaphorical, new production techniques tie synthetic materials to the opulent world of digital forms. In the case of additive production techniques such as 3D printing, laser sintering and stereolithography[4], the products or their parts are produced in layers drop by drop so that formwork or negative moulds are unnecessary for forming curved building components. These production methods only work with materials in liquid or powder form, e.g. plastics or metals, that assume their final form after hardening. The low weight and the possibility of combining them with metals or organic substances to form composites, or equipping them with various properties depending on the chemical composition, is what distinguishes synthetic materials from metals and has already made them the unrivalled material of choice for many unconventional applications in aviation, the automotive industry and shipbuilding. As the building industry does not yet have such production techniques at its disposal, digital, curving architecture is restricted to the much more involved and hence more costly subtractive production techniques[5], or moulding in negative moulds. However, studies of production processes using variable moulds, thermally mouldable plastics and computer-controlled printing methods for multi-component materials are among the key areas of current research. We will have to wait and see whether the architecture of the future with plastics and their composites – furnished with the necessary building performance properties – really can be simply "printed out" on a 3D printer and assembled! Until then, form remains dormant in the virtual world of the computer.

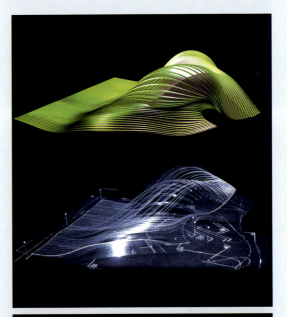

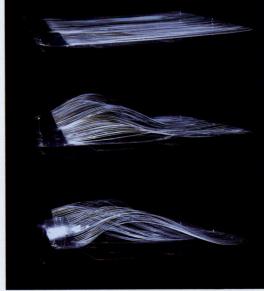

ephemeralMATTER, f-u-r

"12 Reasons to Get Back into Shape", in: Rem Koolhaas, *Content*, Cologne, 2004, pp. 86–87 **4** 3D printing, stereolithography and laser sintering are rapid prototyping production techniques. In 3D printing the raw material in powder form is solidified by the selective addition of an adhesive. Stereolithography involves curing resins (photopolymers) in ultraviolet light. And laser sintering uses materials in powder form (plastics or metals) that are melted down by a powerful laser and thereby solidify. **5** In subtractive production techniques, the final shapes are cut from a larger block. Another way of

PLASTICS AND BIONICS /// One possible design and form-finding method for "self-generating", digital forms consists of the imitation of biological processes, phenomena and structures, which results in a marriage between digital architecture and bionics. Transferring the complex structures and geometries of nature to architecture calls for a building material that can be moulded into any shape, is extremely efficient and adaptable in terms of statics, and can also provide numerous properties. Plastics are suitable for this, not only because of their "programmability" – the possibility of an almost infinite chemical composition and adaptation to natural materials – but also in the form of so-called bionic building materials. Designed as composites or provided with functions, the spectrum of potential material properties is almost inexhaustible and, in addition, the favourable ratio of weight to stability is similar to the optimised constructions of nature. As both the new generation of plastics and the digital production techniques are still undergoing development, the complicated geometries in architecture are frequently implemented in the form of ultra-thin synthetic membranes. In doing so, these lightweight, tensile membrane structures come close to the efficient, minimal constructions of nature in terms of both form and construction. Seemingly effortlessly, they are used to span great distances and remind us of the building principles of insect wings, soap bubbles or spiders' webs.[6] /// Young architectural practices such as raumlabor_berlin have taken up the idea of pneumatic minimal construction with their "mobile kitchen monument" in order to redefine the relationship between public and private. Within the scope of the arts festival "Akzente", which was held in Duisburg and Mülheim in 2006, the architects realised a project that was situated somewhere between a performance and an experiment, and created an inflatable room made from transparent plastic which can protrude from a metal sculpture as required, not unlike a soap bubble. Depending on its surroundings, the transparent enclosure can take on different forms: whereas on a "green-field site" it can develop unconstrained into a regularly shaped air bubble, in an urban context it tends to cling to its surroundings and becomes deformed. This temporary space can be used as a kitchen and dining room, or as a dance hall for social communication, and becomes a place in which public and private are fused together. /// Nicholas Grimshaw's Eden Project, a group of nested domes made from transparent air cushions covering a large part of the landscape, is a reference to the geodesic domes of Buckminster Fuller, which he devised based on his search for "nature's geometry", and which in formal-constructional terms find their counterparts in the miniature lifeforms of the diatomes and radiolaria.[7] Werner Nachtigall sees in the hexagonal honeycomb structure of the Eden Project an analogy to the honeycomb structure of foams in which the competition for space leads to a hexagonal flattening of the sides and creates an optimised lightweight

Kitchen monument, raumlabor_berlin, 2006

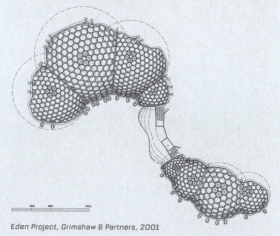

Eden Project, Grimshaw & Partners, 2001

shaping panels in double curvature is to produce a negative mould using a subtractive method.   **6** This is a development that started in the 1950s. Frei Otto was inspired by soap bubbles, spiders' webs or insect wings when trying to optimise the loadbearing structures of efficient minimal constructions.   **7** Joachim Krausse, Claude Lichtenstein (eds.), *Your Private Sky*, Baden, 1999, p. 442. Diatomes are siliceous unicellular algae whose shells consist of hexagonal elements of silicon dioxide; radiolaria are single-celled marine creatures with a perforated, shell-like skeleton of silicon dioxide with a

structure.[8] MO STUDIO's "Curved Building" – their design for a sports centre for extreme sports – also makes use of the construction principles of foams or sponges. The project, which is similar to an oversized, solidified foam, consists of a shell or cave-like 3D loadbearing structure with surfaces in double curvature. Inside, the outcome is a continuous, endless surface and complex spatial relationships, which are further enhanced by the use of transparent plastics and become obvious to the users of the building. Borrowed from boat-building, the space-forming loadbearing structure is made from prefabricated, vacuum-formed, fibre-reinforced plastic composites with varying cores. MO STUDIO has used the optimised constructions of nature for the design of a complex, spectacular interior layout which can only be attributed to the spirit of the age and a society craving for entertainment. /// Besides formal-constructional borrowings from nature, there are more and more attempts to transfer the structures of biological systems to architecture. So-called "intelligent" façade systems and building structures is the fashion here. Looked at from the point of view of sustainability, the "responsive" architecture of Thomas Herzog relates primarily to the way biological systems can adapt to their environment.[9] The adaptive envelope, like human skin, should acclimatise ideally to the climatic conditions. Besides providing the usual protective functions expected of an enclosing element, the envelope should control the light and air permeability autonomously and regulate the energy balance through storing heat and absorbing or reflecting solar radiation. As a media façade or energy provider, the façade takes on functions alien to its original purpose and becomes a complex "machine". Multilayer and movable envelope constructions in which the individual layers are assigned specific tasks, equipped with functions, printing or high-tech coatings turn the façade into an adaptive skin. So-called eco-intelligent[10] architecture is like a living organism. "Cycle Bowl", the EXPO 2000 pavilion designed by Atelier Brückner, illustrated this type of approach with its cooling, ventilation and solar-control system. The use of synthetic materials for such adaptive façade systems is based on the low weight, the thin materials and the possibility of equipping them with any properties. Experiments such as SmartWrap™ or the cocoon "Paul" exploit the versatile options of synthetic materials and pose radical questions regarding conventional wall constructions and assemblies. /// SmartWrap™, developed by Kieran Timberlake Associates, is an "intelligent" plastic composite which was tested and presented for the first time on an outdoor pavilion within the scope of the SOLOS exhibition[11] in New York. This synthetic material, with transparent polyethylene terephthalate (PET) as the backing for different functional layers, illustrates the potential of an electronic building envelope. Ultra-thin coatings act as photovoltaic cells, thin-film batteries, conducting circuits and thin-film transistors, organic LEDs and

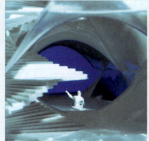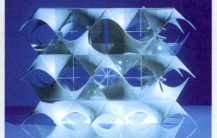

Curved Building, MO STUDIO, 2001

Cycle Bowl, Atelier Brückner, 2000

SmartWrap™, Kieran Timberlake Associates, 2003

honeycomb structure.   **8** Werner Nachtigall, Kurt Blüchel, *Das große Buch der Bionik*, Stuttgart, 2001   **9** Thomas Herzog in an interview with Petra Hagen Hodgson and Rolf Toyka, *Archithese*, No. 2, 2002   **10** The heading "eco-intelligence" embodies concepts such as responsive, functional, easy-to-repair, resources-sparing, long-lasting and recyclable.   **11** SOLOS took place in August 2003 in the Cooper Hewett National Design Museum, New York.   **12** A phase change material (PCM) is a substance in which heat is stored by means of a phase transition (e.g. solid to liquid). The temperature of the

electrochromic solar control. They supply, store and conduct energy, act as sensors, light sources and screens, and control the entry of heat and light. Designed as a multi-layer envelope, with the "intelligent" layer of plastic providing protection from the weather, a hermetically sealed air cavity as insulation and an inner lining of quilted aerogel pockets with integral PCM (phase change material)[12] as additional thermal insulation and latent heat store, the thin, energy-giving media façade exhibits the storage and insulation values of a masonry wall.[13] Its appearance changes with the incoming sunlight like a chameleon. Similar storage and insulation values are achieved by the multi-layer membrane construction that was developed at the ILEK[14] at the University of Stuttgart, which is just a few millimetres thick and was tested on the cocoon "Paul", a cave-like enclosure.[15] The construction of the wall is similar to that of real skin: several layers of PTFE sheeting form a system of several tiers each with a specific function. From outside to inside, the sheets take on the following functions: weather protection, lighting, insulation and heat storage. Depending on their function, they are equipped with fibre-optic lighting, which is responsible for the colour changes, highly insulating ceramics or PCMs. In contrast to conventional solid wall construction, the "skin" is characterised not only by its thinness and low weight, but also by its translucency. The conventional solid wall has been replaced by a movable, thin membrane which reacts to its environment.   ///   Projects by Kas Oosterhuis or f-u-r, with their dynamic architecture, are aimed at a different form of "intelligence". Kas Oosterhuis developed the concept of the trans-ports pavilions as data-initiated spaces that take on the real, substantial part of a hybrid "hyper bodies" consisting of virtual and real spaces. Linked digitally, the virtual and real spaces communicate and interact with each other and react to the influences of their surroundings (access by Internet users or the actions of passers-by) by changing their form and content. The pavilions consist of pneumatic strips arranged in groups like human muscles; their elongation and contraction converts the digital information into motion and changes the form of the pavilion. The synthetic membrane forming the outer layer and the electronic inner layer must be flexible enough to be able to follow the movements of the pneumatic construction.[16]   ///   The TechnoClouds from f-u-r are likewise intended to be artificial, movable super-organisms. The TechnoClouds are spatial structures that can be installed in existing buildings to house concerts or similar events. Designed as pneumatic plastic constructions, the spatial structure consists of several parallel, endless strips which form loop-like formations. The strips are divided into segments like links in a chain in the longitudinal and transverse directions, and are connected to a computer by means of sensors. Controlled by computer, the individual segments can be moved so that each strip can take on many different forms and in doing so also influence the forms of

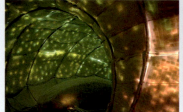
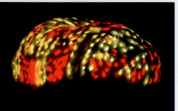

Cocoon "Paul", Markus Holzbach, ILEK Stuttgart, 2004

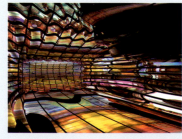

trans-ports pavilion, ONL Oosterhuis_Lénárd, 2000

material remains constant until the phase transition has been completed. The stored heat (or cold) is invisible, but present in a latent state. This reduces summertime temperature peaks and improves the interior climate; paraffins and salt hydrates are currently used as PCMs.   **13** See *Arch+*, No. 172, 2004, pp. 75–76 and www.kierantimberlake.com   **14** Institut für Leichtbau Entwerfen & Konstruieren (Institute of Lightweight Design & Construction)   **15** The cocoon "Paul" is result of research into adaptive, textile building envelopes; see the dissertation by Markus Holzbach at ILEK Stuttgart

its neighbours. Depending on the particular event, a multitude of plan layouts is therefore possible which can be carried out on several levels. /// These examples symbolise the growing convergence between biology and architecture and show the potential for using synthetic materials in building. Delicate membrane constructions, free forms and interconnected spaces, three-dimensional walls, unstable, movable spaces and envelopes that react to their environment, set new standards and distance themselves from a traditional and per se static architecture.

PLASTIC, THE SENSUAL MATERIAL /// Other architects are more interested in plastics for their visible features such as structure, texture and facture, aimed at achieving a sensual effect, than for their data-initiated contents of the chemical composition with the function potential. Japanese architects such as Shigeru Ban or the SANAA practice use the sensual qualities of synthetic materials for their architecture, the prime features of which are the playing with transparency and translucency, specific lighting effects and visual references, the removal of barriers between inside and outside, or their versatile and changeable relationships. Totally in keeping with Peter Sloterdijk, they use the lightness, movability and versatility of the plastics to define mankind's relationship with the world.[17] /// At the same time, the effects and possibilities of synthetic materials go hand in hand with the latest trends in contemporary architecture, the main idea of which is the unconventional use or alienation of materials. Herzog & de Meuron consider form, structure and materials as variables to be developed independently. Sensuality is the crucial aspect of their architecture, which is conveyed by the materiality and the interest in the surfaces, among other things. Printed or illuminated plastic envelopes lend their architecture the desired sensual character. In doing so, the experimentation with material is intended to break with traditions and lead to "subtle irritations". By using materials alien to architecture, or by converting and alienating traditional building materials, and by including immaterial elements such as photography and light, the envelope becomes a medium for a direct architectural language not dependent on context.[18] This design approach is reminiscent of minimalist architecture; Donald Judd was advocating the autonomy of form, substance, colour and surface in 1968. He claimed that forms and materials may not be changed by their context. The removal of context is emphasized by the use of unusual materials (plastics, chromium, electric light), which have no reference to the past but do not point to the future either." The material becomes an information medium with the appearance of the surface acting as the focus. This can lead to form being banished to the marginality of the subservi-

TechnoClouds, f-u-r, 2002

Naked House, Shigeru Ban, 2000   *Museum of Paper Art, Shigeru Ban, 2001*

16 Kas Oosterhuis and Ilona Lénárd presented their trans-ports project for the first time at the Biennale 2000 in Venice; their idea of a network of virtual and real spaces was incorporated into the "Real Time Evolution Game" in which the public could take part via the internet and thus alter the structures of the rooms; a prototype with a pneumatic, movable envelope was erected at the Centre Pompidou in Paris in 2003. **17** From the philosophical viewpoint, the material determines the relationship between being outside and being inside – the ecstatic and the enstatic. The architect philosophises

ent function – relegated to a support for the envelope, which can be replaced on a whim as times and fashions change and in terms of the effects and statements desired.[20] Or, alternately, material and form can be fused together as an apparently inseparable combination, as is impressively demonstrated by the Allianz Arena in Munich – a design approach that occurs more frequently as the form concept is introduced in architecture. The form-material relationship has replaced the form-function relationship and places architecture closer to the visual arts and design. Just like artists and designers, architects are seeking a material adequate for the form, and vice versa. It is not constructional considerations and cultural contexts that are deciding the choice of material, but rather the coherence of form and material. /// Besides the sensual effect, other architects are using the image of plastics as cheap materials quite deliberately for their architecture, trying out unconventional design approaches with new concepts. Here, the cheap industrial product, as an experiment in aesthetics, reflects the experimental nature of the design concepts. Projects by Rem Koolhaas or Lacaton & Vassal demonstrate the cost-effective but nevertheless highly effective possibilities of synthetic materials that result from clever and unexpected applications. Lacaton & Vassal employ inexpensive, untreated industrial products for their houses, which question traditional European housing forms and resemble the notion of the territorial, nomadic lifestyle. Transparent plastic panels offer not only the chance of enclosing spacious living accommodation on a low budget, but at the same time also create intermediate climatic zones that can be closed off from the outside world, or provide an uninterrupted transition between interior and exterior. /// At his art gallery in Rotterdam, Rem Koolhaas uses the indifference and ambiguity of translucent and transparent plastic panels for a room setting whose surprising spatial and visual references make demands on the visitor. A tour of the museum is not unlike a theatrical experience in which the sequence of rooms resembles the scenes in a play which, however, are repeatedly interrupted by retrospective views where the respective other world seen through the plastic panels appears either

Catholic Church in Radebeul, Staib Architects with Günter Behnisch, 2003

Ricola warehouse,
Herzog & de Meuron, 1993

Allianz Arena, Herzog & de Meuron, 2005

accordingly in the material. "Speaking and building normally create so much security in human relationships that one can occasionally allow a little ecstasy. Therefore, in my opinion the architect is actually someone who philosophises in the material. He who builds a house or a building for institution makes a statement about the relationship between the ecstatic and the enstatic, the being outside and the being inside." Peter Sloterdijk in conversation with Sabine Kraft and Nikolaus Kuhnert, *Arch+*, No. 169/170, 2004, pp. 16–23 **18** Jacques Herzog in an interview with H. Adam, M. Heuser and C. Bürkle,

clear and unmistakable or distorted and ambiguous. Different, contrasting materials meet unexpectedly, rooms and walls are like material collages, and standard industrial products contradict the conventional qualities of a museum. /// Visual customs are put to the test, emotions are awakened, the effect governs: synthetic materials are used in shocking, provocative and surprising ways – fitting for a society in which only extreme stimuli gain attention. Trash culture becomes part of civilised culture; plastics, and primarily plastic panels, cultivate "bad taste" – a method art has been using for many years. In this sense, plastics architecture is approaching the visual arts and in the form of material collage or architectural experiment is itself becoming art.

Cité Manifeste, Lacaton & Vassal, 2005

Housing Projects in London, Ash Sakula, 2004

Art Gallery in Rotterdam, Rem Koolhaas, 1992

Archithese, No. 5, 1998, and in: Marianne Brausch, Marc Emery [eds.], *L'Architecture en Question*, Paris, 1995, pp. 28–43   **19** Richard Weston describes this relationship between form and material as follows: Very much clearer than at that moment when Gottfried Semper published his theses, the building envelope can today be understood as 'clothing', as a sort of fabric we choose at random and change according to needs. Richard Weston, *Materials, Form, and Architecture*

PROJECTS

ABB ARCHITECTS | BERNHARD FRANKEN

BMW BUBBLE

MATERIAL_ TRANSPARENT ACRYLIC SHEETS IN DOUBLE CURVATURE /// **FAÇADE TYPE_** SINGLE-LEAF ///

USE_ EXHIBITIONS, TEMPORARY /// **LOCATION_** FRANKFURT AM MAIN, GERMANY /// **COMPLETED_** 1999

The building of the BMW Pavilion at the International Motor Show in Frankfurt represented a new direction in architecture. This relatively minor construction project enabled the architects to approach one step closer to the architectural visions of the new age, the so-called mass customisation (the mass production of one-off articles). /// The starting point for the design was the concept of "clean energy". BMW uses this slogan for its development of vehicles powered by renewable energies, e.g. hydrogen-powered engines. In order to imprint this complex theme on the minds of visitors as an intellectual and visual experience, the architects developed an exhibition consisting of a circular water tank and a solar cloud (an amorphous cable net with LED solar panels) housed in a pavilion shaped like a drop of water.

FORM-FINDING /// The pavilion had to have the form of a *real* drop of water and express the condition of the unstable equilibrium between internal pressure and surface tension. So instead of simply sketching the form of a drop of water and transferring this to the computer, the architects simulated the merger of two drops of water using an animation program normally found in the film industry. The starting point and parent substance of the simulation was the ideal form of one drop of water, which in reality can only exist in a vacuum and assumes the form of a perfect sphere. The laws of physics mean that the force of attraction of a second drop of water, the force of gravity of the Earth itself and the surface tension of the water cause force fields to act on the parent substance, which lead to changes in its shape. These force fields were simulated on the computer and thus generated the final shape. /// The final shape therefore emerged interactively from the parent substance, the form-forming principle, the boundary conditions and the applied forces through specific changes to the parameters selected. Through the interaction of designers and computers, data became form.

001

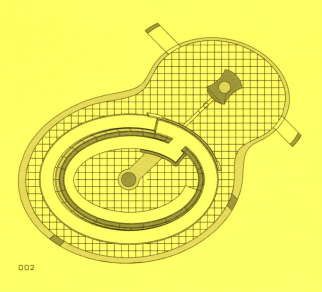

002

001_ As a metaphor for the use of low-resources energy forms, the pavilion is shaped like two drops of water. /// **002_** Plan

The simulation force field is therefore not simply a design method, but also leads to a coding of information in three dimensions. The outcome of this approach was a computer-generated form that corresponds to that of a drop of water which, however, could never actually exist. The *fictitious* drop of water!

CONCEPT /// The digital form generated by means of force-field simulation was designated the "master geometry" by the architects. This network of data curved about two axes is the two-dimensional computer representation of the reality and may not be changed in any way in the subsequent planning and production process. What this means is that even the structural calculations or the building's usage are subservient to the form as generated. And in the digital design process of the force-field simulation, even the selected – but not arbitrary – laws of physics take on a priority normally reserved for the structural engineering theories. At the same time, the generation of the form becomes rational and comprehensible. /// The master geometry is

the foundation for the following planning, and every stage of the planning is a derivative of the form that has been obtained. These derivatives can take the form of CAD renderings, stress calculations or 2D sections as CAD drawings. Every drawing and every component that is not derived directly from the master geometry but instead from a derivative is a higher-order derivative. This leads to derivatives of various orders. The final building is made up of numerous derivatives and represents just one image of the reality of the digital master geometry in an nth derivative.

CONSTRUCTION /// Originally, the "drop of water" was supposed to be realised as a transparent, self-supporting envelope. Glass, transparent membranes and, finally, transparent acrylic sheets were the materials examined by the architects together with the structural engineers. A decision was made to use transparent acrylic because it has advantages over glass in the production of double-curvature elements, in the use of adhesives for jointing and in terms of cost. /// The in-

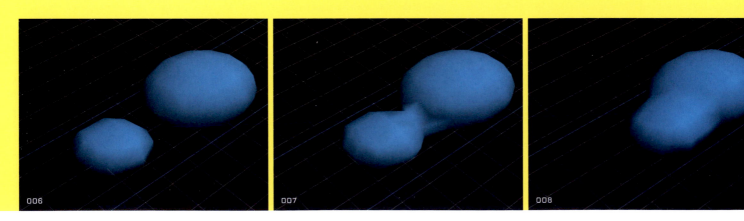

003_ A grid of aluminium ribs forms the loadbearing structure for the pavilion. /// **004_** The curved entrance door slides in a system of rails. /// **005_** Interior ///
006-008_ In order to generate the form, the merger of two drops of water was simulated on the computer with the help of animation programs normally employed by the film industry.

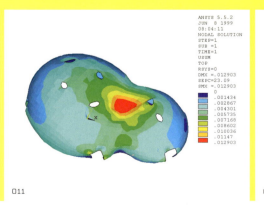

009_ Overall view   ///   **010**_ Smoothed master geometry   ///   **011**_ FEM simulation of stress distribution   ///   **012**_ FEM generation with shell elements

tention was to build the Bubble in separate parts, glue them together and then transport it to its final location by helicopter. However, time constraints forced the architects to abandon the idea of a self-supporting construction. Instead, the drop of water became a single-leaf transparent acrylic envelope supported by a grid of aluminium ribs. Some 305 differently shaped transparent acrylic panels – every one unique – were required. The plastic panels were moulded on CNC-milled rigid PU foam blocks and afterwards trimmed to size with CNC machinery.   ///   The almost dimensionless panels 8 mm thick were attached to the loadbearing construction with tiny individual fixings to form a single-leaf envelope; joints were sealed with silicone. No additional components (e.g. sunshades, thermal insulation, gutters, etc.) disturb the perfectly shaped enclosure. To prevent solar gains overheating the interior, a diecast aluminium floor similar to those used in industry was installed. Perforations in the floor plates enable cold air to flow into the Bubble. (The same principle could be used to heat the interior as well.)   ///   The pavilion was developed and built in a continuous digital design and manufacturing process – a method that has long since been standard in the aircraft and yacht industries. If this design and production method was to become established in the building industry, it would mean a stupendous change. Buildings could then be prefabricated individually and would then only need to be simply erected on the building site.

016

013

014

015

013-015_ The double-curvature transparent acrylic sheets were moulded on CNC-milled rigid PU foam blocks.

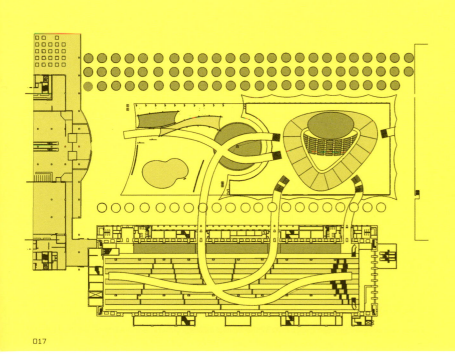

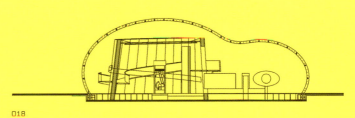

017

MCA – MARIO CUCINELLA ARCHITECTS

EBO BOLOGNA

MATERIAL_ TRANSPARENT ACRYLIC TUBES WITH INTEGRAL LED LIGHTS /// **FAÇADE TYPE**_ MULTI-LEAF /// **USE**_ EXHIBITIONS, TEMPORARY /// **LOCATION**_ BOLOGNA, ITALY /// **COMPLETED**_ 2003

Their minimalist, glass pavilion enabled Mario Cucinella Architects to set an unambiguous sign and establish a counterpoint to the historic city backdrop. With its multi-layer façade built from a hardly perceptible all-glass construction and rows of transparent acrylic tubes forming a second leaf, the pavilion forms a sublime outdoor sculpture whose play with light and transparency suggests a futuristic quality.

CONCEPT ///   Whereas the historic heart of Bologna is a focal point for activities and attention, the outskirts of the city are showing signs of dilapidation following years of neglect. In order to rectify this deficiency, the local authority gathered ideas and initiated numerous reports and competitions. Since 2003

the results of these planning activities have been on show in an exhibition in the subterranean passageways of a former pedestrian precinct, which as a relic of the misguided urban planning of the past, was for a long time a hotbed of criminal activities. The architects redesigned this uninviting space into an exhibition area and covered it with a glass pavilion to act as temporary access and a communication platform.   ///   The pavilion is made up of two elliptical cylinders joined together at one point by a small glazed entrance zone. During the hours of daylight the enclosure appears insubstantial, fluid. When the circular acrylic tubes reflect the sunlight playfully, the façade is reminiscent of a shimmering layer of water, an association that is deliberate because the plan shape is intended to

001

001_ At night-time, the pavilion becomes an illuminated sculpture.   ///   **002**_ The modern, minimalist pavilion forms a contrast to its historic surroundings.

represent two water droplets splashed from the famous Neptune Fountain nearby. In this way the modern, minimalist structure gains a poetic link to its historic surroundings.   ///   The interior of the pavilion, continuing the theme of the external appearance, is also minimalist and unambiguous. White surfaces and glass fittings dominate the aesthetic of the interior, reminding the observer of a futuristic scene from a Stanley Kubrick film.   ///   The pavilion forms the starting point for the underground exhibition in terms of both access and information. A film informs visitors about the city's activities concerning the most important aspects of the planned, sustainable urban redevelopment. Further information and publications are avail-

able at a service desk before visitors disappear underground to visit the exhibition itself.

CONSTRUCTION ///   The fluid-looking envelope is designed as a double-leaf façade. The outer leaf consists of a self-supporting all-glass construction made from bent laminated glass panes that are fastened at the top and bottom only. They form a weatherproof enclosure but remain almost invisible. However, the external appearance is characterised much more by the inner leaf of transparent acrylic tubes. These 120 mm diameter tubes, which were specially developed and manufactured for this project, are lined up in a row following the plan shape. They are joined together by satin-finish

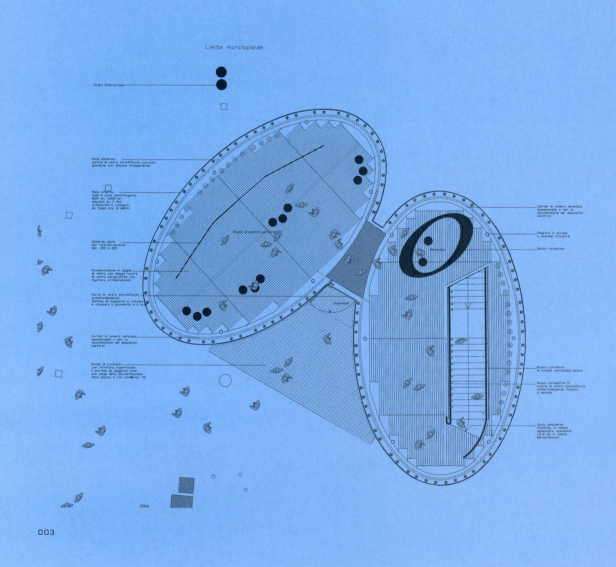

003

004_ White surfaces and glass fittings dominate the aesthetic of the interior.

acrylic glass caps fitted into the ends of the tubes. Despite their transparency, they offer only a distorted view through the façade, an intentional effect due to the curved geometry of the tubes. At the same time, this curvature refracts and redirects the incoming solar radiation and thus prevents the pavilion from overheating in summer. A mechanical cooling system is used only during extreme temperatures. During the winter the pavilion is heated with warm air via floor inlets positioned along the façade. The rising warmth also helps to combat condensation.   ///   At night, the glass pavilion becomes an illuminated sculpture, thanks to blue and white LED lights installed at the base of the tubes. The blue and white lighting effect accentuates the immateriality of the pavilion and lends the scene a degree of unreality.   ///   In this play of light and transparency, the plastic, in contrast to its reputation as a cheap material, turns the pavilion into an urban jewel, a conspicuous, staged interface between city and citizens, between the worlds above and below ground.

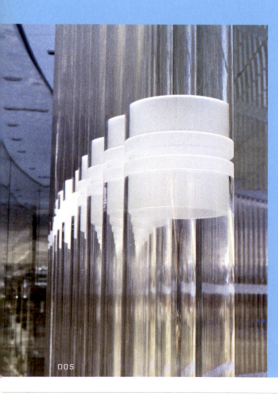

005

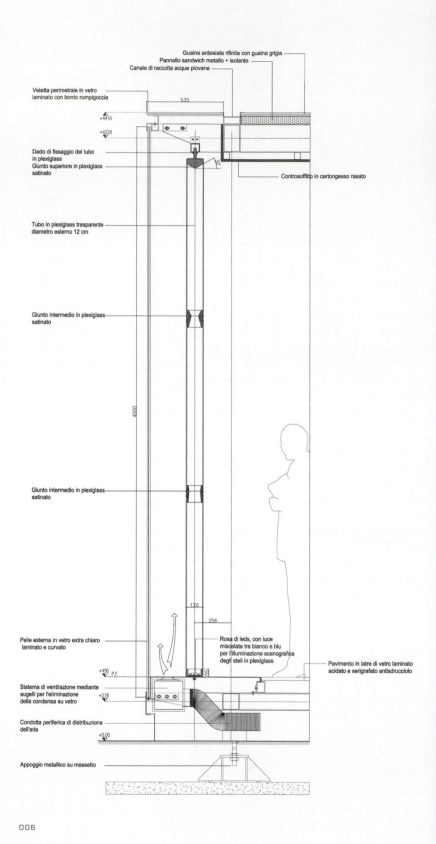

006

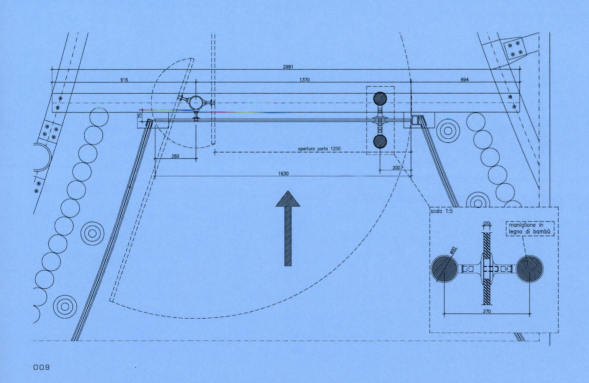

ATELIER KEMPE THILL

»LIGHT BUILDING«
MOBILE PAVILION

MATERIAL_ TRANSLUCENT BEER CRATES /// **FAÇADE TYPE_** SINGLE-LEAF /// **USE_** EXHIBITIONS, TEMPORARY ///

LOCATION_ MOBILE /// **COMPLETED_** 2001

The ephemeral, mobile pavilion belonging to the Dutch travelling theatre troupe "De Parade" is a successful example of the architectural use of a standard plastic product. The young architects Oliver Thill and André Kempe simply stacked empty beer crates on top of each other to create the walls, laid trapezoidal profile metal sheeting on top and the mobile pavilion was finished!

CONCEPT /// The motivation for this charming "mis-use" of an everyday product was a competition organised by the BNA (Royal Dutch Institute of Architects). The purpose of the competition was to find solutions for temporary exhibition buildings that could be built for just 25,000 guilders (about EUR 11,350). This was a task that could not be solved using conventional methods and therefore was rife for experimentation. The parameters *low-budget* and *ephemeral* gave the architects the idea for an unusual but consequential answer. They devised a pavilion built from existing, standard products that are obtained by paying a deposit, i.e. they can be returned to the supplier if the building is dismantled! Walls made from stacks of beer crates and a floor of wooden boards were the result of these deliberations. ///Schoeller Wavin Systems agreed to cooperate with the architects. The company produced a special batch of their stan-

dard beer crates out of colourless, translucent plastic exclusively for the pavilion. More than *objets trouvés*, these mundane items were presented in a new light with their own aesthetic. /// The modular, lightweight but at the same time stable plastic crates could be regarded as a LEGO system for adults, turning building into child's play! /// The individual crates were to be simply stacked and bonded together to form an unadorned, rectangular room measuring 15 x 4 x 6 m. The jury liked the idea and awarded the architects second prize and an order for one pavilion.

CONSTRUCTION /// A buyer for the pavilion was found in the shape of the Dutch travelling theatre troupe "De Parade", which visits Dutch towns and cities every summer with a new theatre programme. The beer crate pavilion has become a regular attraction in their activities since 2001. They use it as an art gallery, as a bar or for jazz concerts. The temporary pavilion has become a multifunctional mobile building that can be erected or dismantled within a day – a requirement that could not have been met if adhesive had been used as originally envisaged. /// To enable fast and easy erection and dismantling, the architects developed a standard module consisting of 18 beer crates (6 crates long x 3 crates

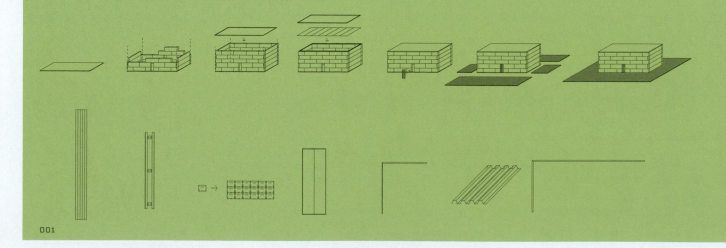

001

002

001-002_ The simple box-like enclosure consists exclusively of standard, rented elements that can be assembled by two persons in a few hours.

high) which are joined together with steel plates and threaded rods to form a stable "wall panel". The modules, some with electric cables already pre-installed, are stacked loose according to an erection drawing. A steel channel at the base of the wall prescribes the positions of the walls and at the same time acts as a ring beam. Its counterpart at roof level is a steel angle. Tying the two ring beams together with vertical threaded rods and the plate effect of the trapezoidal profile metal roof stabilise the beer crate construction. Reinforcing bars, driven into the ground like tent pegs, anchor the pavilion to the ground to resist the effects of wind forces. Spring force measurements – a tent erection method familiar to the theatre troupe – are used to check the tensile strength of the anchorage. /// Like any other mobile structure,

the pavilion does not satisfy any thermal or sound insulation requirements and is also not entirely rainproof. Instead, the pavilion is a "light building" in the truest sense of the word: a room of light in a light(weight) enclosure. /// The translucent, semi-permeable walls filter and scatter the light in different ways, depending on the weather conditions. As the cloud formations move across the sky, so the sunlight creates ever-changing patterns of colour, light and shade inside the pavilion. /// The construction of a 300 mm thick loadbearing wall that is at the same time light-permeable has resulted in an ambiguity that unites traditional and modern architectural thinking. The space is both enclosed and permeable, the construction both substantial and lightweight.

003

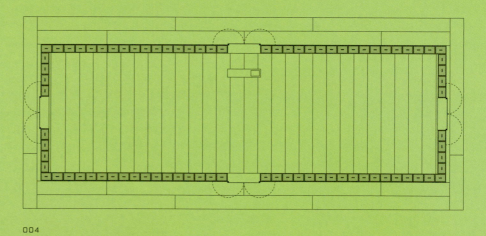

004

005

003_ The basic module of the pavilion is a standard beer crate. /// **004_** Plan /// **005_** Elevation

006

007-008

009

006_ An even, diffuse light fills the mobile pavilion, which can be used as a bar, museum or housing for various events.   ///   **007-008**_ Plan and longitudinal section; the master assembly module consists of 18 beer crates.   ///   **009**_ Section through wall; the beer crates are tensioned between ring beams at the top and bottom of the wall, and reinforcing bars anchor this lightweight building to the ground.

ATELIER BRÜCKNER

CYCLEBOWL

MATERIAL_ ETFE MEMBRANE, TRANSPARENT AND PRINTED, THREE LAYERS /// **FAÇADE AND ROOF FORM**_ PNEUMATICALLY PRETENSIONED, SINGLE-LEAF, INTEGRAL SUNSHADING /// **USE**_ EXHIBITIONS, TEMPORARY /// **LOCATION**_ HANNOVER, GERMANY /// **COMPLETED** _ 2000

The exhibition pavilion of the "Duales System Deutschland" (a nationwide recycling scheme for packaging materials) at EXPO 2000 in Hannover was a futuristic structure in more ways than one. The pneumatic membrane construction of the external envelope could adapt "intelligently" to different requirements and situations, and the internal climate concept centred around natural processes. The role models for the design team were living organisms which could adapt to their environment and react to changing situations, and thus exist in a dialogue with their habitats. This interaction between inside and outside followed a defined dramatic plot which was intrinsic to the staging of the exhibition. /// "Form follows content." This, a reformulation of the maxim of the Modern Movement, was the guiding principle for the planners – a multidisciplinary team of architects, stage designers and scenery specialists. They therefore paid homage to the transformation of "content" into tangible settings which were generated by the interaction of exhibition scenes and architecture.

CONCEPT /// The theme of EXPO 2000, "Humankind – Nature – Technology", can be seen as a concise expression of the ecological and economic relationships that culminate in a cradle-to-grave economy. The cradle-to-grave economy is not just the *raison d'être* of the Duales System; instead, it is primarily a visionary economic system. Just like in nature, there are no waste products in this system, only beneficial materials. The principle of the cycle was the starting point for the design of the pavilion. It dictated the architectural language, the staging and the internal climate concept. /// The cycle was reflected in the three-dimensional spiral form, which at the same time can be seen as a type of *Weltanschauung* in which the return, the movement and the development constitute constants in the framework. The spiral also represented the three-dimensional translation of the logo of the Duales System – two Yin-Yang-style intertwined arrows. Accordingly, the planners presented the theme of the exhibition on spiralling ramps, an organised tour telling a story which at the end returns to its starting point. A maze of

001

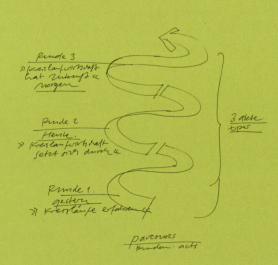

002

003

001_ Conceptual sktech /// **002_** The spiralling exhibition tour is a symbol for the cradle-to-grave economy. /// **003_** The funnel-shaped pavilion made from air-filled ETFE membrane cushions on its storey-high plinth.

hedges as the springboard and the spiral stairs as the conclusion of the tour also made references to the spiral form and pointed out its symbolic significance.

CONSTRUCTION /// Enclosed in transparent ETFE membrane cushions, the spiral appeared from the outside as a funnel-shaped pavilion standing on a square plinth. Both the three-dimensional, spiralling tour and the setting of the exhibition itself were evident in the transparent membrane construction. As part of the staging, the transparency of the envelope could be changed, at the click of a mouse as it were, to transform the pavilion – according to a structured, recurring sequence – from a brightly lit room to a black box. This allowed the entire spectrum of multimedia presentation forms to be exploited – display panels, installations for all the senses, films, etc. The envelope mirrored the drama and the architecture was part of the production.

/// Simple physical laws were responsible for this effect. The vertical enclosure consisted of three-layer, transparent, pneumatic ETFE membrane cushions measuring 18 x 3 m which were welded together along their edges and stretched between aluminium frames. Two of the layers were printed with a leaf motif, but one layer was a reverse of the other. Controlled pressure changes in the two chambers of the air-filled cushions altered the position of the centre membrane, which either merged with the upper membrane and darkened the interior or was pressed against the lower membrane to allow more daylight to enter. /// Besides this staged effect, the printing on the membrane also acted as a sunshade and therefore prevented excessive temperatures inside the building. /// The transparent, circular roof measuring 25 m in diameter consisted of one single, three-layer ETFE membrane cushion. In addition to the internal air pressure, two radial cable nets

004_ The exhibition was staged on a spiralling ramp; the light-permeable envelope changes in a predetermined cycle.

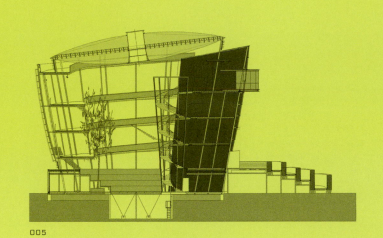

005

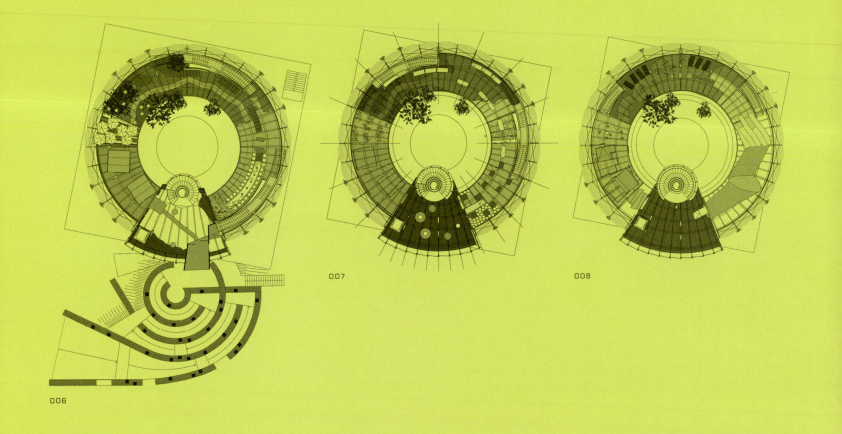

006

007

008

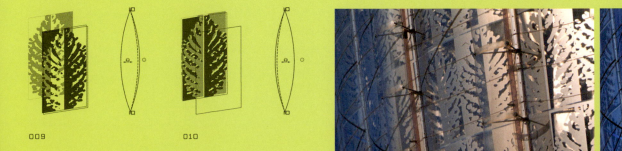

009

010

011

012

– between which the membrane roof was stretched – helped to stabilise the giant cushion. Another, central cable net prevented the upper membrane from sagging – and possibly leading to a huge pond of incalculable weight – should the air supply fail. Textile, louvre-type air-filled tubes integrated into the transparent membrane cushions were used to control the light. When inflated, the air-filled louvres spread out and prevented daylight entering through the roof. Once the air was extracted, the louvres collapsed and the roof became transparent again. /// The centre of the membrane roof was marked by an oversized fan some 4 m in diameter. It was this fan that was primarily responsible for generating the artificial tornado – the once-an-hour highlight of the exhibition. /// Plastics, or rather the recycling of plastics, is one of the principal lines of business of the Duales System. It was therefore no surprise to discover that the company had no problem when it came to using plastics. Indeed, a whole range of plastics was used in and on the pavilion for effective advertising. Besides the membrane façade, the outer layer of the square plinth made use of multi-web acrylic sheets (filled with transparent paper). The double-leaf façade of the Blue Box (the rigid special part of the pavilion from which the membrane funnel projects) was treated to a cladding of multi-web polycarbonate sheets filled with fragments of blue glass, and in the exhibition areas transparent plastics were used generously and in many forms.

CLIMATE CONCEPT /// Another special feature of this pavilion was its air-conditioning system. All temporary and transparent structures that do not possess any storage mass always present a challenge for the internal climate. The planners solved the problem by taking nature as their example and by using various cycles. ///

013_ At the end of the tour, visitors could relax in transparent plastic shell armchairs.

014

015

015

014_ Cable-supported membrane cushion roof with integral pneumatic sunshading louvres /// **015_** Roof open /// **016_** Roof closed

Like the leaves of plants, the cooling system functioned by exploiting evaporation. During the day, cooled water fed from huge underground tanks circulated through a fine network of pipes fitted to the underside of the ramps. As the water evaporated, so the cooling effect led to a local drop in the temperature and to an improvement in the microclimate. Another cycle ensured that the heated water cooled down during the night. The water was sprayed via fine nozzles into open, vertical, channel-like acrylic shells which were fixed to the outside of the membrane façade. The water cooled as it ran into the collecting tank and was then fed back into the underground tanks. At the start of the next day, the daily cycle of cooling the air started again. The third cycle ensured circulation of the air for the night-time cooling of the interior. During the day, sensor-controlled louvre openings, which were enlarged or reduced depending on the internal temperature, the humidity of the air and the carbon dioxide content of the air, regulated the circulation of the air. Thanks to this approach, which was based on the three factors air circulation, sunshading and water cooling, no mechanical air-conditioning systems were required in the pavilion. /// The Cyclebowl told the story of a visionary economic form by exploiting natural effects while integrating innovative technologies. It therefore united economy, ecology and technology and became a symbol of EXPO 2000.

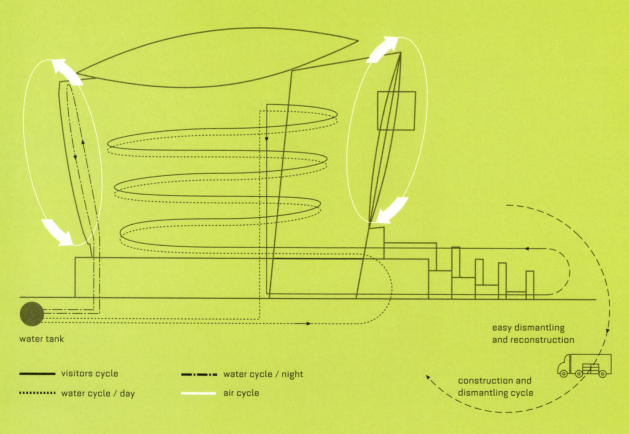

water tank

—————— visitors cycle   —•—•— water cycle / night

•••••••••• water cycle / day   —————— air cycle

easy dismantling
and reconstruction

construction and
dismantling cycle

017

018_ Night-time photo /// **019_** Open transparent acrylic channels on the façade for water cooling at night /// **020_** A network of water-filled "capillaries" fixed to the underside of the ramps ensured cooling by evaporation to lower the interior temperature.

B & K+

APARTMENTS AND STUDIOS IN COLOGNE

MATERIAL_ TRANSLUCENT, GLASS FIBRE-REINFORCED PLASTIC SHEETS, PIGMENTED   ///   **FAÇADE TYPE_** MULTI-LAYER, INSULATED OR DOUBLE-LEAF   ///   **USE_** RESIDENTIAL/COMMERCIAL   ///   **LOCATION_** COLOGNE, GERMANY   ///   **COMPLETED_** 2000

In this project the architects solved the task of creating attic-type living quarters and studios – in other words, transforming characteristic features of 19th-century industrial architecture into contemporary architecture, via an indirect route by using a module. For their design, Messrs Brandlhuber and Kniess chose a modular, abstract framework as an information medium which in reality is transformed into the spatial qualities of a factory floor whose benefits are spaciousness (both horizontally and vertically) plus good illumination and flexibility.

CONCEPT ///   The architects devised complex L-shaped modules to realise the specified spatial qualities. Each module is made up of two rectangular blocks that are joined together at a right-angle. Through mirroring and rotation about all three axes in space plus horizontal and vertical offsets, 12 of these modules have been fitted together like building bricks to form a straightforward, block-like construction.   ///   In use, the abstract modules become room modules with a floor space

of 140 m², and form an L-shape both on plan and on elevation. So this results in two-storey maisonettes with dissimilar floor areas on their lower and upper floors, with two-thirds of the total area as single-storey accommodation, and one-third as two-storey.   ///   Although the 12 modules are identical, the rotations and mirroring give rise to different layouts, which are further enhanced by the different access arrangements. Seven different types of apartment have therefore been created from one single module. Optional horizontal or vertical combinations of several units result in further layout and room variations. To achieve this, parts of the loadbearing reinforced concrete walls were omitted and these areas closed off with lightweight materials which can be removed at any time in the future. To avoid restricting the combination options unnecessarily, the architects placed the access arrangements on one side of the building as an open, cantilevering reinforced concrete structure. The spacious, open stairs are conceived in such a way that they also offer space for external activities. Further

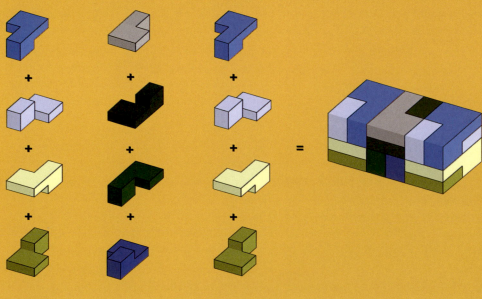

001

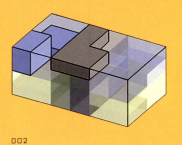
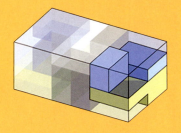
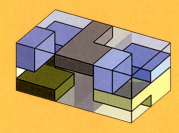

002

003

001_ A total of 12 L-shaped basic modules, each made up of two rectangular volumes, are rotated and mirrored about all three axes in space – according to the modular principle – to produce a rectangular structure. /// **002_** Possible arrangements and combination options of the room modules within a rectangular volume /// **003_** View of road side

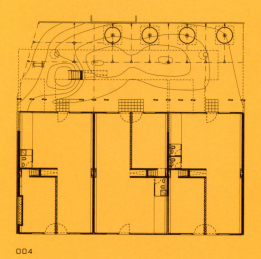

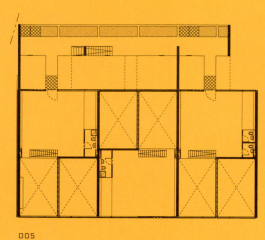

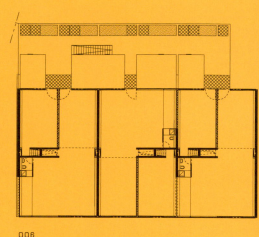

004

005

006

space outside is provided by the rooftop terraces with their extensive planting. /// The attic-type apartments were offered for sale as no more than empty "shells", i.e. as open, spacious units without partitions, kitchens or bathrooms, which could then be fitted out according to the individual wishes of the buyers. Many different fitting-out options were available: partitions that could be positioned as required, open galleries for later installation, and bathrooms in three different sizes. In essence, the building consists of multifunctional room modules which can be fitted out specifically to suit the intended use – as apartment, dental laboratory, artist's studio or office. Thanks to the flexibility of the interior design, the open, spacious units are ideal for combining workspaces and living quarters. This design takes into account changes in society and offers single-parent families and those starting a business the option of harmonising work and family commitments.

CONSTRUCTION /// It is not only the three-dimensional concept, but also the influence of materials and surface finishes that achieve the overall effect. The uniform use of high-quality oak wood-block flooring and full-height glazing gives the apartments their high-class character. At the same time, the untreated, exposed reinforced concrete walls and soffits and the façade cladding of plastic sheets generate the intended experimental, improvised workshop character of a factory floor. ///

007

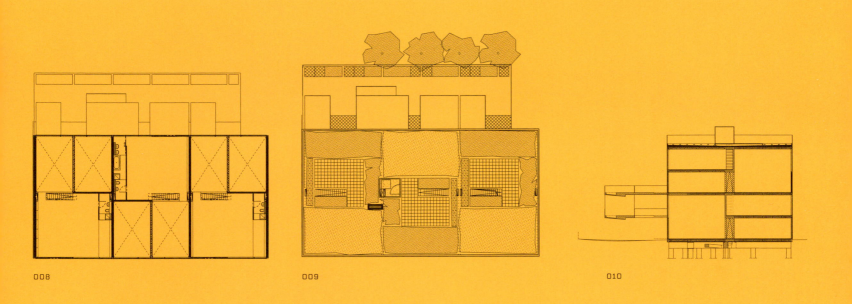

008

009

010

011

008_ Plan of 3rd floor   ///   **009**_ Plan of roof   ///   **010**_ Section   ///   **011**_ The three-dimensional realisation of the L-shaped module results in a large variety of open-plan, two-storey interior space relationships.

The architects used plain glass fibre-reinforced plastic sheets with a yellow-green shimmer as the weather protection to various façade assemblies. The gable ends of the building consist of a multi-layer façade: thermally insulated concrete walls on the inside, an air cavity and Scobalit sheets as the outer leaf. The façade is broken up only by the rectangular grid of the framework which can be discerned through the translucent sheets. The interlacing and stacking of the various apartment modules can be seen on the longitudinal sides of the building: irregular bays filled with transparent, translucent and opaque panels. The opaque bays are made from vapourtight panels of glass fibre-reinforced plastic with a timber inner lining, specially devised for this project.

Clamped into the post-and-rail façade construction, these panels alternate with transparent glass panes. The translucent bays indicate the bathrooms. These panels consist of double glazing with an outer layer of plastic to guarantee privacy. Depending on the construction, the façade panels were glued, screwed or clamped to the supporting structure.   ///   The architects deliberately restricted the choice of materials to concrete and plastic; even the safety barriers and floor finishes outside are made from glass fibre-reinforced plastic gratings. One special feature is the yellow-green colouring of the plastic sheets, which was achieved by mixing in fluorescent pigments during manufacture, and allows the building to "glow" at dusk.

012_ The smooth Scobalit sheets are in some cases simply glued to the supporting construction.   ///   **013_** The balustrades and spandrel panels are also made from green-tinted glass-fibre reinforced plastic.

014

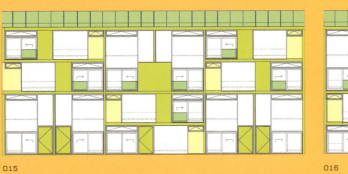

015

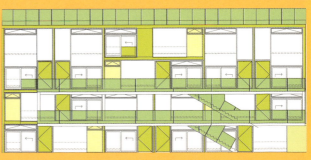

016

014_ The irregularity of the façade panels reflects the interwoven arrangement of the room modules.   ///   **015**_ Elevation of road side   ///   **016**_ Elevation of courtyard side

SHIGERU BAN

NAKED HOUSE

MATERIAL_ EXTERNAL: GLASS FIBRE-REINFORCED PLASTIC SHEETS, CORRUGATED; INTERNAL: NYLON MEMBRANE   ///

FAÇADE TYPE_ MULTI-LAYER, INSULATED   ///   **USE**_ RESIDENTIAL   ///   **LOCATION**_ KAWAGOE, JAPAN   ///   **COMPLETED**_ 2000

Again and again, Shigeru Ban awakens the interest of the public with his experimental houses. The experimentation with spaces and layouts, their movability, flexibility and delimitation runs like a thread through his work. Very often, the re-interpretation of these themes involves a new definition of building components and elements. In Shigeru Ban's houses, the movable furnishings take on a statically relevant function, or they form compartments. Materials are used apparently in contradiction to their physical properties; for example, lightweight, unstable, water-soluble paper, which in the form of cardboard is used for the loadbearing structure, or curtaining materials which are transformed into a façade. The delimitation of the space, i.e. the spatial fusion of interior and exterior, a dominant theme in his architecture, has its roots both in Japanese tradition and the Modern Movement. Whereas the architecture of the Modern Movement achieves a suggestion of interconnected spaces by means of full-height glazing, Shigeru Ban goes beyond the visual delimitation to cre-

ate an additional "physical transparency", an openness that encompasses more than just the visual sense. Definitions and boundaries are blurred. Naked House is his 10th Case Study House, which can be interpreted as the latest variation of these architectural themes.

CONCEPT ///   The house unites three generations – grandmother, parents and two children – under one roof. The family wanted a house in which they could live as a group instead of separately. Each should be able to carry out his or her activities but without being isolated. The house was built some 20 km north of Tokyo near the Shingashi River, in an area surrounded by paddy fields and greenhouses.   ///   Like the nearby greenhouses, Naked House is a single, large, two-storey enclosure. Four cardboard boxes mounted on rollers, an idea akin to the paper-covered sliding walls (shoji) of traditional Japanese architecture, form the family's private accommodation. Depending on needs and usage, the boxes can be moved around and combined, which leads to

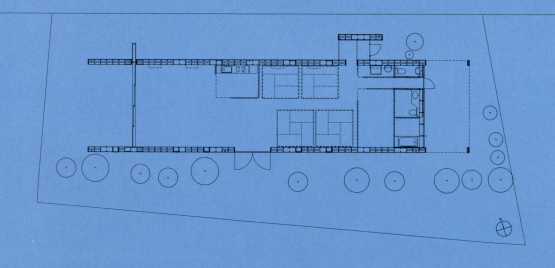

001

002

001_ Plan /// **002_** The mobile bedrooms can be positioned anywhere within the interior, and the children can even play on top.

a multitude of layout options. When placed against the walls of the house, they can be connected to radiators, air conditioning and power sockets. Sliding doors are provided on two sides of each box; these can be closed or left open or even removed completely to determine the visual interaction of the room units with the overall layout and guarantee the occupants a degree of privacy. Removing the sliding doors and joining the boxes together creates one large room of 24 m² which can be positioned anywhere within the two-storey volume. Large openings in the façade enable the boxes to be rolled out onto the terrace if required, enabling the occupants to use the full floor space of the house or to extend their living space to the outside. The roofs of the boxes can also be used by the children as additional

play areas. In order that the flexibility of the plan layout and the movability of the rooms does not just remain a grand theory, the weight of the boxes was reduced to a minimum. This resulted in somewhat compact dimensions: the children have a little under 5 m² and the parents just over 7 m². The loadbearing timber frame was covered with lightweight honeycomb cardboard panels and the occupants restricted the furnishings and fittings to essentials. The only permanent installations in the house are the kitchen, the wardrobes and the bathroom, which are separated from the open-plan layout by half-height walls or white curtains.   ///   In essence, Naked House with its room boxes mounted on rollers is a radical continuation of the traditional Japanese house with its sliding paper walls.

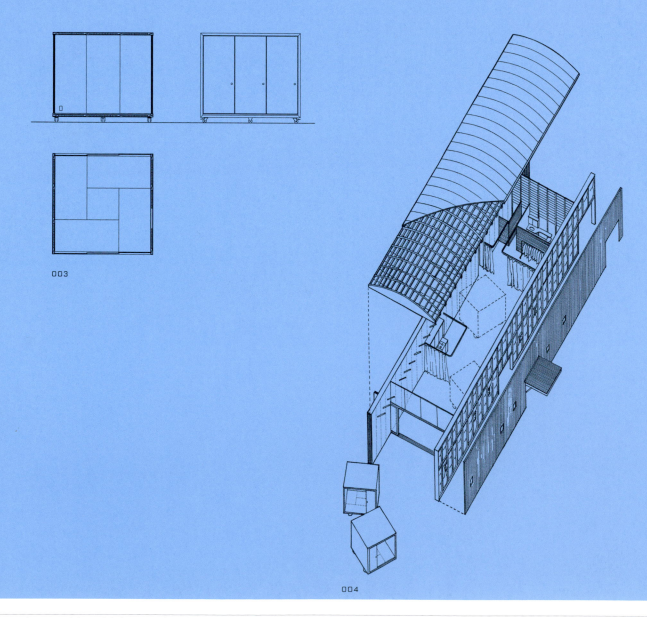

003

004

003_ The sizes of the mobile boxes are based on the dimensions of *tatami* mats.   ///   **004_** Isometric view

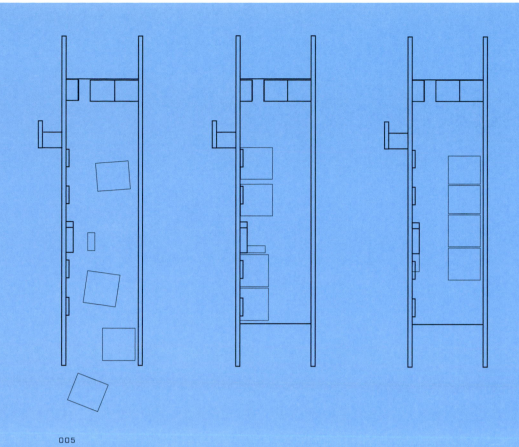

005

006

CONSTRUCTION /// The unusualness of the plan layout is matched by the multi-layer, translucent plastic façade. The weatherproof outer layer consists of corrugated, glass fibre-reinforced plastic panels. The inner layer, which forms the interior wall surface, is formed by a nylon membrane which is attached to the loadbearing timber construction by means of touch-and-close fasteners and can therefore be taken down at any time for washing. In between these two layers there is a layer of translucent plastic thermal insulation, which was developed by the architect himself and actually put together by members of his team. When searching for suitable thermal insulation, the architects tested various materials, such as wood chips, paper cuttings, glass fibres and eggboxes, until they finally decided in favour of extruded polyester fibres, which are normally used for packaging. They stuffed the synthetic fibres, impregnated with a fire retardant, into more than 500 transparent plastic bags which were divided into individual compartments to prevent the filling dropping to the bottom. The plastic bags are fixed to the frame with another synthetic film to provide fire protection. /// This translucent wall construction refracts the sunlight and bathes the interior in a low-level, even glow – a way of controlling light that is anchored in Japanese culture and has been employed for many centuries in the traditional paper walls. Small, square, transparent windows accentuate the long, milky external walls and permit discrete, specific views to the outside world. However, their primary function is ventilation. The necessary reference to the exterior is provided by the fully glazed gable walls. At the west end the glass façade is made up of sliding elements that can be stored in a housing in the wall. The interior and the covered terrace therefore merge into one space that continues into the greenery of the surroundings.

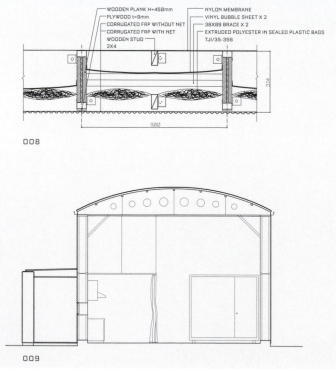

007

008

009

007_ The linear structure of the surrounding paddy fields is reflected in the lines of the plastic façade. /// **008_** Section through external wall /// **009_** Section

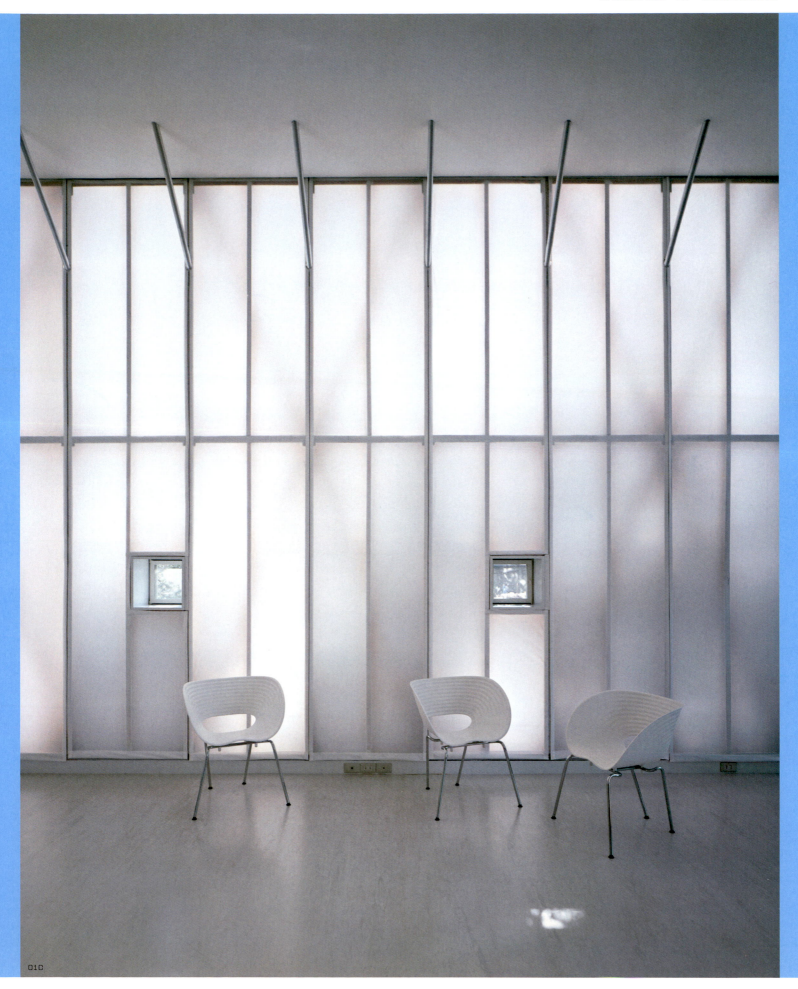

010_ The small square windows permit limited, but specific views of the surrounding countryside.

TEKUTO ARCHITECTURE STUDIO

LUCKY DROPS

MATERIAL_ EXTERNAL: TRANSLUCENT, GLASS FIBRE-REINFORCED PLASTIC SHEETS; INTERNAL: PLASTIC FILM /// **FAÇADE TYPE**_ MULTI-LAYER, INSULATED /// **USE**_ RESIDENTIAL /// **LOCATION**_ SETAGYA-KU, TOKYO, JAPAN /// **COMPLETED**_ 2005

A new land survey in a suburb of Tokyo revealed a long, thin piece of no man's land in the shape of a trapezium, just 700 mm wide at one end and 3.2 m at the other, a total of a little under 60 m². Placing a house on this curious remnant of land posed a challenge even for Japanese architects, who are used to dealing with small plots, especially in view of the regulation requiring a house to be positioned at least 500 mm from the boundary of the plot! The architects took on this challenge and attempted to turn the peculiar characteristics of this plot to their advantage. In a setting dominated by the structures so typical of Japanese city suburbs, the result was a highly unusual family home.

CONCEPT /// Above ground, the house tracks the boundaries of the plot at the legally required distance. Below ground, in the basement, the architects were able to use the full width of the plot. This led to a tube-like, trapezoidal plan shape with a length of about 17 m and

room widths varying from 800 mm to 2.2 m. The structure that rises from this unusual plan form has the shape of a pointed arch; its slender, high proportions remind the observer of a Gothic church window. This long, thin house has a sloping ridge which rises from the single-storey garden end to a height equal to two storeys at the narrow entrance end. /// The extremely confined plan area is compensated for by a generously proportioned volume, an open-plan layout and the bright, even illumination of the whole interior thanks to a translucent envelope. The living area including the kitchen amenities and dining area is located underground in the basement. The floors in the two/three-storey volume above this area make use of metal open-grid flooring, a delicate form of construction that saves space and also allows the daylight shining through the translucent, curved external walls to reach the basement. There is no acoustic or visual disruption to the open-plan layout. The bathroom at the narrow end of the basement is the

001

002

001 The structure in the shape of a pointed arch is covered in a translucent, thin plastic membrane. /// **002** This narrow, tall building is only 2.2 m wide at the entrance end!

sole enclosed room within the entire house. /// The entrance zone raised above ground level is constructed as a small gallery. From here, a narrow single flight of stairs descends into the living area and a steep ship's ladder provides access to the sleeping gallery on the upper floor. This sleeping gallery is connected to the rear door at the garden end via a sloping platform running the full length of the house. Following the line of the ridge, the platform slopes over virtually a complete storey height and thus reinforces the linear structure of the house. This narrow, sloping passageway is used by the occupants as additional storage space.

CONSTRUCTION /// One condition for building on this sliver of land was that the wall construction had to have practically zero thickness! The architects designed an extremely thin external envelope of high-tech materials no more than 69 mm thick to cover the entire building from ground level to ridge. The multi-layer façade construction consists of 3 mm thick glass fibre-reinforced plastic panels as the outer layer, a translucent high-tech thermal insulation layer, an air cavity and a plastic film on the inside for fire protection. Fixed to the steel structure in vertical, narrow strips, the façade emphasizes the verticality of the construction and lends the building a rhythmic impulse. As the house has no windows, the plastic façade conveys the impression of a calm, homogeneous surface. Mechanical fans ensure adequate ventilation of the interior and the reference to the outside world is created exclusively via the doors at each end. /// The plastic envelope fulfils three essential requirements. Firstly, it allows daylight to enter and illuminate the interior of this windowless building, distributing the indirect diffuse light evenly throughout the house. Roller blinds fitted inside can be used to regulate the amount of incoming light. Secondly, it screens the interior from the inquisitive looks of the neighbours, which – considering the closeness of the

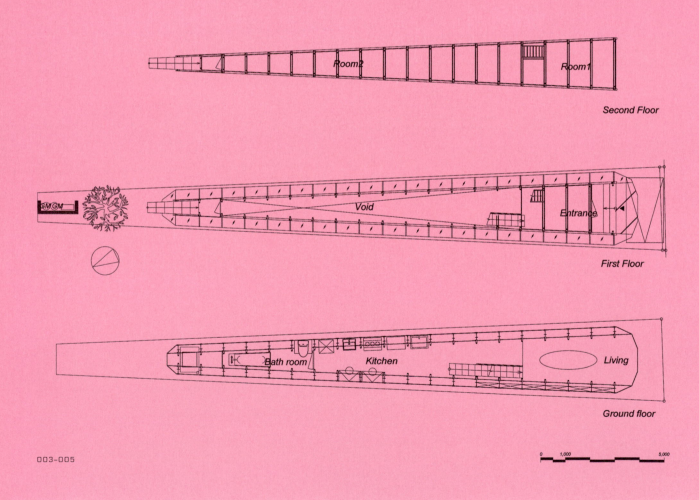

Second Floor

First Floor

Ground floor

003–005

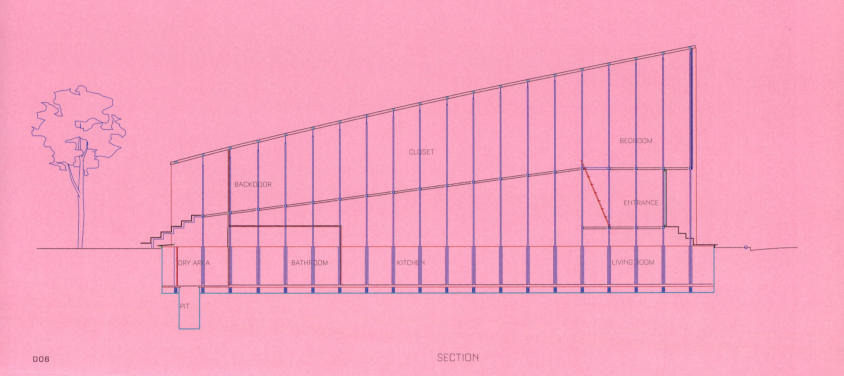

006

SECTION

006_ Longitudinal section /// **007_** View from the entrance gallery into the living area in the semi-basement; the ladder leads up to a gallery that serves as a bedroom. ///
008_ The semi-basement contains living area, kitchen and bathroom; services and cupboards are housed in the niches behind the steel columns. /// **009_** Light can penetrate the open-grid flooring used in the house.

surrounding buildings – is not as trivial as it sounds. Thirdly, its minimal thickness helped make a house feasible in the first place on this narrow building plot and thus gain valuable floor space. /// At night, the simple, introvert building looks like a paper lantern with the shadows of its occupants vaguely discernible. However, this tiny house is much more than just an interim solution to an apparently insoluble task. Instead, the architects have given the confined interior spaciousness and character and transformed it into a home that has earned the name "Lucky Drops"! ("Lucky Drops" is the translation of an old Japanese proverb which means, more or less, "And the last shall be first.")

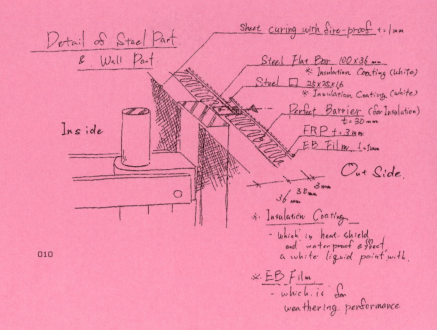

010

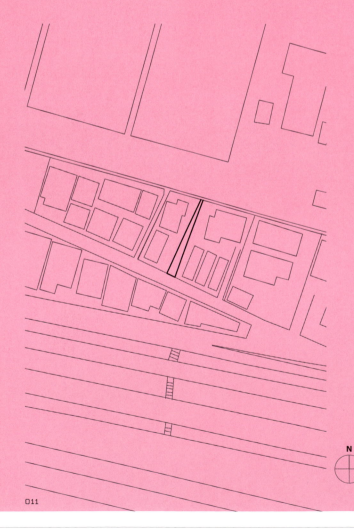

011

012

013

013_ At night, the translucent walls of the house allow the building to shine like a lantern.

ASH SAKULA

HOUSING PROJECT IN LONDON

MATERIAL_ GLASS FIBRE-REINFORCED CORRUGATED PLASTIC SHEETS, TRANSLUCENT OR PALE YELLOW   ///   **FAÇADE TYPE**_ MULTI-LAYER, INSULATED   ///   **USE**_ RESIDENTIAL   ///   **LOCATION**_ LONDON, UNITED KINGDOM   ///   **COMPLETED**_ 2004

Always on the lookout for new, experimental housing solutions, the Peabody Trust Housing Association has been organising competitions regularly for a number of years. The housing project in Silvertown, a development area in East London, called for low-budget housing units each with 65 m² floor space for a four-person household. Peabody Trust specified the price per square metre and also the target group – young families with two children who were looking for a low-cost first home.   ///   Based on these clear but restrictive conditions, which left little leeway, the architects responded by reorganising the typical apartment layout and by using unconventional building materials.

CONCEPT   ///   Ash Sakula designed two small blocks each with two apartments. By shifting the space and function priorities, the architects redefined living in a small space. The apartments are characterised by variance and a number of "communal spaces" ideal for family life. The arrangement of kitchen, dining and living areas plus the hall and an external terrace provide ample "meeting points" with varying qualities. By reducing the size of the bedrooms to a minimum (they are hardly larger than sleeping berths), the architects were able to allocate more floor space to the other rooms. The living room is no longer the focal point of family life, but rather has been redefined as a sort of quiet corner, which may

also be used as a guest room or study. The social hub is the generously sized, brightly lit kitchen. It provides enough space for a large table and chairs, but also for comfortable armchairs and a television. Thanks to the bulge in the plan shape, the hall widens towards the entrance to form a space equipped with a number of built-in cupboards. The cupboards can be used for clothing, food or general storage and also include a fold-out table, which can turn the hall into a temporary utility room or office. In summer the family on the ground floor can make use of a terrace outside the kitchen, and the family on the upper floor a large platform between the access stairs and the entrance.

CONSTRUCTION   ///   The special character of the interior of the apartments is reflected in the unconventional external appearance. The two small blocks look like they have been packaged in wrapping paper! A reflective, crinkly aluminium foil shimmers, sometimes golden, sometimes silvery, behind the glass fibre-reinforced polyester corrugated sheets which rise beyond roof level. These varying nuances of colour are generated by the corrugated plastic sheeting, which is either transparent or pale yellow.   ///   The plastic envelope, with the corrugations running either vertical or horizontal, is the outermost layer of a multi-layer external wall construction. The unconventional envelope

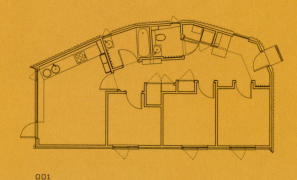

001

002

003

001_ Plan /// 002_ Section /// 003_ Access to the upper apartments takes the form of spacious timber terraces.

conceals a timber building which was completely pre-fabricated and merely assembled on site, a choice of construction dictated by cost and time savings. The external walls consist of prefabricated, insulated, aluminium-laminated timber panels with plasterboard on the inside and, separated via a ventilation cavity, glass fibre-reinforced polyester corrugated sheets to provide protection from the weather. The façade was given a final artistic touch by Vinita Hassard, who installed twisted, recycled electric wires behind the polyester sheeting. /// The façade with its contemporary, youthful-looking approach is not the only reason why these apartments appeal specifically to young first-time buyers. A house is no longer just a house, but instead joins the ranks of the design world and challenges the perceptions of the man in the street.

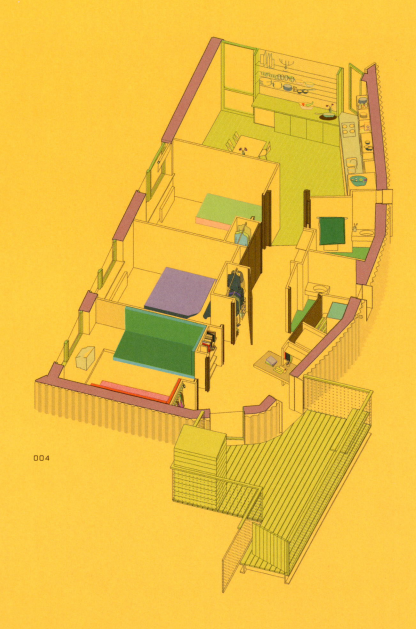

004

005   006

004_ Isometric view /// **005_** The experimental nature of these buildings is reflected in the external envelope made from aluminium foil and plastic. /// **006_** Twisted, recycled electric wires – an artistic touch by the artist Vinita Hassard – decorate the elevations.

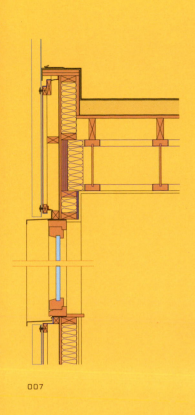

007

008

LACATON & VASSAL

CITÉ MANIFESTE

MATERIAL_ TRANSPARENT CORRUGATED POLYCARBONATE SHEETS /// **FAÇADE TYPE**_ SINGLE-LEAF OR MULTI-LAYER, INSULATED ///

USE_ RESIDENTIAL /// **LOCATION**_MULHOUSE, FRANCE /// **COMPLETED**_ 2005

The realisation of the Cité Manifeste project in Mulhouse – an experimental housing development – celebrated the 150th anniversary of *Société mulhousienne des cités ouvrières* (SOMCO), a housebuilding company. The beginnings of the company can still be seen on the adjoining site, where SOMCO built France's first housing estate for factory workers in the company's founding year of 1853. Architect Jean Nouvel drew up the masterplan for Cité Manifeste and included references to the urban planning contours of the former workers' housing estate. He conceived four rows of terrace houses based on a strict, orthogonal grid which are linked by one transverse block. /// Besides Jean Nouvel, four young French architectural practices worked on the designs for the individual rows of terrace houses. SOMCO allowed the architects considerable freedom. The masterplan and a very tight budget based on publicly assisted housing norms were the only conditions with which the architects had to comply. One of the rows of houses was designed by Lacaton & Vassal.

BACKGROUND ///   The architectural practice of Lacaton & Vassal is well-known for its experimental low-budget houses in which half of the floor space usually consists of an unheated conservatory. These two French architects have been searching for new housing solutions for more than 10 years. Inspired by their many years in Africa, the architects have redefined living accommodation to suit their own ideas. In some regions of Africa (and this is particularly true of the nomadic peoples), living quarters is synonymous with appropriation – and not the dominating possession and reconfiguration – of a

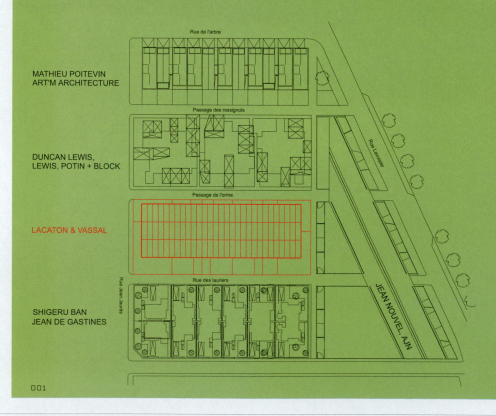

MATHIEU POITEVIN
ART'M ARCHITECTURE

DUNCAN LEWIS,
LEWIS, POTIN + BLOCK

LACATON & VASSAL

SHIGERU BAN
JEAN DE GASTINES

PLAN MASSE

0 5 10   50

001

002

PARTIE ISOLEE   JARDIN D'HIVER

Ⓐ   Ⓑ   Ⓒ   Ⓓ

003

001_ Location plan /// **002_** Section /// **003_** The reinforced concrete structure forms a storey-high plinth for the lightweight plastic construction of the upper floor.

territory. The living quarters is the undefined space in the lee of the tent, under the shade of the trees or around the warmth-giving open fire. The location of household activities is determined by the respective time of day and time of year. /// Transferred to the climatic conditions of Europe, this becomes an approach that calls for the occupied "territory" to be enclosed in an envelope that can react to the changing climate. The house becomes a multifunctional group of spaces consisting of a loadbearing structure and several layers (some of which enclose the spaces) that – like clothing – can be changed to suit the weather and the needs of the occupants. This definition of living accommodation overturns the conventional, European concept of housing and its relationship with the outside world. Whereas housing in Europe normally entails the screening-off from a "threatening" outside world (thermal insulation, double glazing, airtight assemblies and the avoidance of thermal bridges are given maximum priority), the architecture of Lacaton & Vassal is determined by the absence of boundaries and the opening-up of the space through the layer-by-layer dissolution of the house. The architects took as their role models the intelligent systems of glasshouses, which guarantee an optimum environment for plants at all times – an obvious transfer of technology and typology.

CONCEPT /// The theoretical approach described above also forms the conceptual foundation for the terrace houses of the Cité Manifeste project. Laying aside the normal standards for publicly assisted housing that fix the room numbers and sizes, their utilisation and even the internal furnishings (stipulations based on traditional, conventional values and concepts), the architects strived to redefine these values and create living accommodation characterised by unencumbered, open layouts and references, flexible, bright interiors and a "permeability" from inside to outside – akin to the idea of the appropriation of a "territory". /// The terrace houses were conceived according to this definition of living space. They occupy almost the entire depth of the building plot, which has reduced the front gardens so typical of terrace houses to room-size, asphalt-paved external seating areas. The row of houses comprises 14 two-storey, 20 m deep units with eight different plan layouts, all of which, however, adhere to the same principles. Each house is essentially just one single room. Only the bathroom and the garage, which at the same time serves as an entrance zone, are separated from the layout and divide the house into functional areas, but with uninterrupted, open transitions. However, this one-room-house principle only works because of the unequal division of floor space between ground floor and upper floor. Varying the widths of the houses results in different room sizes to suit the different internal functions. In addition, positioning the party walls at an angle on plan explores the possibilities between the prescribed minimum room size and the desirable maximum room size.

CONSTRUCTION /// The construction, too, was to a large extent dictated by the desire to achieve the

004_ Large façade openings, untreated fair-face concrete surfaces and delicate, greenhouse-type conservatories in plastic determine the character of these terrace houses.

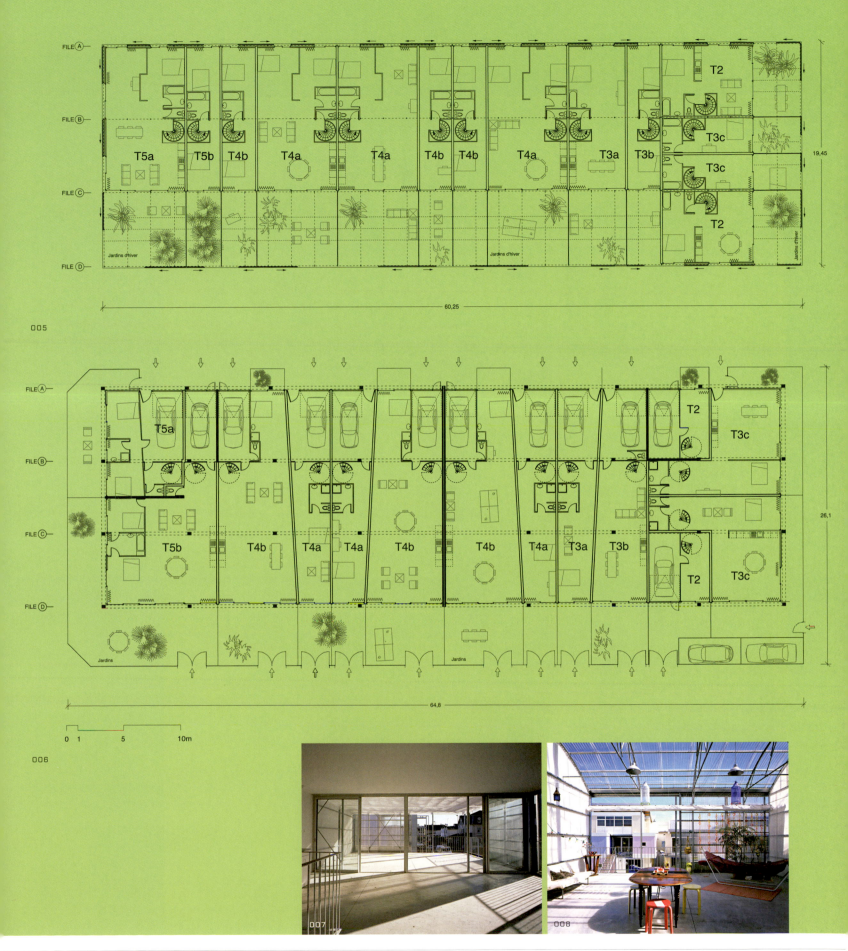

FILE Ⓐ
FILE Ⓑ
FILE Ⓒ
FILE Ⓓ

T5a   T5b   T4b   T4a   T4a   T4b   T4b   T4a   T3a   T3b

T2

T3c

T3c

T2

Jardins d'hiver   Jardins d'hiver   Jardins d'hiver

19,45

60,25

005

FILE Ⓐ
FILE Ⓑ
FILE Ⓒ
FILE Ⓓ

T5a

T5b   T4b   T4a   T4a   T4b   T4b   T4a   T3a   T3b

T2

T3c

T2

T3c

Jardins   Jardins

26,1

64,8

0 1   5   10m

006

007

008

005_ Plan of upper floor /// **006_** Plan of ground floor /// **007_** The open-plan layouts of the houses are interrupted only by the stairs and the sanitary blocks; large areas of glazing and glass doors link interior and exterior. /// **008_** In the summer, the outside becomes part of the living area.

maximum volume. The architects selected mainly prefabricated, standardised elements for the construction and left the surfaces untreated. Precast concrete elements form the loadbearing framework for the ground floor and punctuate the generous transparency of the façade. The upper floor on top of this 3 m high, table-like concrete plinth is formed by a lightweight glasshouse structure made from steel sections clad in corrugated transparent polycarbonate sheets. These plastic walls consist of multi-leaf insulated or single-leaf uninsulated assemblies depending on the internal uses. The spacious, uninsulated area functions like a conservatory. During spring and autumn it supplements the accommodation and in summer it is almost transformed into an external area. Large openings in roof and façade can be opened up to 50 %. A fabric sunblind can be extended horizontally if required. /// In order to guarantee permeability between inside and outside, the boundary between conservatory and living quarters is characterised by large areas of glazing and glass doors. Multi-leaf plastic external walls were used on the north side. The lightweight façade construction with their air cavity were given an additional double layer of insulation and finished internally with a lining of plasterboard. Special, highly reflective curtains on the inside or sliding panels of corrugated polycarbonate sheets on the outside form an integral part of the façade concept and protect against overheating in summer. These movable elements can be deployed as required. /// The architects remained loyal to their material concept in the interior as well. They used the plastic sheeting for the internal partitions too and left the concrete wall and floor surfaces exposed. This mixture of materials, untreated surfaces, open-plan layout and unusual wall constructions resulted in housing units that are nearly twice the size of those normally found in publicly assisted housing. The quality of the accommodation benefits from this gain in space, but at the same time requires the tenants to rethink their living habits. Functions are no longer tied to confined internal spaces; they start to migrate and the house itself becomes a territory which is not screened off from its environment, but rather remains permeated by it and enters into an intensive dialogue with it.

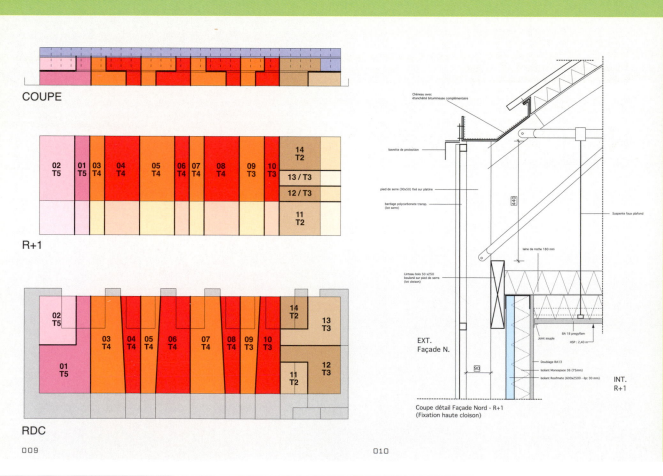

009_ Schematic plan layout and section /// **010**_ Section through eaves

011

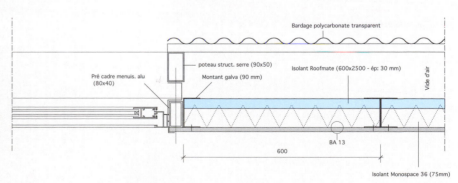

EXTERIEUR (façade Nord)

Bardage polycarbonate transparent

poteau struct. serre (90x50)

Isolant Roofmate (600x2500 - ép: 30 mm)

Pré cadre menuis. alu (80x40)

Montant galva (90 mm)

Vide d'air

BA 13

600

Isolant Monospace 36 (75mm)

INTERIEUR (Espace isolé)

Plan détail sur cloison périphérique - R+1

012

011_ The conservatory adds another room to the accommodation. /// **012**_ Horizontal section through façade

ARCONIKO

HOUSE AND STUDIO IN ALMERE

MATERIAL_ TRANSLUCENT MULTI-WEB POLYCARBONATE SHEETS /// **FAÇADE TYPE**_ SINGLE-LEAF /// **USE**_ RESIDENTIAL/STUDIO ///

LOCATION_ ALMERE, THE NETHERLANDS /// **COMPLETED**_ 1998

The house and studio project in Almere demonstrates that low-budget building and high aesthetic demands is not necessarily a contradiction in terms. The successful collaboration between the clients (two artists) and the architects resulted in a house with a special character based on an unpretentious loadbearing structure, a straightforward plan layout and the use of "cheap materials" such as corrugated sheet metal and plastic. High ceilings, an open-plan arrangement and, above all, the treatment of light have resulted in high-quality accommodation.

CONCEPT /// The choice of materials and form of construction can be understood from the architectural context. Located on the boundary between industrial and housing districts, this house is surrounded by, from the architectural viewpoint, simplistic, everyday commercial structures. The architects "borrowed" the cheap materials and the standardised building components from the nearby greenhouses and industrial sheds and turned them into a more sophisticated but nevertheless clear-cut design. /// Corrugated sheet metal and plastic dominate the external appearance of the simple, rectangular building. The corrugated sheet metal, which is actually a thermally insulated sandwich panel, is placed over the steel structure like a wide, upturned "U" to form the roof and the gable ends of the house. However, the corrugated sheet metal has been placed at an angle to form a monopitch roof, which results in a different number of storeys inside. On the southern side, facing the garden, the house has two storeys, whereas the northern side, which includes the entrance, is just one tall single storey. Opaque plastic panels form the longitudinal elevations spanning between the gable ends. /// Just like the building envelope, the plan layout also employs an uncomplicated approach. There are essentially just two rooms separated by a zone containing the stairs and ancillary rooms. On one side an open gallery and built-in cupboards divide the living area into

001

001_ At night, the "internal workings" of the building are discernible through the translucent façade.

functional zones; cooking, eating, relaxing and sleeping take place in an open-plan arrangement. On the other side, the sculptor has set up his workshop with a separate room for dust-free working and a gallery to present a view of his works. The interior atmosphere is dominated by the exposed steel frame, which reminds the observer of an old industrial building, and the untreated surfaces of the materials employed.

CONSTRUCTION /// The search for the zero point, the absolute minimum in architecture, led the architects to devise an unconventional façade construction: a single layer of multi-web polycarbonate sheets was bonded directly to the steel structure using a special double-sided adhesive tape. This amazingly simple method of erection was tested for the first time on this project in conjunction with the manufacturers. The butt

joints were subsequently filled with silicone. There are therefore virtually no details on this house. Even the junctions between the plastic sheets and the wooden frames to the double-glazed windows and between the frames and the primary structure make use of adhesive tape and silicone. This unusual form of construction created a new aesthetic with a remarkable appearance utterly free from any disturbing fixings. The façade is a flat skin, which is accentuated by the reddish brown wooden frames of the windows.   ///   Another special feature of the façade construction is the way it controls the incoming light, or rather provides the interior with daylight. The opaque plastic sheets bathe the interior in a low-level, even light without creating a link between interior and exterior, a function reserved for the transparent glass windows which are positioned to provide specific views into and out of the house. The use of

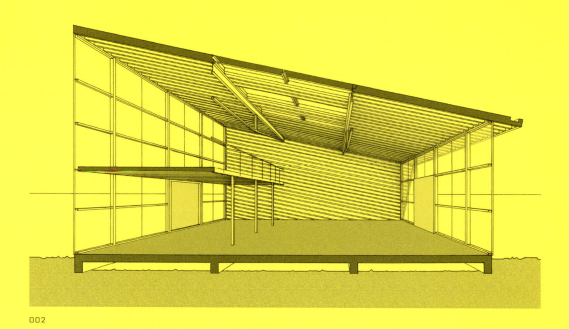

002

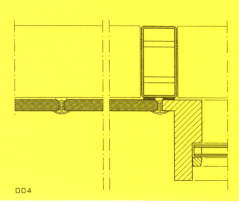

004

002_ Section   ///   **003**_ There is a seamless transition between the corrugated sheet metal forming the roof and the end walls of the building.   ///   **004**_ Horizontal section through façade

005_ The flush façade is accentuated by the dark wooden frames around the openings.   ///   **006**_ Plan of ground floor   ///   **007**_ Plan of gallery

plastic sheets over most of the façade alters the significance of the windows. /// Standard elements from builder merchants' catalogues add detail to the house without disrupting its clarity and strictness. For example, a standard garage door was used to provide access to the studio, and the steel stairs as well as the sliding doors on the elevation facing the garden are likewise standard products. /// Owing to the simplicity of the construction and the details, the clients were able to carry out some of the work themselves and thus keep the costs down. Contractors were brought in only for the concreting works, the steel structure and the metal roof and gable ends. The plastic façade was erected and the interior fitting-out completed by the artists themselves. /// The merits of the simple plastic façade are not just limited to the fact that it employs a low-cost, easy-to-handle material. During the daytime the special character of the plastic sheets means that the interior is lit by an even glow, which is important for the studio but also lends the living areas a special quality. And conversely, the house is turned into an illuminated sculpture at night when lit from within.

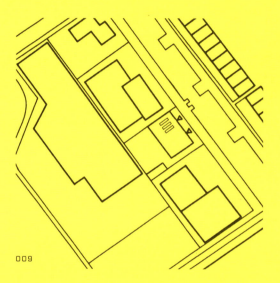

008_ Standard industrial products and the unpretentious structural steelwork determine the atmosphere of the studio. /// 009_ Location plan /// 010_ Night-time photo

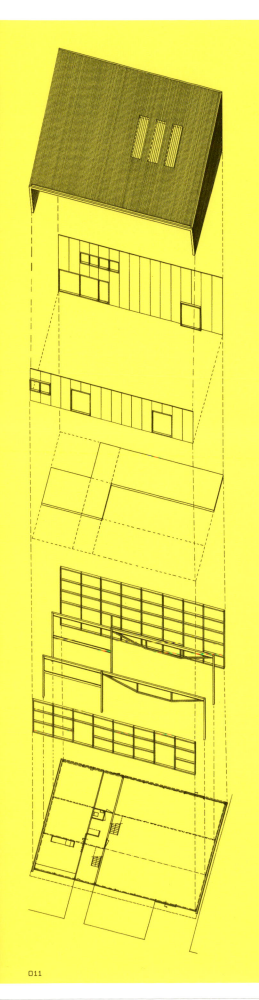

011

012

011_ Exploded drawing /// **012**_ Windows and glazed façade elements are integrated into the external envelope very sparingly and specifically.

PFEIFER.KUHN

SEMI-DETACHED HOUSES IN MÜLLHEIM

MATERIAL_ TRANSLUCENT MULTI-WEB POLYCARBONATE SHEETS /// **FAÇADE TYPE**_ SINGLE-LEAF OR MULTI-LAYER ///

USE_ RESIDENTIAL /// **LOCATION**_ MÜLLHEIM, GERMANY /// **COMPLETED**_ 2005

At first sight this house looks just like any other in this area; the local design guidelines prescribe the form of such a single-storey building with a duopitch roof. However, in this case appearances are deceptive. It is not only the synthetic envelope, but also the plan layout and the energy concept that bear witness to the unconventional building culture behind this design. /// The client, a biologist, was used to sleeping in a tent on her many research expeditions and therefore wanted a house with a "tent-like character", one that would be light and airy. At the same time, it should provide more than just a small family home and instead should be designed for two parties who want to live together under one roof without sacrificing any of their independence.

CONCEPT /// The architects turned this brief into an unusual plan layout that is not readily apparent in the form of a standard two-dimensional drawing and requires the third dimension to reveal the architects' in-tentions. The house provides a volume in which the individual rooms are stacked like boxes, grouped around a large atrium-like central hall to form closed, semi-open and open spaces like galleries. At any time the occupants can therefore choose to withdraw into one of the closed rooms or remain available for communication in one of the open spaces. In order that both parties profit from the sunshine, the storeys of the housing units are turned through 90°. This approach resulted in a layout that spirals around the central hall. Straight stair flights facing in opposite directions in the multi-storey hall create independent access to the respective housing units but at the same time create an area for communication.

CONSTRUCTION /// The enclosing volume in the form of a duopitch-roofed house is built from multi-web polycarbonate sheets. Following the house-within-a-house principle, the façade to the central hall consists

001

001_ Location plan /// **002_** At night-time, when the building is lit from within, the different wall constructions become visible.

exclusively of a single-leaf, uninsulated wall assembly, whereas the cubes of the living accommodation have a multi-layer façade. This enabled the more costly, multi-layer wall construction to be used specifically for the heated rooms only. The façade to the living quarters consists of translucent, airtight, waterproof plastic sheets, an air cavity and a solid leaf of edge-fixed timber elements as the inner lining. Owing to the relatively good U-value of the plastic sheets and the adjoining air cavity, the façade construction achieves a level of thermal insulation that satisfies the strict regulations without any additional thermal insulation. Their low weight-per-unit area, the simple construction details and the low capital outlay mean that the polycarbonate sheets have many advantages over conventional glazing. /// During spring and autumn, the ingenious façade system changes to a functional façade – a supplier of energy which forms a substantial component in the building's energy concept.

CLIMATE CONCEPT /// The fundamental idea behind the energy concept is to use a low-tech approach: heat losses are to be minimised, energy requirements reduced and solar gains exploited. These premises resulted in a design concept in which the plan layout and the building services are inextricably linked. /// The open hall and the façade construction are intrinsic to the internal climate concept. The hall, around which the rooms spiral, takes on the function of a conservatory. It exploits solar gains for heating and reduces heat losses. In winter it forms a buffer zone between the cold outside air and the heated habitable rooms, in spring and autumn the heat stored in the hall reaches the adjoining living quarters via open doors, and in summer roof vents help to prevent overheating of the interior. Just like the hall changes its function through the seasons, the multi-layer façade also behaves differently depending on the external climatic conditions. During spring and autumn the multi-layer external walls function as air collectors and supply additional heat to the interior: the solar radiation heats up the air behind the translucent outer leaf and convection currents drive this air into the roof space from where it can be channelled via a duct into the central hall. In summer the heated air escapes to the outside via roof vents and in winter the "stationary" layer of air acts as thermal insulation. Vents at ground level and

003_ The accommodation is grouped around a three-storey circulation and communication atrium. /// **004_** The spacious, open atrium, with its single-leaf polycarbonate walls, functions as a conservatory. /// **005_** Straight stair flights facing in opposite directions provide independent access to the two houses under one roof.

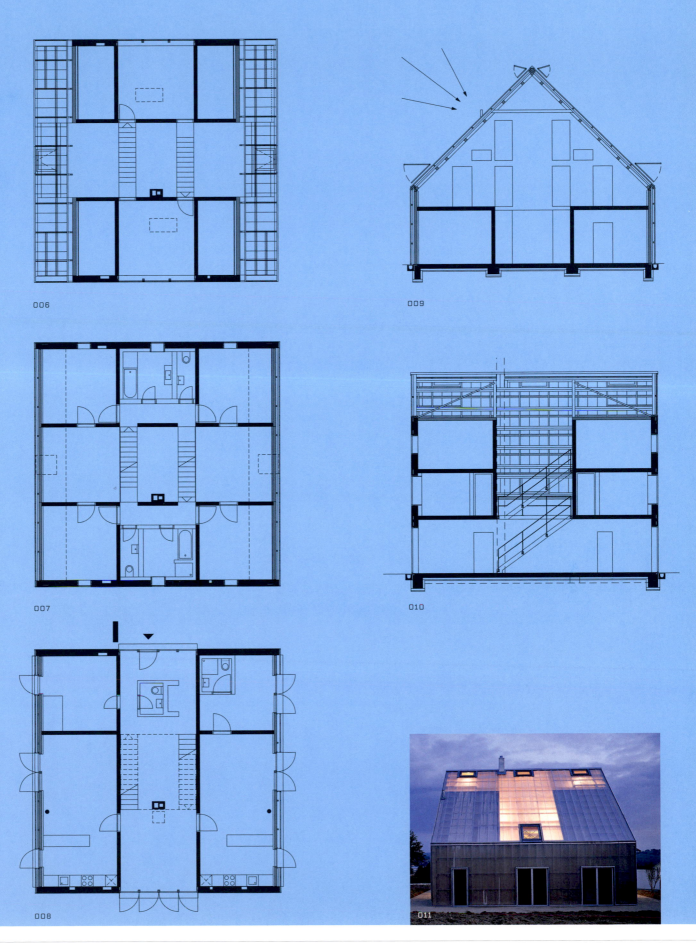

006

007

008

009

010

011

006_ Plan of roof   ///   **007_** Plan of upper floor   ///   **008_** Plan of ground floor   ///   **009_** Section   ///   **010_** Longitudinal section   ///   **011_** Brightly illuminated roof surfaces denote the three-storey atrium.

ridge are responsible for the functionality of the façade. In winter the vents remain closed so there is no flow of air. During the rest of the year the roof windows can be opened to create a negative pressure in the façade cavity, which automatically opens the vent at ground level and thus generates a convection current. This is a form of construction that the architects have already employed in a number of variations. /// The zoning of the house into rooms with different temperatures, the "energy garden" and the collectors reduce the heating requirement to such an extent that heating in a form of activating the components in the concrete floors is sufficient. /// This new building is an impressive demonstration of contemporary housing. Instead of traditional semi-detached houses, the architects created a form of accommodation with a complex interlacing of common and private zones which benefits from new materials and innovative energy concepts.

012

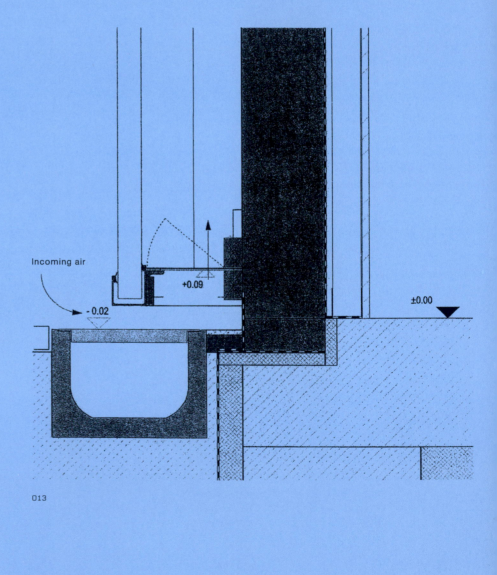

Incoming air

+0.09

- 0.02

±0.00

013

012_ The plastic sheets form a thin outer leaf in front of the solid timber walls. /// **013**_ Detail of base of wall in living area

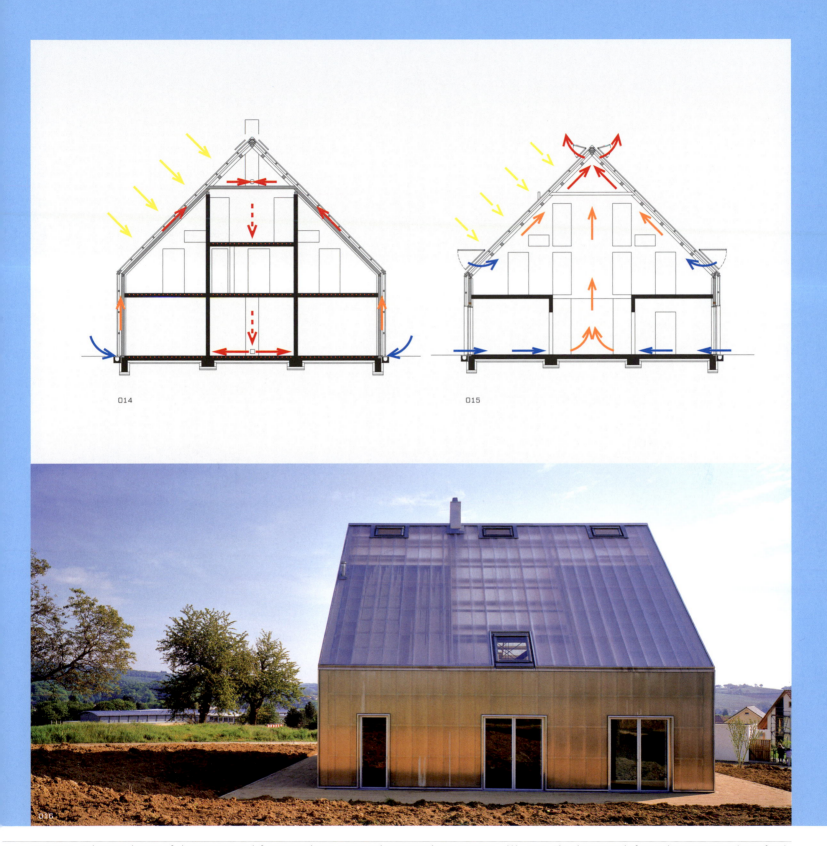

014

015

016

014–015_ Schematic diagram of climate concept: left energy scheme, winter; right energy scheme, summer   ///   **016**_ The plastic panels form a thin covering to the roof and external walls.

SHIGERU BAN

MUSEUM OF PAPER ART

MATERIAL_ TRANSLUCENT GLASS-FIBRE REINFORCED PLASTIC SHEETS /// **FAÇADE TYPE_** SINGLE-LEAF OR MULTI-LEAF ///

USE_ EXHIBITIONS /// **LOCATION_** SHIZUOKA, JAPAN /// **COMPLETED_** 2001

In Japan, paper production and paper art are based on traditions stretching back thousands of years, and enjoy worldwide acclaim. Just recently, a museum of paper art, of which there are only a handful in Japan, opened in Shizuoka, not far from Tokyo. This private museum, set up by one of Japan's leading paper manufacturers, contains a comprehensive collection of traditional paper art and in the adjoining gallery, a converted old factory building, shows examples of contemporary, avant-garde tendencies in Japanese paper art. Tradition and avant-garde, the thematic foundations of the exhibition, also enjoy a congenial relationship in the museum design by Shigeru Ban. The architect used new materials to create contemporary modern spaces, but at the same time he creates a reference to the traditional architecture of Japan with his re-interpretation of and variation on the *shitomido*, a vertical window shutter common in traditional Japanese architecture, or the thematic treatment of the space continuum.

CONCEPT ///   In climatic terms, the new museum structure – a square, three-storey block with a glass pavilion on the roof – follows the building-within-a-building principle. A steel frame provides the loadbearing structure and weatherproof simple double-web sheets made from glass fibre-reinforced plastic form the outer building. Inside this three-storey building there are two more three-storey blocks, each of which covers one-third of the plan area. The two blocks are separated by a three-storey multifunctional atrium in the middle. Narrow bridges span this void and link the two internal blocks. The southern block houses the museum offices, archives and a lecture theatre; the northern block is reserved for the museum's exhibits. Only those rooms that require air conditioning, e.g. offices and exhibition areas, have a second, inner leaf to the façade. The atrium and circulation areas, on the other hand, are separated from the outside merely by the single-leaf plastic façade.

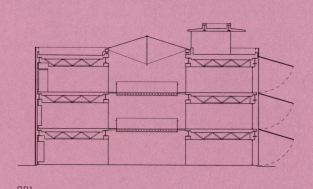

001

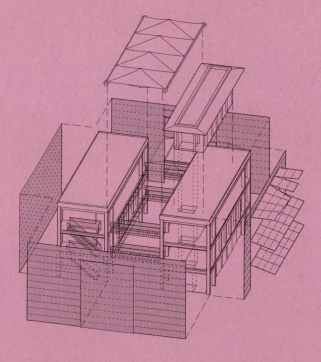

002

001_ Section   ///   **002_** Isometric exploded view   ///   **003_** The exhibition and administration areas are climatically separate entities located within a three-storey volume according to the building-within-a-building principle; large sections of the façade can be opened up to the outside.

CONSTRUCTION /// At first sight the museum appears to be hermetically sealed and introvert. But a closer inspection reveals that the building is a transformable organism with many facets. The idea of a flowing, unmarked transition between inside and outside governed the design and construction. The re-interpretation of the traditional *shitomido* helped the architects to realise their idea. The lightweight plastic façade can be easily opened, rolled aside or lifted up in different ways. For example, the storey-high façade panels to the offices on the southern side can be raised to the horizontal position so that they also act as sunshades. Furthermore, the inner leaf (storey-high single glazing) can be slid sideways almost completely so that on mild summer days the museum staff are virtually working out-

doors. In the three-storey atrium the plastic panels can be opened over their full height of nearly 10 m. The sole rigid façade is located on the north side of the exhibition area. Calcium silicate panels as the inner leaf provide both thermal insulation and, at the same time, a surface for exhibits. /// The adjoining gallery in the converted factory building adheres to the same principle: it was given a single-leaf façade comprising six-part, translucent, glass fibre-reinforced plastic panels. With the panels closed, the wall reminds the observer of *shoji* screens, the traditional Japanese sliding paper walls. The 5 m high façade elements are opened by rolling them upwards onto cantilevering horizontal external steel beams, where they form a generous sunshade. This feature enables the façade to be opened over the

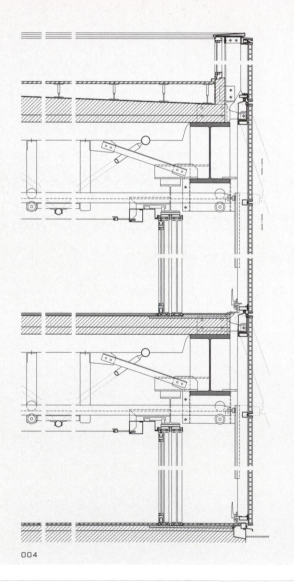

004

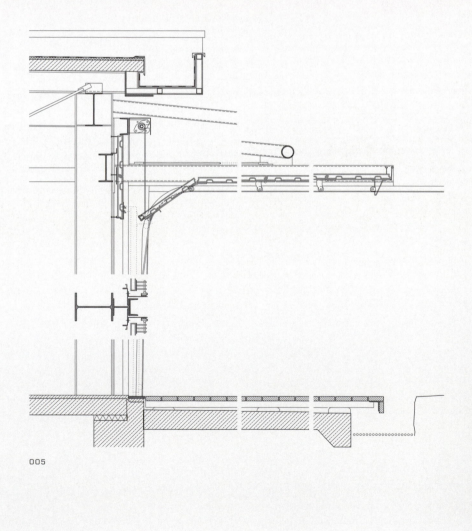

005

004_ Section through façade, museum /// 005_ Section through façade, gallery

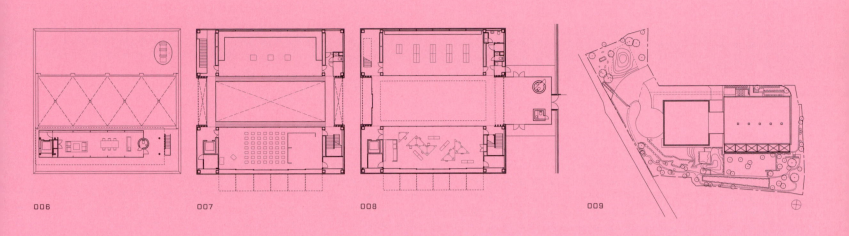

006   007   008   009

010

006_ Plan of roof   ///   **007**_ Plan of 2nd floor   ///   **008**_ Plan of ground floor   ///   **009**_ Location plan   ///   **010**_ Large sections of the lightweight plastic façade in each storey can be swung upwards to link interior and exterior as well as to provide generous sunshading.

full height and length of the building. The interior of the gallery can thus be extended into its surroundings and becomes embraced by the landscape. /// The movability and large openings of the lightweight plastic façade leads to a transformation of the interior spaces and creates a spatial continuity that blurs the boundaries between interior and exterior.

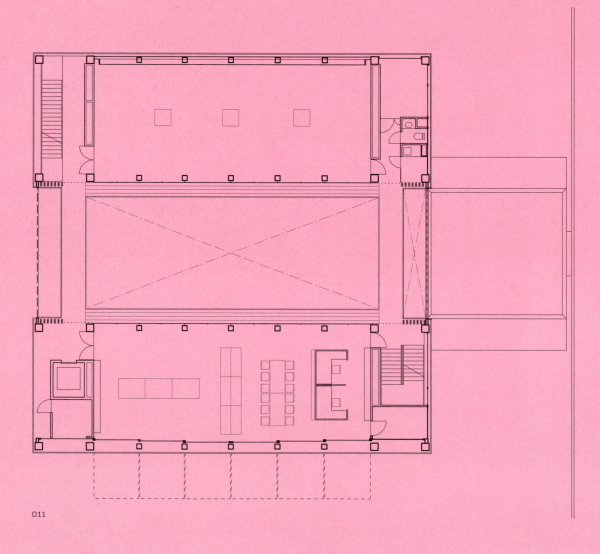

011

011_ Plan of 1st floor

012

013

012_ When closed, the plastic façade forms an uninterrupted, plain surface.   ///   **013_** The atrium façade can be opened over its full height, turning interior and exterior into one continuous space.

STAIB ARCHITECTS WITH GÜNTER BEHNISCH

CATHOLIC CHURCH OF JESUS CHRIST THE KING, RADEBEUL

MATERIAL_ TRANSLUCENT MULTI-WEB POLYCARBONATE SHEETS WITH COLOURED GLASS OR TRANSPARENT ACRYLIC INSERTS ///

FAÇADE TYPE_ SINGLE-LEAF /// **USE_** WORSHIP, TEMPORARY /// **LOCATION_** RADEBEUL, GERMANY /// **COMPLETED_** 2001

CONCEPT /// Surrounded by a park-like landscape and impressive villas dating from the late 19th century, this simple, triangular glass edifice that forms the Catholic place of worship in Radebeul could be mistaken for a garden pavilion. However, this new building does not try to curry favour with the existing built environment, but rather aims – through its strict, lucid architectural language – to evade any comparison. /// The rigid, triangular plan shape is relieved somewhat at ground floor level by a curving fair-face concrete wall. The completely random line of the wall separates the entrance area and the vestry from the place of worship itself and at one end includes the confessional box – on plan in the shape of an ear. The wall supports the choir, which protrudes through the façade to form a canopy over the entrance. /// Inspired by the nearby vineyards and the surrounding large residences, the architects pursued the idea of an open-air church enclosed within a bower overgrown with dense, wild vines – an idea reminiscent of Laugier's primitive hut. It is not the façades that demarcate the place of worship, but rather the internal curving wall and the foliage of the trees and vines in front of the façade. (However, the external planting has not yet been realised.) The façade itself offers protection against the weather and is also responsible for the look and feel of the interior – through specific lighting and visual effects achieved through the multifaceted construction of the façade, which includes the whole range of nuances from transparency to translucency.

CONSTRUCTION /// Like a patchwork quilt, the panels of the façade alternate between customary, transparent insulating glass units and cellular plastic sheets in various colours with different cell widths and different degrees of transparency. The arrangement and types of façade infill panels are a response to the surroundings. The presence of the outside world and the atmosphere and colouring within the church depend

002

001

001_ The coloured plastic and glass inserts in the façade lead to a colourful play of light in the interior.   ///   **002_** The fully glazed façade permits an uninterrupted view of the surrounding landscape.

on the choice of panel – transparent, translucent or coloured. /// The effect of this façade design is especially evident on the two-storey main façade facing south-east, which is divided in two horizontally. The upper section consists of polycarbonate sheets intended as a modern interpretation of mediaeval church windows with their hand-blown glass in clear, illuminating, primary colours. The sunlight generates zones of coloured light in the interior of the church and brings to life the structure of the façade. The lower section contrasts with this by employing transparent insulating glass units and translucent plastic sheets, thus allowing the exterior to be specifically included in or excluded from the church service. /// The entrance façade follows the same principle. But this time the selection of colours – from yellow to green – matches the yellow sunlight and the green foliage covering the pergolas and trellises that will be added later. To reduce the costs, coloured acrylic strips were integrated into the cellular plastic sheets. /// Again and again, the churchgoers encounter this

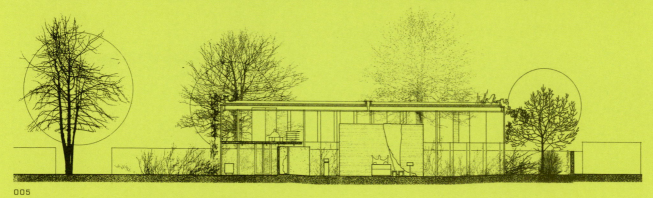

005

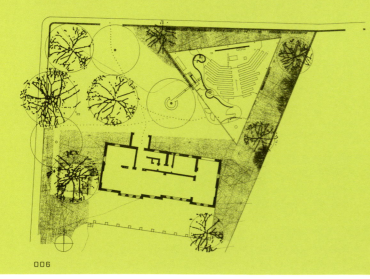

006

007

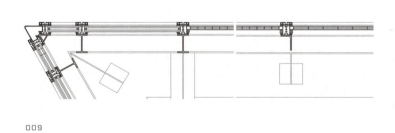

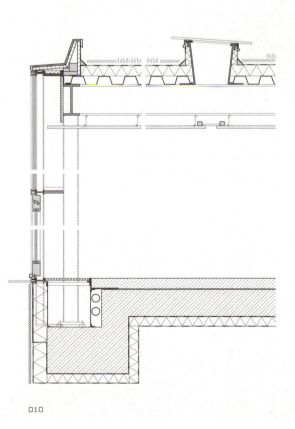

008_ The unadorned triangular glass block is reminiscent of a garden pavilion. /// **009_** Horizontal section through façade /// **010_** Vertical section through façade

011

play of light and colour. For example, the architects have incorporated a rooflight between the rooftop planting on the flat roof. On the outside, the rooflight comprises transparent polycarbonate sheets but on the inside it takes the form of a narrow slit in the suspended ceiling with an infill of yellow acrylic sheets. This allows a ray of bright, yellow, overhead light to reach the interior of the church which, as the position of the sun changes, moves across the wall behind the altar. /// As the sun moves across the sky, so the colouring and hence also the atmosphere within the church alters. The architects have used the versatility of the polycarbonate sheets to generate a bright, friendly atmosphere in the interior through the play of light, shadows and colours.

011_ The façade, with its multitude of different coloured inserts, resembles a patchwork quilt.

012_ Close-up of pews /// **013**_ Confessional box in the shape of an ear with backlit plastic ceiling

HERZOG + PARTNER

DBU CONFERENCE AND EXHIBITION PAVILION

MATERIAL_ ETFE FILM, TRANSPARENT, ONE LAYER   ///   **ROOF FORM_** SINGLE-LEAF OR MULTI-LAYER, MECHANICALLY PRETENSIONED   ///

USE_ EXHIBITIONS/OFFICES   ///   **LOCATION_** OSNABRÜCK, GERMANY   ///   **COMPLETED_** 2002

When the Deutsche Bundesstiftung Umwelt (DBU – German Environmental Foundation) undertakes a building project, then you can expect the end result to be innovative and environmentally compatible. Accordingly, when planning its new conference and exhibition pavilion, the DBU specified an environmentally friendly but at the same time low-budget solution which should take into account technical innovations and allow for the exemplary use of new materials. Energy-efficient and recycling-compatible forms of construction plus the use of natural building materials had to be coupled with engineering innovations and new materials to create a permanent, simple and flexible building satisfying high architectural demands.   ///   The architects responded to this apparently contradictory and all-embracing brief with a multifunctional, two-storey structure with a roof comprising one layer of transparent ETFE film to provide protection from the weather.

CONCEPT ///   Besides the constructional and technical requirements outlined above, maximum flexibility of the interior was another factor that dictated the design. Both the plan layout and the size of the building

had to be adaptable for future, changing needs. The new building was initially designed to accommodate an exhibition area and foyer, conference rooms and offices – three different forms of utilisation that place different demands on the design.   ///   The architects provided a modular framework in the form of a rectangular, two-storey loadbearing timber structure on a 10 x 8.1 m grid, which resulted in 21 identical modules on plan. Each individual two-storey bay can accommodate different usages as required and can be closed off horizontally and vertically, or left open as an exposed loadbearing structure, linking interior and exterior. For example, the exhibition area comprises four bays extending the full height of the building, interrupted in one bay by a gallery at first-floor level. The offices zone extends over five bays and two levels. Depending on the utilisation required, the modules can be closed off with lightweight partitions or façades, floors or roofs. The roof was designed in such a way that the individual bays are independent in terms of layout and construction, which means that the roof construction can be varied from transparent to opaque separately for each bay.

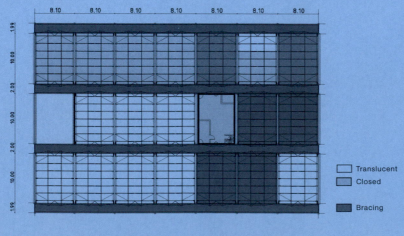

001

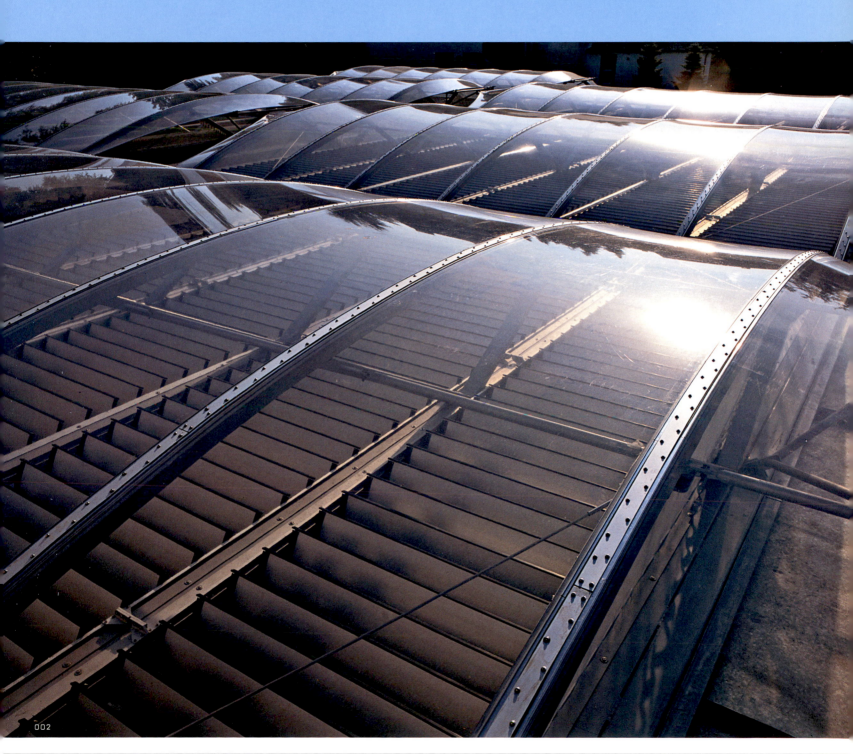

002

001_ The bays between the members of the two-storey-high timber framework result in 21 identical modules which can be fitted with different roof forms. /// **002_** One layer of transparent ETFE film forms the weather-resistant roof covering.

003

CONSTRUCTION /// Irrespective of the internal utilisation, the bays were provided with a single layer of transparent ETFE film as the outermost, weatherproof roof. Beneath this weatherproof membrane, numerous multi-layer roof constructions are conceivable, which can be matched to the respective uses of the interior spaces below. Four different types of construction were implemented. The conference rooms required high thermal and sound insulation values and so were given translucent roof panels made from horizontal double glazing with integral translucent thermal insulation and incorporating adjustable sunblinds in the cavity. The overhead light, which provides a higher level of illumination than lighting from the side, is exploited to illuminate the inte-

rior. In the exhibition area, on the other hand, the thermal insulation was omitted. Here, the roof bays were closed off with matt-finish obscured double glazing. Over the offices and storage areas the inner roof layer consists of laminated veneer lumber panels which help to brace the roof and are covered with temporary waterproofing material and thermal insulation. The simplest form of roof construction can be found over the terraces, where the single layer of film forms a transparent canopy. /// The film is not only the water run-off layer for the roof; it also carries the snow and wind loads. Consequently, the roof constructions below the plastic outer membrane could be constructed considerably simpler than is usually the case. The panes of double glazing were able to

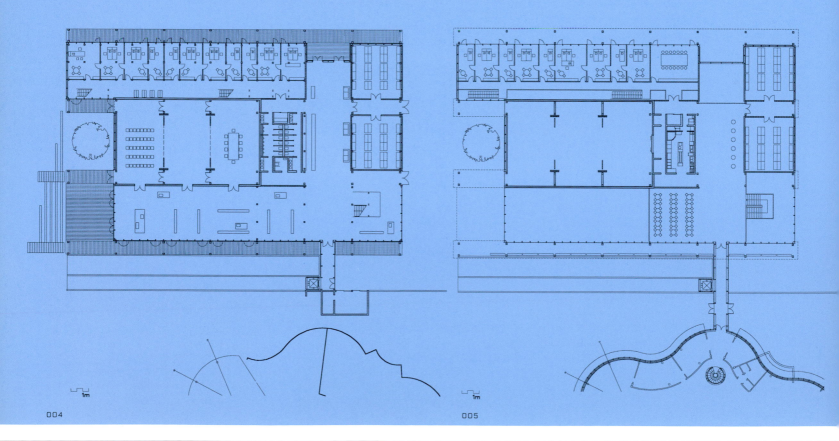

004

005

003_ Overall view /// **004**_ Plan of ground floor /// **005**_ Plan of upper floor

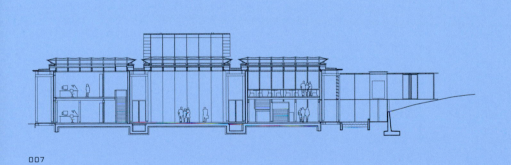

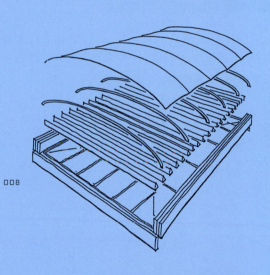

006_ Conference room /// **007**_ Section /// **008**_ Construction principle of roof bay /// **009**_ The multi-layer construction of the roof bays can be adapted to suit the use of the rooms below. /// **010**_ The roof is divided into individual bays, each one of which can have a different construction.

be installed horizontally without falls and did not have to satisfy the usual safety standards. The sunblinds are virtually zero-maintenance and the thermal insulation to the closed roof bays is protected against rain. /// Looking beyond the concept itself, the single-layer plastic membrane roof curving about both axes is also a technical and constructional innovation. Whereas pneumatic film assemblies have been sufficiently researched to date, the behaviour of single-layer, prestressed plastic membrane roofs under normal loadings was unknown up to now. /// The transparent ETFE film is stretched over arched beams made from steel hollow sections spaced 1.5 m apart and supported on the primary timber structure. To provide stability, the individual pieces of film were prestressed along the edges and fixed to the steel arches and along the longitudinal edges with specially designed clamp fasteners. The saddle shape that ensues in the membrane as it spans between each pair of arches is due to the prestress. Special tensioning arrangements, which tighten the membrane at certain points, were devised for the end pieces making up the transverse sides of the bays. /// The design of the clamp fasteners and the calculation of the prestress, which may not decrease even in the case of long-term or frequent loading by snow and wind, had to be determined empirically. Numerous experiments were carried out especially for this project at the former Essen Polytechnic (since 2003 known as the University of Duisburg-Essen) in order to discover the creep and relaxation behaviour, the behaviour of the film when subjected to repeated loads and the deformation progression as the load is relieved. In addition, the film was investigated for its behaviour when subjected to biaxial actions with strains

that exceed the serviceability conditions. The membrane construction as built with its curving saddle-shaped, mechanically prestressed plastic film was the outcome of these studies and experiments.

CLIMATE CONCEPT /// Resource-sparing and energy-saving concepts were realised under the heading of energy efficiency. The provision of light-permeable roof surfaces reduced the cost of heating and artificial lighting because the windowless conference rooms and the deep exhibition and foyer area can be lit by daylight throughout the year. In winter solar gains via the roof glazing and the preheated incoming air back up the underfloor heating. /// In the summer, louvres in the roof, which are controlled depending on the light, protect against excessive temperatures in the rooms below. However, if the interior does have to be cooled on hot summer days, the incoming air can be precooled or the underfloor heating used as a cooling system. The circulating water required for this is cooled in underground collectors. Another special feature is the combined fresh- and exhaust-air duct which functions as a heat exchanger and utilises the heat in the outgoing air to precondition the incoming air in summer and winter. Solar cells and vacuum-tube collectors on the roof supply further energy. Thanks to these comprehensive and diverse measures, the new pavilion achieves a specific annual heating energy requirement of 29 kWh/m²a, which is substantially lower than the low-energy house standard. /// In the DBU's new conference and exhibition pavilion, innovation and environmentally compatible building are fused into one by the new type of membrane roof construction.

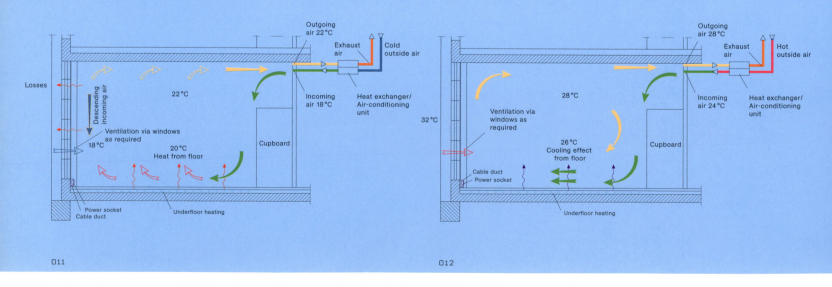

011

012

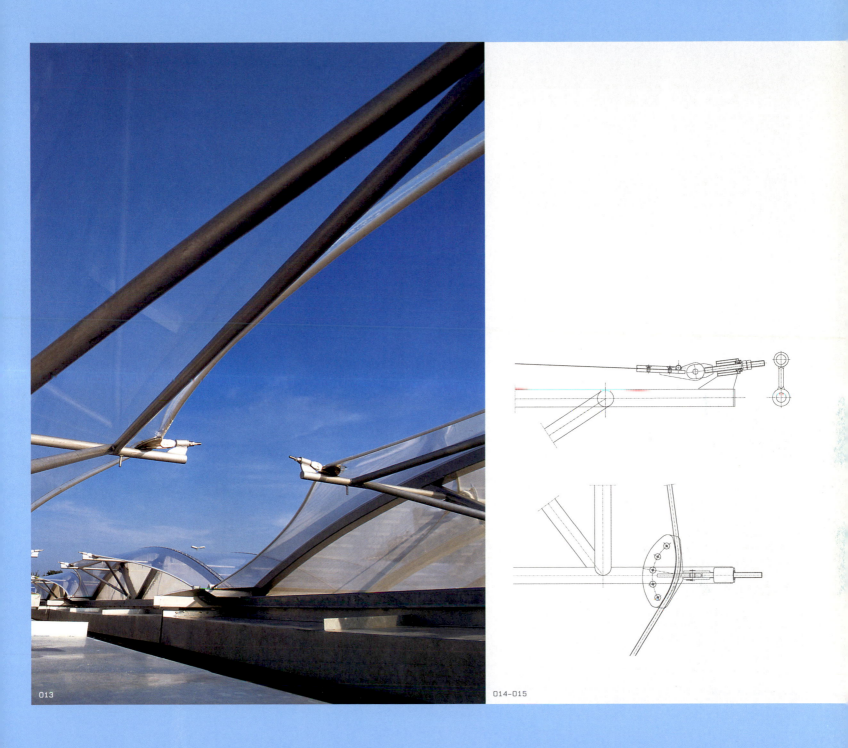

013

014–015

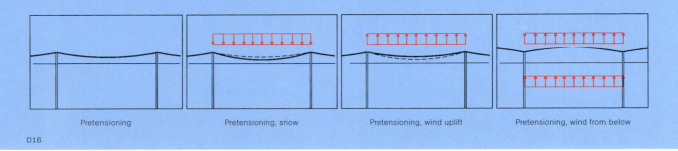

| Pretensioning | Pretensioning, snow | Pretensioning, wind uplift | Pretensioning, wind from below |

016

013_ In the end bays, the ETFE film is stabilised via a special tensioning arrangement.   ///   **014–015**_ Detail of tensioning apparatus   ///   **016**_ Schematic diagram of the loading cases for determining the pretension in the film.

HERZOG & DE MEURON

ALLIANZ ARENA

MATERIAL_ TRANSPARENT AND TRANSLUCENT ETFE-FILM, TWO LAYERS /// **FAÇADE TYPE**_ SINGLE LEAF OR MULTI-LAYER, PNEUMATICALLY PRETENSIONED /// **USE**_ SPORT /// **LOCATION**_ MUNICH, GERMANY /// **COMPLETED**_ 2005

The building of stadiums, alongside bridge-building undoubtedly one of the most important tasks for the structural engineer, is usually dominated by the issue of spans and ingenious loadbearing structures, which sometimes result in pioneering constructions, like in the case of the Olympic Stadium in Munich. But in designing a new football stadium for Munich, the architectural practice of Herzog & de Meuron abandoned the constructivist approach of its famous predecessor and devised a large-scale emblematic form which places football in its multimedia mass entertainment setting and in doing so itself becomes part of the spectacle. Looking like an oversized, out-of-scale, apparently monolithic air-filled cushion, the new stadium appears to float over the landscape and against the dark night sky takes on the appearance of a colourfully illuminated UFO!

CONCEPT /// One year before the kick-off of the World Cup 2006, Munich's two professional football clubs – FC Bayern Munich and TSV 1860 Munich – took possession of their new stadium on the edge of the city in surroundings dominated by waste sites, motorways, waste-water treatment works, wind turbines and wide expanses of undeveloped space. Basel-based Herzog & de Meuron prevailed against seven other competitors in a type of expert appraisal. Their proposal was for a structure that revels in itself and turns its back on this relatively desolate environment. /// Three dominating issues – the movement, the space and the envelope – form the focus of the design and constitute the framework, set the stage as it were, for the sporting event. A 600 m long x 133 m wide plateau-like ramp, with winding, asphalt-paved pathways and green lawns, leads up to the stadium structure. This Esplanade links the stadium with local public transport and coach parking spaces and skilfully conceals the parking for nearly 10,000 vehicles, which is distributed over the four storeys beneath the plateau. The fans who arrive for sporting

001

002

events in the frequent trains and overfilled buses and coaches or climb up from the low-level car parks then progress towards the stadium en masse along the Esplanade; a procession of the masses reminiscent of a Hollywood epic. Once they reach the stadium itself, the fans switch to the Promenade, which surrounds the stadium two storeys above the level of the pitch. From here, the staged movement continues into the four-storey staircases positioned directly behind the organic membrane façade, distributing the masses of spectators as far as the highest terraces in the sixth storey.

SPACE ///   All aspects of the introvert interior focus on the sporting event in an outstanding way. A total of 66,000 closely packed seats are stacked up on three terraces around the football pitch, rising to a height of about 40 m (roughly the height of a 14-storey building!). The density is, on the one hand, a result of the sporting

complex itself, which is designed exclusively for football matches and hence – in contrast to stadiums designed for light athletics as well – does not have to provide a perimeter running track which puts distance between spectators and players. On the other hand, the steepness of the seating increases as we go higher; indeed, the angle of the highest terrace is 34°, which is on the limit of acceptability. But this steepness enables the fans to get closer to the action on the pitch and provides them with an excellent view of the match. In addition, however, this funnel-shaped space creates a three-dimensional compactness whose role model is the traditional Shakespeare theatre, the theatre in the round. This effect is reinforced by the colour scheme of the grandstand. The light grey of the seats and the fair-face concrete surfaces plus the milky white of the membrane roof help to direct attention to the rectangular patch of bright green grass in the centre.

003

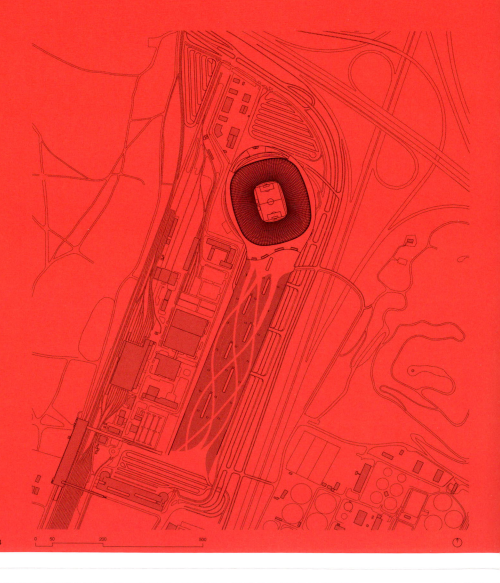

004

005

006

005_ The introverted interior with the steeply rising terraces creates a compact three-dimensional space that focuses attention on the football pitch. /// **006_** The 600 m long Esplanade steers the football fans towards the stadium and, with its curving network of pathways, is the ideal platform for the coming football event.

CONSTRUCTION /// This compact space is enclosed in diamond-shaped, two-layer ETFE membrane cushions placed like a bubbly skin over the roof structure and the outer walls of the stadium structure – like an oversized inflatable ring. /// The stadium enclosure consists of 2,760 air-filled cushions (with more than 1,400 different pieces) which are clamped to a grid of steel sections and fixed to the respective primary loadbearing system. /// The roof to the grandstand is formed by the grid of steel members plus the cushions supported on pinned columns on curving, cantilevering steel girders. To provide shade for the spectators, the cushions are either transparent or printed depending on the compass orientation. Horizontal fabric blinds, which can be extended as required, provide additional sunshading. The roof drainage incorporates a special feature: in order to prevent ponding (and hence incalculable roof loads) in the case of failure of the air supply to the cushions, each horizontal roof cushion is fitted with a special emergency roof outlet in the form of an aluminium tube which penetrates both layers of the plastic membrane. /// The rings of horizontal, diamond-shaped cushions on the double-curvature façade extend over five storeys right around the stadium. The membrane façade is attached to the reinforced concrete frame of the stadium structure but is independent of the roof construction. On the three lower storeys the cushions form the outer leaf of a double-leaf façade construction, concealing an inner leaf of double glazing with roller blinds or a multi-layer lightweight wall construction. There is enough space in the intermediate cavity for the travelling maintenance cradles. The inner leaf is omitted on the upper two storeys, the plant floor and the access level for the seats of the uppermost terrace, so the air-filled cushions here form the entire wall construction. Views of the surrounding Munich suburbs vary depending on the density of printing on the membrane material.

ENVELOPE /// However, it is not the construction and the technical details that are the main attraction in this design, but rather the dramatic multimedia effect of the envelope. Just the oversized

Diamond-shaped Cushions
ETFE-Foil, two-part

Stadium
(227m / 258m/ 50m)

Upper Tiers (22,000 seats)

Middle Tiers (24,000 seats)

Lower Tiers (20,000 seats)

Northern Ramp

Gallery

Field
(68m / 105m)

Access Esplanade / Parking

E7
E6
E5
E4
E3
E2
E1
E0

Esplanade
(134m / 600m)

E7 - Mechanical

E6 - Small Promenade, Kiosks, Fan Shops, Access Upper Tiers

E5 - Boxes, Event Boxes, Foyers, Catering

E4 - Business Club, Guests of Honour, Catering

E3 - Sponsor Lounges, Restaurants, Fan Meeting Points, Leisure Areas, Daycare, Offices

E2 - Large Promenade, VIP Access, Kiosks, Fan Shops, Access Lower Tiers, Access Middle Tiers

E1 - VIP Access , Parking Garage

E0 - Media Facilities, VIP Access, Security, Police, Ambulance, Lawn Maintenance, Mechanical, Parking Garage

007

007_ Isometric view

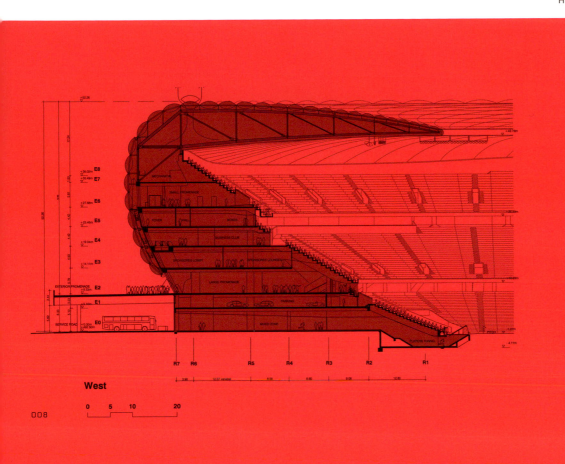

West

0   5   10   20

008

009

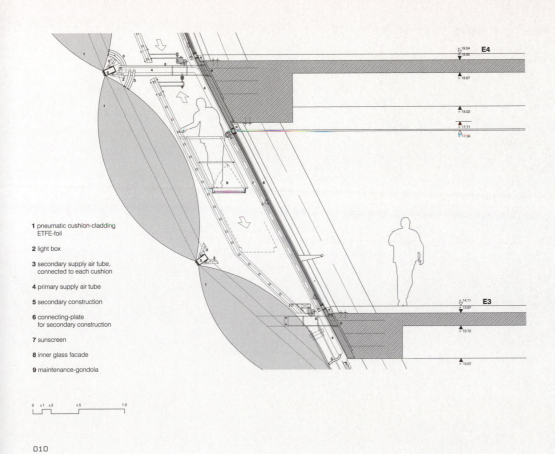

E4

E3

1 pneumatic cushion-cladding
ETFE-foil

2 light box

3 secondary supply air tube,
connected to each cushion

4 primary supply air tube

5 secondary construction

6 connecting-plate
for secondary construction

7 sunscreen

8 inner glass facade

9 maintenance-gondola

0 0.1 0.2   0.5   1.0

010

011

012

013

air-filled cushions themselves drew the attention of the public, perhaps for the first time, to the use of ETFE film as a form of façade construction. The climax of the dramatic setting is, however, the use of lighting effects to turn the entire structure into an illuminated display – red or blue to match the colours of the two clubs. This impressive show is achieved with three-colour lamps positioned directly behind the membrane cushions. More than 4,000 computer-controlled lamps – every cushion is equipped with four lamps – generate either a monochromatic object in white, blue or red, or dual-colour patterns. /// The stadium as a changing illuminated object rising from this insipid landscape generates the constructional programme for the sporting event as a multimedia mass spectacle.

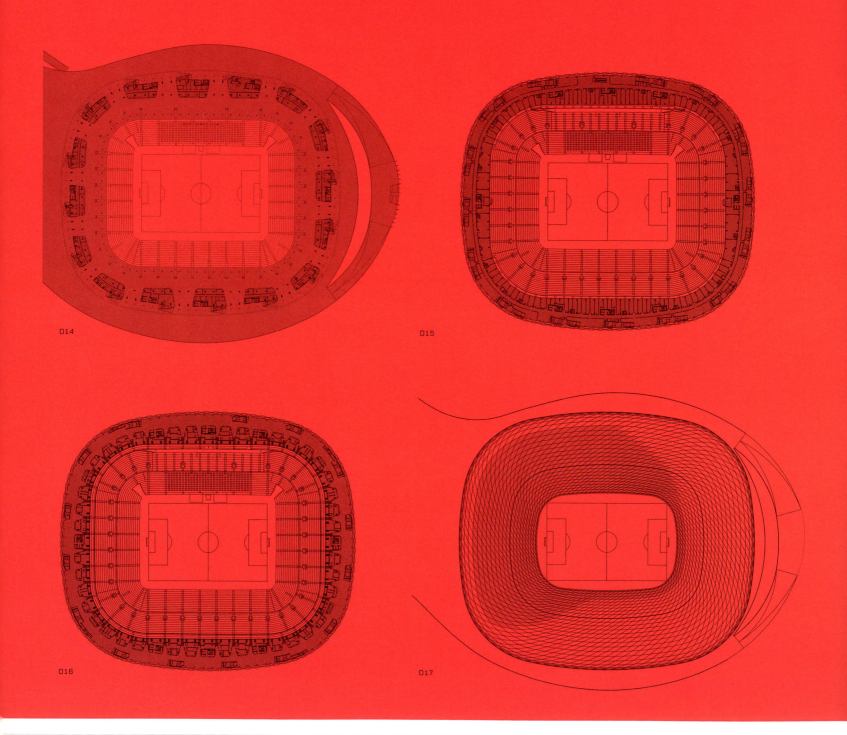

014

015

016

017

018

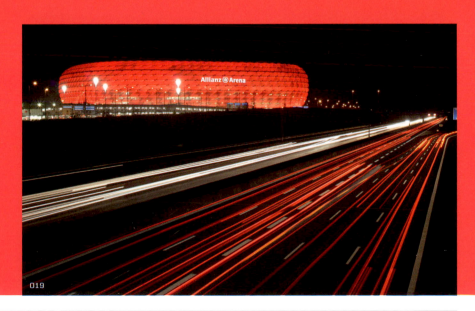

019

018-019_ As a dramatic but at the same time an alluring gesture, the envelope can be illuminated in the colours of the football club.

D. J. SIEGERT

GERONTOLOGY TECHNOLOGY CENTRE, BAD TÖLZ

MATERIAL_ ETFE FILM, TRANSPARENT, ONE LAYER /// **FAÇADE TYPE**_ SINGLE-LEAF, MECHANICALLY PRETENSIONED /// **USE**_ RESEARCH/ CIRCULATION /// **LOCATION**_ BAD TÖLZ, GERMANY /// **COMPLETED**_ 2004

The Gerontology Technology Centre (GTZ) in Bad Tölz is the first building in the world to use a single layer of transparent film for its façade. It is not only the physical properties of this extremely thin material that make this a highly unusual façade design; the double curvature of the façade lends the building a new aesthetic and presents a challenge to conventional perceptions of architecture. At the same time, the planning and production process of this complex configuration called for a rethink in the building industry.

CONCEPT /// To create a focal point for and at the same time also a contrast to the rigid, box-like arrangement of the former American army barracks, the architects designed a spiral-shaped building to house the new Innovations Centre. The spiral can be seen as a symbol of renewal, of development, or as a symbol of life it-

self, reflecting the work of the centre, which aims to promote interdisciplinary scientific projects in the relatively new field of gerontology. For this purpose, the GRP (Generation Research Program) Institute, an off-campus section of Munich's Ludwig Maximilian University, was housed in the centre of the spiral, forming in terms of both content and location the nucleus from where new impulses will radiate. In order to promote synergy effects, the offices and retail premises in the ensuing spiral are reserved for companies whose activities are directly linked to the areas of research. /// This geometrically complex building evolves like a ramp from the three storeys at the start of the spiral to the four storeys at the (provisional) end of the spiral. In addition, behind the façade each storey is stepped back and includes an open walkway at each level. The walkways link the individual office/retail units and can also be used by

001

002

001_ The ETFE film in double curvature forms the external envelope and spans the complete building from top to bottom. /// **002_** The transition from flat to curved columns gives the façade its structure.

003

the businesses for exhibitions and presentations, or for additional seating areas, thus encouraging informal communication between the various companies.

CLIMATE CONCEPT /// The external envelope in front of these open walkways is formed by a transparent ETFE film curving in two directions. A new development at the time of its erection, the film spans the complete height of the building. It provides protection against the weather and at the same time controls the internal climate. Although the façade consists of just one layer of this thin film, the open access zone behind, acting as a kind of conservatory, forms a climate buffer between the building itself and the exterior, just like its glazed predecessor. In winter, spring and autumn, the intermediate zone stores the solar radiation and therefore reduces the heating requirements and hence the heating costs – a factor that is becoming more and more relevant as energy costs rise. Contrastingly, during the summer the printing on the film and screens on the inside serve as protection against excessive solar gains. In addition, sensor-controlled vents open in the night to ensure an exchange of air.

The stack effect in the multistorey void between walkways and façade is responsible for the airflow which replaces the warm interior air with cold night air. Furthermore, the storage capacity of the solid floor slabs is exploited to reduce daytime temperature peaks. Another advantage is the generous transparency of the façade; daylight can be exploited to the full and energy costs for artificial lighting minimised.

CONSTRUCTION /// The curve of the membrane façade gives it a natural look, like a row of bird feathers. The single layer of ETFE film forms a complex, twisted surface geometry due to the spiral-shaped, terraced and, at the same time, ramp-like arrangement of the building. However, this unusual shaping of the membrane façade is not just the result of the building's geometry; it is more the result of the two-way spanning, which is necessary in order to stabilise the single layer of material. Consequently, the loadbearing structure over which the film is stretched is not simply a supporting framework, but rather determines the very shape of the façade. The architects chose steel circular hollow sections for the façade structure. The circular steel

004

003_ The building has a spiral form on plan and rises like a ramp.   ///   **004_** Location plan

005_ Plan of ground floor /// **006**_ Plan of 3rd floor /// **007**_ Section; the passages are circulation and climatic intermediate zones between offices and external envelope.

columns follow the spiral shape of the plan layout. Inclined in two directions, they form trapezoidal bays on elevation and in section follow the terrace-like outline of the building. Owing to the ramp-like increase in height, every column is positioned at a different angle to the building. In addition, every trapezoidal bay includes a diagonal member which curves outwards. This framework, alternating between straight and curved members inclined in different directions, forms the geometry and dictates the curvature of the façade film.

FABRICATION /// The façade planning and production process was remarkable. Instead of the conventional detailed draft design, sketches and technical detail considerations formed the basis for the fabrication of the loadbearing structure. Only after erecting the loadbearing structure and with the help of special computer programs was it possible to draw the actual double-curvature membrane geometry and hence the elevation. A three-dimensional laser survey of the most important fixed points provided the necessary input data for this. The expansion parameters of the film, which were determined from trials, had to be taken into account for the conversion into an exact two-dimensional geometry. Only in this way was it possible for the

manufacturer of the film to cut the material pieces exactly to size and weld them together. /// Therefore, the planning and production process did not proceed in the usual sequence from the accurate, detailed planning and then to production, but instead the drawings were first produced after erection and served only for the computer-aided determination of the façade material. This meant that there were no drawings, as design aids, with which to check, fine-tune and adjust the configuration. The laws of statics and physics replaced the drawings and, in the end, the as-built structure determined the final form. /// Another special feature of the construction results from the relaxation angle of the film. This property requires the cutting of the material to be adjusted (compensation) and the installation of a (re)tensioning facility. Unknown in conventional membrane construction, the (re)tensioning facility necessary was devised in empirical trials on a 1:1 model – a world first. Finally, the circular aluminium bars with adjustable screws responsible for the final tension in the film were mounted on the curved diagonal members. /// Not unlike the use of the building itself as a centre for innovations, the double-curvature membrane façade itself represents an innovation in façade engineering.

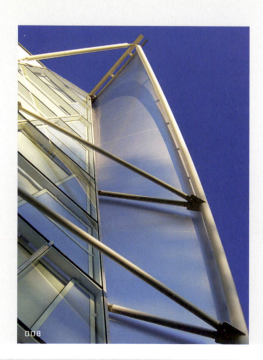

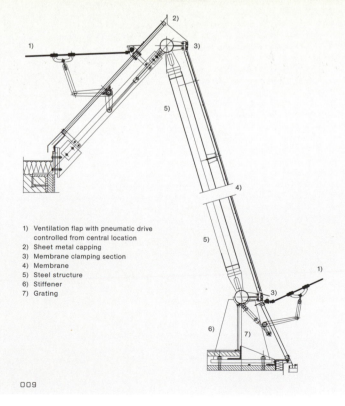

1) Ventilation flap with pneumatic drive controlled from central location
2) Sheet metal capping
3) Membrane clamping section
4) Membrane
5) Steel structure
6) Stiffener
7) Grating

008

009

008_ Film tensioning, end bay /// **009**_ Detail section through membrane façade

010_ The curving diagonal structural members tension the single layer of ETFE film. /// **011_** The underlying framework determines the geometry of the film.

NICHOLAS GRIMSHAW & PARTNERS

ROCKET TOWER

MATERIAL_ TRANSPARENT ETFE FILM, THREE LAYERS   ///   **FAÇADE TYPE_** SINGLE-LEAF, PNEUMATICALLY PRETENSIONED   ///

USE_ RESEARCH/EXHIBITIONS   ///   **LOCATION_** LEICESTER, UNITED KINGDOM   ///   **COMPLETED_** 2001

Since 2001 British rocket and space scientists have had a new meeting point. Their new research centre, the National Space Centre (NSC) designed by Nicholas Grimshaw & Partners, is located on the north bank of the River Soar in Leicester, in the disused stormwater tanks of the historic Abbey Pumping Station. The NSC brings together university institutes for teaching and research in the field of rocket technology and combines them with a planetarium, the Challenger Learning Centre and a museum of space travel.   ///   A conspicuous local landmark and the spectacular symbol of the centre is the transparent 10-storey tower situated at the entrance to the complex and made from air-filled cushions.

CONCEPT ///   The various different uses of the centre are accommodated in a group of three buildings framed by the rectangular stormwater tank. The main building is a square, two-storey shed-type building housing the university institutes, offices, generous exhibition areas and the planetarium. The planetarium forms a special circular element within the building whose position is revealed by the dome on the land-scaped roof. Next to the main building is the Challenger Learning Centre, accommodated in a rectangular, single-storey temporary building which previously stood on the university campus.   ///   Forming the highlight in terms of both content and architecture is the so-called Rocket Tower, situated at the south east corner of the main building. The tower houses the most spectacular exhibits of the space travel exhibition: two 35 m high rockets, looking as though they are standing on the launchpad ready to blast off! Two lifts, which travel up and down the outside of a steel mast reminiscent of a rocket launch tower, take visitors to the (on plan) trapezoidal steel platforms at various levels within the convex, circular tower. Here, visitors can see smaller exhibits of satellite and space stations and also gain a close-up view of the rockets.

CONSTRUCTION ///   The technical achievements of space travel are presented in an airy exhibition tower made from triple-layer air-filled ETFE film cushions. These storey-height, transparent "tyres" are stacked like rings, but each ring has a different diameter. The effect of this is to create an organic, bulging effect,

001

002

001_ Elevation of National Space Centre with exhibition tower /// **002**_ The spacious rocket tower is the symbol and architectural highlight of the NSC.

larger in the middle than at the top and bottom. Owing to this "natural" tower geometry curving in two directions (a geometry that would have been extremely complicated and expensive in glass), the cutting of the film for the façade had to be calculated exactly by means of three-dimensional computer simulations before the material could be fabricated and attached to the loadbearing structure. /// Thirteen horizontal, concentric, approximately circular (on plan) steel beams form the loadbearing structure for the plastic envelope. These are positioned 3 m apart, corresponding to the maximum span of the air-filled cushions, and are fixed to the primary structure. The primary structure of the tower consists of a rigid reinforced concrete staircase tower, which acts as a stiffening vertical "backbone", and two curved columns made from steel circular hollow sections, which span the full height of the tower and bend back over the roof to link up with the staircase tower. /// The air supply and the control systems for the air-filled cushions are housed in the staircase tower and are visible by way of the large metal pipes on the outside of the staircase tower. Only minimal measures are taken to control the

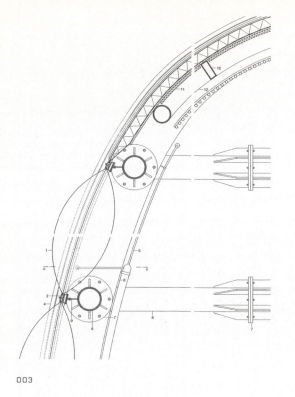

003

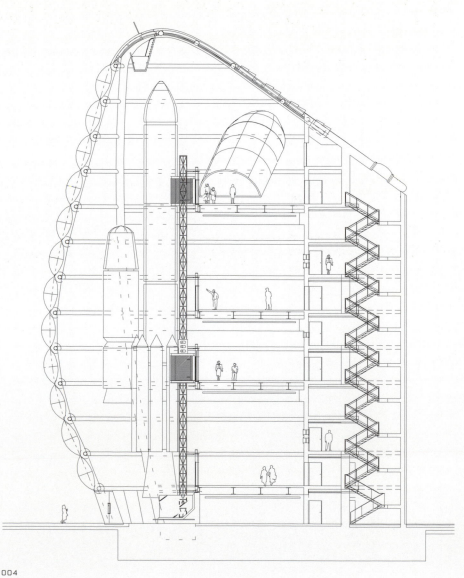

004

003_ Detail section through façade /// **004_** Section

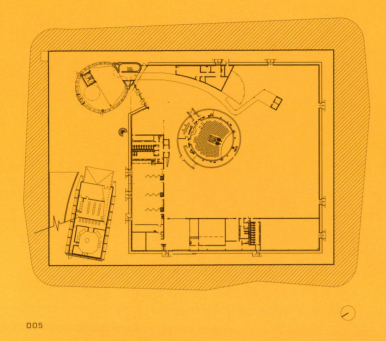

005

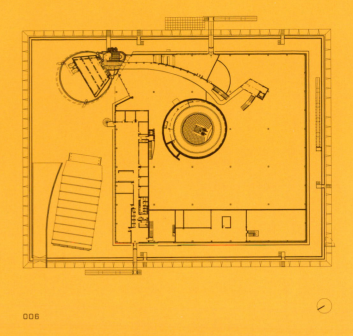

006

007

005_ Plan of entrance level   ///   **006**_ Plan of upper floor   ///   **007**_ Interior view during assembly of the exhibits

interior climate. The sole protection against solar radiation is provided by the silver dots printed on the film on the east and west sides of the tower. Vents are provided at the top and bottom of the tower for ventilating and cooling the interior. Rectangular heating panels, which look like solar panels, are distributed over the full height, attached to the horizontal façade beams. These panels guarantee a minimum temperature of 10 °C in the winter and prevent condensation forming on the façade. /// Thanks to the use of innovative technologies, the almost weightless, airy façade construction and, of course, also its appearance make the Rocket Tower a symbol of space technology in more ways than one.

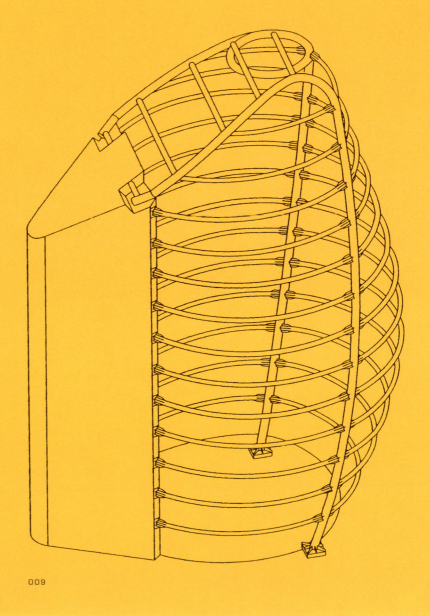

009

008_ Storey-height, ring-shaped air-filled cushions made from ETFE form the "bulging" tower. /// **009_** Isometric view of loadbearing structure

PGM 17
THOR

010_ The rockets look like they are ready for take-off!

JASCHEK & PARTNER

FESTO AG TECHNOLOGY CENTRE

MATERIAL_ PRINTED ETFE FILM, THREE LAYERS   ///   **ROOF FORM** _ SINGLE-LEAF, PNEUMATICALLY PRETENSIONED, INTEGRAL

SUNSHADING   ///   **USE_** RESEARCH/ATRIUM   ///   **LOCATION_** ESSLINGEN, GERMANY   ///   **COMPLETED_** 2002

The new Technology Centre of the Festo company in Esslingen near Stuttgart features spacious atria with roofs of pneumatic membrane constructions. The plastic membranes enclose non-air-conditioned conservatories which act as buffer zones and are intrinsic to the energy concept.   ///   Originally, the six four-storey glazed office blocks, which spread out like a fan, were to be enclosed in one shell-type, transparent synthetic membrane envelope. At least that is what the competition drawings showed. However, during the course of further planning, the impressive, large-format pneumatic structure shrunk to three separate atria.

CONSTRUCTION ///   The use of air as a structural material was an important aspect for this company, whose main line of business is the production of pneumatic drives for all forms of industrial automation. Within the company, air is regarded as a sixth building material alongside stone, timber, metal, glass and membranes. Festo puts this belief to the test in its research work as well. Consequently, the roofs to the three atria were built from air-filled ETFE membrane cushions. The transparent cushions measuring 2.5 m wide are placed transverse to the office blocks on a grid of steel members arranged like a barrel vault spanning from eaves to eaves. The trapezoidal plan shape of each atrium results in a roof of plastic tubes with lengths ranging from 14 to 28 m. Each tube consists of three layers of plastic film which are welded together airtight along the edges and stretched between an aluminium frame. The tubes are filled with air to give them their form; a fan maintains a marginal overpressure inside the tubes so the synthetic film remains permanently taut.   ///   The special feature of this construction is the integral, pneumatically adjustable sunshading. The centre and upper layers of plastic film are printed with a chessboard-type pattern, but with the black squares offset. A fully automatic control mechanism regulates the pressures in the two chambers of the cushions depending on the position of the sun and in doing so changes the position of the central layer of synthetic material which thus regulates the amount of incoming light. Depending on the position of the central layer, it is possible to vary the degree of sunshading from 50 % to 93 %. It takes about 15–20 minutes to move the film from its lowest to its highest position.   ///   In contrast to air-supported buildings in which the compressed air plays a loadbearing role, the air supply in this air-inflated building is subsidiary in structural terms and therefore does not require elaborate emergency back-up arrangements. The geometry of the roof is such that minor snow loads can be carried by empty cushions, i.e. by the plastic film itself, for a limited period. Therefore, the layer of air is in the first instance relevant for the insulation properties of

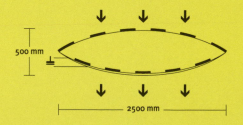

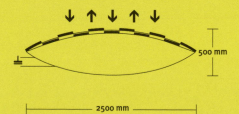

001

001_ Schematic diagram of sunshading: left, open; right, closed   ///   **002**_ The chessboard-type pattern of the air-filled ETFE cushions functions as a pneumatically controlled sunshade.

003

the construction. /// The advantages of the pneumatic cushion assembly compared to a glazed roof construction are readily apparent: the air-filled cushion is very light in weight so the long-span roof structure can employ a much more delicate construction than would otherwise be the case. A gently curving, orthogonal grid of slender steel sections – secured against wind uplift by a network of thin steel cables – spans over the four-storey void. The steel cables form an arch from the edge of the roof on the north side to the base of the atrium glazing on the south side and therefore act as a truss for the roof, which also stabilises the all-glass façade and, in addition, carries walkways that are suspended elastically from the cables. The gable end of each atrium is formed by an all-glass façade which slopes inwards; the panes of glass are held in place by discrete fixings.

Large fabric "sails" in front of the atrium façades can be unfurled by a hydraulic mechanism to provide shade from the sun as required.

CLIMATE CONCEPT /// The open walkways within the spacious atria provide internal circulation routes and areas for relaxation during break periods, but can also be used temporarily for events or customer information displays. /// In terms of the energy audit, the atria with their membrane roofs function like fully glazed conservatories, which create a Mediterranean climate in winter. Even when the outside temperature is low, the temperature in the atria remains stable at about + 12 °C. This effect is due to the solar heat gains and the layer of air in the plastic cushions, which achieve a U-value of about 2.5 W/m²K. /// Like with all conservatory

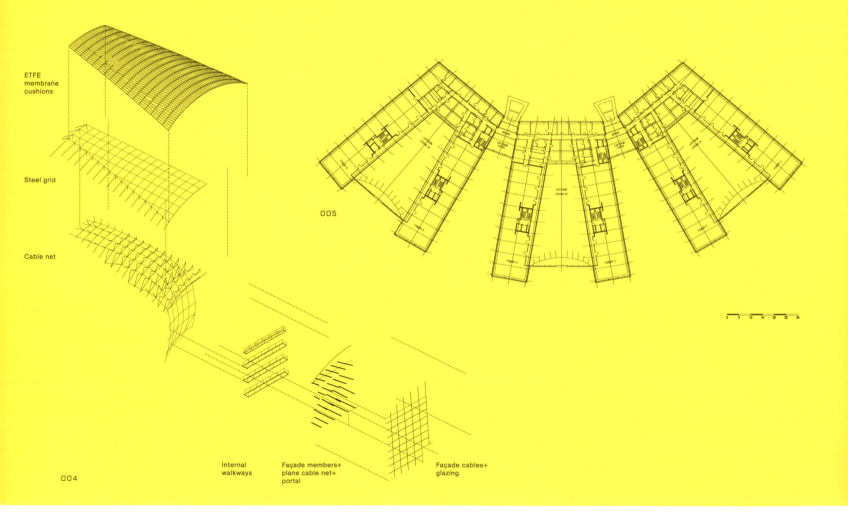

ETFE membrane cushions

Steel grid

Cable net

005

Internal walkways

Façade members+ plane cable net+ portal

Façade cables+ glazing

004

003_ View at night /// **004**_ Atrium construction /// **005**_ Plan of standard floor

006_ Delicate walkways are suspended from the cable trussing to the atrium roof; hydraulically controlled fabric "sails" form sunshades.

designs, the real problem is the undesirable overheating effect in summer. To avoid overheating in the atria, the fabric "sails" described above are used as sunshades; in addition, air can be pumped through the roof cushions to prevent a build-up of heat. Permanent ventilation and night-time cooling of the atria are ensured by the louvre openings above the edges of the roofs to the adjoining office blocks; this system is backed up by mechanical ventilation. The water-filled solid components of the adjoining concrete walls and gallery floors provide additional cooling. These comprehensive measures mean that even on hot summer days the temperature in the atria is about 5 °C lower than that of the outside air. /// Thanks to the use of heat from the soil and exhaust air plus solar energy, the use of daylight control systems, component cooling, intelligent building automation, triple glazing, extensive planting on the roofs and, last but not least, the spacious, airy atria, the new Technology Centre obtains 70 % of the energy required to heat and cool the buildings from regenerative sources and therefore counts as a low-energy building. /// Ecology, economy and technology, the three most important criteria in the planning, reflect the principles of this high-tech company.

007

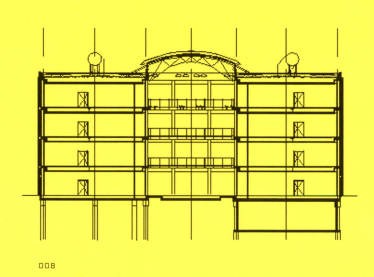

008

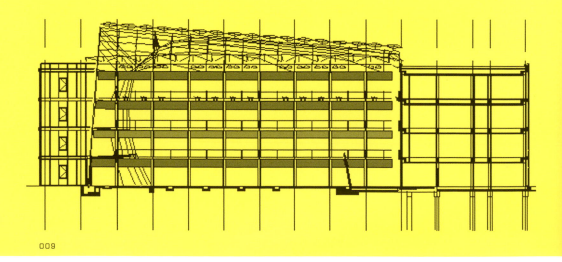

009

007_ Walkways link the spacious glazed offices and serve as meeting points for employees. /// **008_** Section /// **009_** Longitudinal section

010_ The – on plan – trapezoidal form of the four-storey atrium creates a buffer zone between interior and exterior.

VOLKER GIENCKE

GLASSHOUSES, GRAZ

MATERIAL_ CURVED TRANSPARENT ACRYLIC ELEMENTS   ///   **FAÇADE TYPE_** DOUBLE-LEAF   ///

USE_ RESEARCH/EXHIBITIONS   ///   **LOCATION_** GRAZ, AUSTRIA   ///   **COMPLETED_** 1995

Glasshouses have graced the Botanical Gardens in Graz since the 19th century. Attached to the university, they have been used for research and teaching purposes and have also acted as "showcases" to attract the general public. After 100 years of continuous use, the deficiencies of the old glasshouses could no longer be disputed: old-fashioned methods, dilapidated exteriors and cramped interiors were the prime-movers behind the construction of new glasshouses just a few hundred metres away from their predecessors.   ///   Totally in keeping with the tradition of glasshouse design, which again and again has produced pioneering architectural masterpieces, Volker Giencke's glasshouses represent technological and constructional innovations.

CONCEPT   ///   The architect placed three transparent, sloping, parabolic cylinders at acute angles to each other on a plateau-type base. Incorporated into the plateau, which merges imperceptibly into the landscape of the Botanical Gardens, are the offices, seminar rooms,

exhibition rooms and plant nurseries. Only a long pitched glass roof for lighting purposes reveals the presence of the subterranean functions. This approach allows the glasshouses to become exhibits themselves, which appear to spread out uncontrolled across the plateau.   ///   The glasshouses contain exotic or threatened plant species in four separate climatic zones. Ramps, bridges and winding pathways allow visitors to explore the tropical house, Mediterranean cold house, palm house and the desert-like succulents house. The pathways link together the glasshouses in which the plants are placed in landscaped settings designed to match their natural habitats. The route through the exhibition, which illustrates the ecological relationships between the different types of vegetation, is backed up by video installations and information stands.

CLIMATE CONCEPT   ///   Precise control of the internal climatic conditions is crucial to the breeding of exotic plants. Temperature, air humidity, brightness and

001_ The parabolic cylinders are laid out at acute angles to each other on a plateau-type base. /// **002**_ Night-time photo

air circulation must correspond exactly with the climatic conditions of the original habitats of the plants, and must be constantly adjusted to suit the prevailing exterior climate. /// The internal temperatures necessary in winter are achieved by means of solar gains and a system of hot-water pipes. Invisible to visitors, the hollow sections of the aluminium loadbearing structure simultaneously serve as hot-water pipes which distribute the heat evenly over the full height of the building. Hydraulic, sensor-controlled vents at the top and bottom of each structure control air circulation in the interior. During the summer these vents can be used to cool the air and counteract the greenhouse effect. Additional cooling is achieved with the two-component nozzle system developed specially for this project, which simultaneously regulates the humidity of the air. This pressurised system creates a fine mist of microscopic water droplets which instantly lowers the internal temperature by 5 °C. At the time of the planning, NASA was the only organisation using such a "fog system". With such an effective cooling system, sunblinds are rendered unnecessary. /// Although temperature and humidity are important factors for plant growth, it is the intensity of the light that is crucial. The light permeability of the glasshouse construction was therefore a key issue and dictated both the form as well as the structure and façade.

CONSTRUCTION /// The parabolic primary structure of each glasshouse is a structurally optimised arch form, which enables the loadbearing members to be minimised and in turn maximises the area for the incoming

003_ The delicate hollow sections of the parabolic aluminium loadbearing structure simultaneously serve as hot-water pipes.

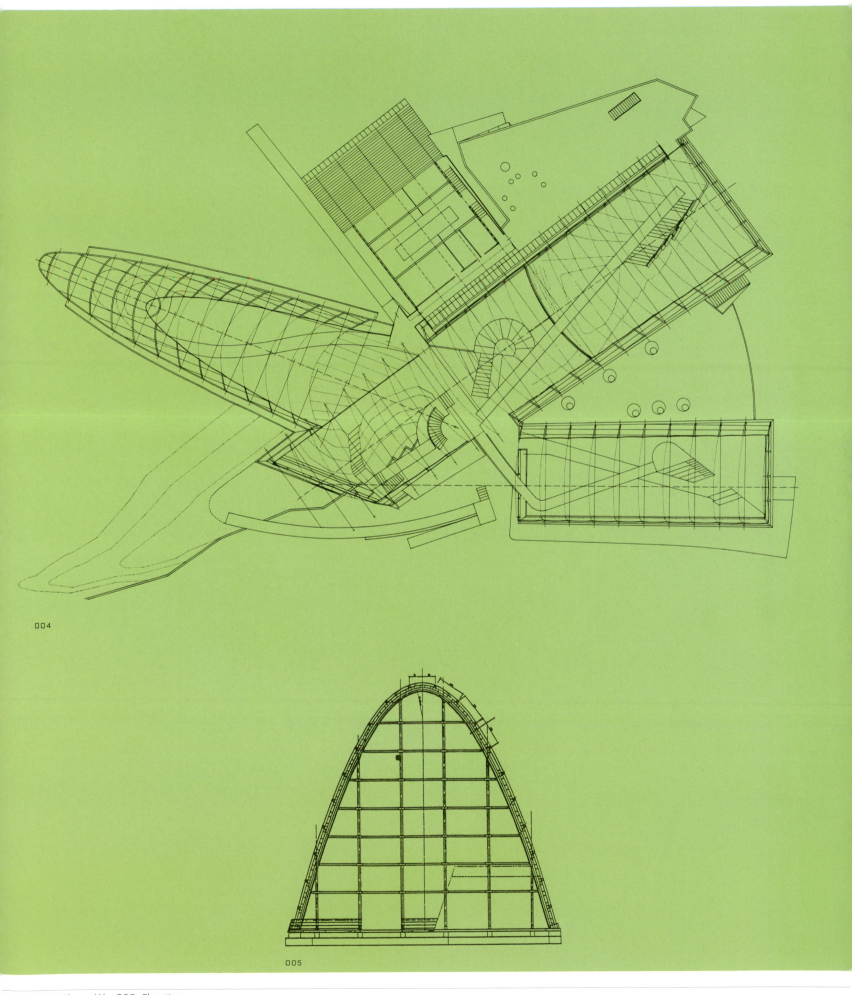

004

005

daylight. A parabola is virtually identical with the so-called catenary curve, the shape of a hanging chain, and is therefore a natural structural form. The lightweight loadbearing members were specially developed for the project from high-quality aluminium alloys – an innovation in structural engineering that would have been impossible without suitable computer programs. Although standard these days, this method of analysis represented completely new ground at the time of the design work back in 1982. The nodes in the loadbearing structure are designed as "plug-in" elements; the horizontal purlins are connected to these and compressed-air lines plus bridge and ramp constructions are "plugged" into place.   ///   The transparent envelope of double-leaf acrylic elements was fixed directly to the loadbearing structure. The transparent façade consists of convex rectangular plastic shells reminiscent of conventional rooflights. Despite the curving geometry of the buildings, the façade elements were able to be standardised because the three glasshouses follow the same parabolic curve. The transparent elements also take into account the minimal structure and the optimisation of the light gains. These lightweight acrylic units reduce the load on the structure and exhibit a better spectral analysis behaviour than conventional soda-lime-silica glasses.   ///   The minimisation of the loadbearing construction and the use of a plastic façade has resulted in a light transmission of almost 98 % – a value that represents an unbeaten record in the history of modern glasshouse construction.

006

006_ The inclination of the structure corresponds to the height of the plants.